radiant textuality

radiant textuality

literature after the world wide web

jerome mcgann

palgrave

RADIANT TEXTUALITY: LITERATURE AFTER THE WORLD WIDE WEB
© Jerome McGann, 2001

First published 2001 by PALGRAVE™
175 Fifth Avenue, New York, N.Y.10010 and
Houndmills, Basingstoke, Hampshire RG21 6XS.
Companies and representatives throughout the world

PALGRAVE is the new global publishing imprint of St. Martin's Press LLC Scholarly and Reference Division and Palgrave Publishers Ltd (formerly Macmillan Press Ltd).

ISBN 0-312-29352-6 hardback

Library of Congress Cataloging-in-Publication Data

McGann, Jerome J.
    Radiant textuality : literature after the World Wide Web / Jerome McGann.
        p. cm.
    Includes bibliographical references and index.
    ISBN 0-312-29352-6
    1. Criticism—Data processing. 2. Criticism, Textual—Data processing.
    3. Hypertext systems. I. Title.

PN98.E4 M39 2001
801'.959'0285—dc21   2001021795

A catalogue record for this book is available from the British Library.

Design by Westchester Book Composition

First edition: November 2001
10 9 8 7 6 5 4 3 2 1

There is a crack in every thing,
That's how the light gets in.
　　　—Leonard Cohen, "Anthem" (1993)

For John Unsworth
Deo Gratias

Contents

Acknowledgements   ix

Preface   xi

Note on the Text   xvi

Introduction. Beginning Again: Humanities and Digital Culture,
1993-2000   1

Part I. Hideous Progeny, Rough Beasts: 1993-1995
1. The Alice Fallacy; or, Only God Can Make a Tree   29
2. The Rationale of Hypertext   53
3. Editing as a Theoretical Pursuit   75
    Appendix to Chapter 3   88

Part II. Imagining What You Don't Know: 1995-1999
4. Deformance and Interpretation (with Lisa Samuels)   105
    Appendix to Chapter 4   131
5. Rethinking Textuality   137

Part III. Quantum Poetics: 1999-2000
6. Visible and Invisible Books in N-Dimensional Space   167
    Appendix to Chapter 6   187
7. Dialogue and Interpretation at the Interface of
Man and Machine   193

Conclusion. Beginning Again and Again: "The Ivanhoe Game"   209
        Appendix to the Conclusion   232

Notes   249

Bibliography   259

Index   267

Acknowledgements

This book transcribes some of the things that happened at the University of Virginia at a certain interesting intellectual moment—the period from 1993 to 2000. The events involved—and still involve—many people. John Unsworth was the chief architect of these events, and so this book is one person's record of what he did and what he made possible.

And then there is another person to be specially singled out—Johanna Drucker, who came to Virginia in 1998 with a new set of interests and energies. This book was completed through her inspiration and encouragement. So many of its ideas and arguments were developed and clarified through our conversations in 1999 and 2000 that I can scarcely recognize many of them as my own.

Those conversations were for me only the intense locus of a much larger set of conversations we were carrying on with a great many other people—some in face-to-face encounters, many through scholarly exchanges. The bibliography cites a core group of those who have been the most immediate presences in this book.

But certain people must be set apart for special thanks. Most important are those who have made up the remarkable intellectual scene at the University of Virginia in the past seven years: Robbie Bingler, Chris Jesse, Worthy Martin, Bethany Nowviskie, Dan Pitti, Steven Ramsay, Thorny Staples, and all my graduate students who have been working with me on *The Rossetti Archive*. To Lisa Samuels and Dino Buzetti I owe a special debt for the stimulating conversations we have had and continue to have. And so many others: Ed Ayers, George Bornstein, Lou Burnard, Doug Duggan,

Morris Eaves, Robert Essick, Neil Fraistat, David Greetham, Steve Jones, Cecil Lang, Marjorie Levinson, Willard McCarty, David Seaman, Michael Sperberg-McQueen, Kendon Stubbs, Will Thomas, Joseph Viscomi. And finally there are some enlightened administrators and supporters who made the Institute for Advanced Technology in the Humanities (IATH) possible: Alan Batson, Gene Block, John Casteen, Mel Leffler, Peter Lowe, Kendon Stubbs, Karin Wittenborg, Bill Wulf. Nothing at IATH— and so nothing in this book—could have been accomplished without them.

The texts of the following chapters are revised versions of essays originally published elsewhere, and I acknowledge with thanks the editors of the following journals for permission to include material here that originally appeared in their publications: *Chain*, fall 1996 (chapter 1); TEXT, 1996-1997, 1998-1999 (chapters 2 and 3); *New Literary History*, winter 1999, spring 2001 (chapters 4 and 6); *Computers and the Humanities*, fall 2001 (chapter 7).

Wallace Stevens poems are reprinted here with permission. From *The Collected Poems of Wallace Stevens* by Wallace Stevens, copyright 1954 by Wallace Stevens. Used by permissions of Alfred A. Knopf, a division of Random House, Inc.

Preface

Knowledge of the world means dissolving the solidity of the world.
    —*Italo Calvino,* Six Memos for the Next Millenium

In one sense the story running through this book is a very old story. We sometimes see it as the story of Faust and Margaret, and it comes again as Beauty and the Beast or as any of that wondrous fairy tale's mutations. A hundred years ago Henry Adams recognized its emergence in a historical tension he named the Dynamo and the Virgin.

The Computer and the Book—their relation has much in common with those three legends. For the book was once upon a time the very emblem of Faustian power. As late as 1870 Emily Dickinson could think that "There is no Frigate like a book." The thought charms us now precisely in its quaintness, since current imaginative voyagings are everywhere traversing digital space. And so bibliographical lamentations begin to arise, "Ou sont les livres d'antan?"

This book is a commentary on that question, and the commentary is organized around two ideas about humanities-based digital instruments. The first is that understanding the structure of digital space requires a disciplined aesthetic intelligence. Because our most developed models for that kind of intelligence are textual models, we would be foolish indeed not to study those models in the closest possible ways. Our minds think in textual codes. Because the most advanced forms of textual codings are what we call "poetical," the study and application of digital codings summons us to new investigations into our textual inheritance.

To date that summons has been slow to develop, which brings me to the second idea that organizes this book. Digital technology used by humanities scholars has focused almost exclusively on methods of sorting, accessing, and disseminating large bodies of materials, and on certain specialized problems in computational stylistics and linguistics. In this respect the work rarely engages those questions about interpretation and self-aware reflection that are the central concerns for most humanities scholars and educators. Digital technology has remained instrumental in serving the technical and precritical occupations of librarians and archivists and editors. But *the general field of humanities education and scholarship will not take the use of digital technology seriously until one demonstrates how its tools improve the ways we explore and explain aesthetic works—until, that is, they expand our interpretational procedures.*

A close genetic relation holds between the book and computer. For textual and digital forms alike, however, this historical continuity has brought questions and problems that have not been studied at all well precisely because the genetic relation between the two media has been too much taken for granted, as if it were simple to see and understand. The situation is emblemized in the dichotomy of enthusiasm and skepticism that marks so much of the current discussion—indeed, that organizes the discussion along two sides.

We have to break away from questions like "will the computer replace the book?" So much more interesting are the intellectual opportunities that open at a revelatory historical moment such as we are passing through. These opportunities come with special privileges for certain key disciplines—now, for engineering, for the sciences, for certain areas of philosophy (studies in logic), and the social sciences (cognitive modeling). But unapparent as it may at first seem, scholarship devoted to aesthetic materials has never been more needed than at this historical moment.

That necessity leaped to one's attention in 1993 with the coming of the World Wide Web (W3). Until that epochal moment, digital technology had moved at the margins of literary and humanistic studies. The tools were taken up largely by some linguists and form-critical scholars, and by specialists interested in problems of storing and archiving scholarly (textual) materials. Even word-processing tools came slowly into the hands of humanities scholars. We forget that ten years ago—I am writing this sentence in late February 2000—the number of humanities scholars who used any computerized tools at all was relatively small.

A discontinuous historical event occurred during those ten years, and in the course of its unfolding emerged W3, the digital environment that organizes and commands the subjects of this book. To the speed and ubiquity of digital intercourse and transaction have been added interface and multimedia, and that, as the poet said, "has made all the difference." Our sense of language will never be the same.

Or rather, perhaps, our sense of it—in every sense—has been renewed, restored to something like the richness that it possessed in the Middle Ages, and that is still available in the works descending to us from that remarkable period—pre-eminently in its greatest invention, the medieval church and cathedral. From Santa Sophia to St. Mark's to Monreale, and across all of Europe and England, the doors of human perception were flung open in those amazing multimedia environments. And not only in Europe. Scattered across the globe from China to New Guinea to Egypt to the Nazca desert in Peru are the remains of human inventions of similar and even more amazing complexity. Next to them, even our most recent and advanced virtual reality tools and constructions seem primitive indeed.

However toddling they appear, contemporary instruments of hyper- and multimedia constitute a profane resurrection of those once-sacred models of communication. To get a clear grasp of their historical emergence one would have to return to the middle and late nineteenth century, when so much of what is apparent today was being forecast: in mathematics and physics, in logic, in the emergence of photography. My own special field of interest, textuality, underwent a great renewal at the same moment. In England, the work of John Ruskin, D. G. Rossetti, and William Morris catalyzed a complex set of historical forces into the Arts and Crafts movement and, more particularly, into the Renaissance of the Book. In the rediscovered "Grotesque" art of the Middle Ages was heard—the metaphor is deliberately mixed—the first premonition of the famous proverb that would define the coming of the digital age a century later: the medium is the message.

This book is a report on some early attempts to understand how that proverb might be read by people interested in humanities education. It is based in certain ideas about language and semiotic systems that recur throughout history—ideas that may seem not to match with many common formulations. In my view, however, the problem here lies in the formulations, not in the actual fact of the matter (so to speak).

Recall that even before we began creating formal systems of visual signs—systems that generate this very sentence-object you are now reading—the language we use is woven from audible and visible elements. And as the syntax of that last sentence is designed to suggest, this textual condition of ours is constructed as a play of incommensurable elements, of which temporality is one. Linguistic units are not self-identical, as even the briefest reflective glance at a dictionary will show. Indeed, they don't even occupy fixed positions within a given textual space—the specialized space of this reading-text, for example—since a variety of overlapping and incommensurable planes transact all textual spaces. Textual space and textual time are n-dimensional simply because they locate embodied actions and events.

Computational systems are not designed like the first sentence of the previous paragraph. They are designed to negotiate disambiguated, fully commensurable signifying structures.

"Indeed! And so why should machines of that kind hold any positive interest for humanities scholars, whose attention is always focused on human ambiguities and incommensurables?"

"Indeed! But why not *also* ask: How shall these machines be made to operate in a world that functions through such ambiguities and incommensurables?"

Both of those questions have set the terms for the work of this book.

Anyone who works with texts in disciplined ways, and especially those interested in their rhetorical and aesthetic properties, understands very well the incommensurability of textual forms. How to gain some clarity and control over our textual condition has been a perpetual human concern and is a central concern of this book as well. It is organized to show how the work at the University of Virginia's Institute for Advanced Technology in the Humanities (IATH) from 1993 to 2000 led to the practical implementation of catastrophe and quantum models for the critical investigation of aesthetic forms. Suggestive as the ideas of quantum mechanics have been for many humanities scholars, the scale of quantum effects has seemed far removed from the apparent scale of textual and semiotic phenomena. The latter involve macroscopic events, the former submicroscopic— indeed, quantum effects are, in the view of many, not objective events at all but simply types of measurements and calculations executed for certain practical ends. It was Roger Penrose, I think, who first argued most effectively against this view. He proposes that "the phenomenon of consciousness is something that cannot be understood in entirely classical terms" and that "a quantum world [might] be *required* so that thinking, perceiving creatures, such as ourselves, can be constructed from its substance" (Penrose 226).

The empirical data of consciousness are texts and semiotic phenomena of all types—"autopoetic" phenomena, in the terms of Humberto Maturana and Francesco Varela. This book will argue that our "classical" models for investigating such data are less precise than they might be and that quantum dynamical models should be imagined and can be built. The book focuses on the historical circumstances that forced this argument into being. It traces the development of certain experiments with textual materials to their unforeseen but, I would now say, necessary consequences: most importantly, the practical illustrations and proposals for new models of critical and interpretational study.

One final comment may be helpful. This book's commitment to a "quantum poetics" may call to mind, for Modernist scholars at any rate, Daniel Albright's stimulating and elegant study of certain strains of twentieth-century writing, *Quantum Poetics* (1997). Albright's book investigates "the appropriation of scientific metaphors by poets" (1) whose work emerged at the same time as the great figures of early-twentieth-century science. Albright argues that these writers exploited certain scientific figures in their imaginative work. My argument is quite different: that quantum and topological models of analysis are applicable to imaginative writing tout court, that these models are more adequate, more comprehensive, and more enlightening than the traditional models we inherit from Plato and Aristotle to Kant and Marx. "Quantum poetics" in this study does not signify certain figures and tropes that stimulated the practices of a certain group of historically located writers. On the contrary, it comprises a set of critical methods and procedures that are meant to be pursued and then applied in a general way to the study of imaginative work.

The final discussion of "The Ivanhoe Game" illustrates the difference very clearly. "The Ivanhoe Game" models a new form of critical method. Its applicability is of a general kind—as much for Yeats and Pound as for Keats and Byron, for Shakespeare or Dante, for Ovid, Lucretius, the Bible. It is a model that we propose to build in a new kind of textual environment—a digital one. Finally, it is only a model—one model. We propose to build it in the hope that it may stimulate others to develop and build more adequate critical tools.

Note on the Text

The idea for this book took shape in 1998 to 2000, when most of it was written. The five chapters comprising Parts I and II were drafted earlier, however. Three of those were written between 1993 and 1995 as a related series of critical reflections on *The Rossetti Archive* and its initial theoretical goals. The two very different chapters titled "The Alice Fallacy" and "Deformance and Interpretation" were written in 1993 and 1996 (respectively). Framing the other three conceptually as well as historically, they define the interpretational issues that had been running through the work we undertook with *The Rossetti Archive*. The full elaboration of this book's arguments only emerged very late, however, when those interpretational topics and problems had been rehearsed and pursued. This happened in 1998 to 2000 when the rest of the book was written. At that point—the spring of 2000, when "The Ivanhoe Game" was conceived in conversations with Johanna Drucker and John Unsworth—I saw how important "The Alice Fallacy" had been for the development of the arguments being made in this book. I then revised and recast the chapters originally written from 1993 to 1995, and I wrote the introduction, "Beginning Again," as well as the series of critical reflections that introduce the different parts of the book. I played several iterations of "The Ivanhoe Game" with Johanna Drucker and some graduate and undergraduate students (May to November 2000) and finished the book by writing up several accounts of those events, including the last chapter of this book, "Beginning Again and Again."

Introduction

Beginning Again: Humanities and Digital Culture, 1993–2000

we're like the man who climbed on a chair and declared
he was a little closer to the moon.
— *Hubert Dreyfus,* What Computers Can't Do

Humanities computing is beginning again. It passed through one coherent period of historical development and, more recently, through an exploratory interlude of considerable importance. This book examines that interlude, the years 1993 to 2000, from the perspective of a project I undertook at exactly the same moment (fortuitously as it happened): *The Complete Writings and Pictures of Dante Gabriel Rossetti. A Hypermedia Research Archive* ("The Rossetti Archive").[1] Working on the archive during those years, I began to see more clearly the kinds of change that are coming to literary and humanistic studies. These changes will bring to the center of scholarly procedures theoretical models that have been perceived until now as odd, idiosyncratic, nonnormal.

Before 1993 the computerized future of our humanistic inheritance was apparent to a relatively small group of librarians and archival scholars and to very few other people in literary and cultural studies. I am speaking here not of loose and speculative cybernetic conceptions and imaginings, which have been widespread for some 15 years or so, but of practical and concrete understandings of the momentous changes that lay in store for our libraries and other archival depositories. Now, however, in 2000, the community of humanities scholars at large has also begun to see that future with greater clarity and to feel the pressure of its demands. In 1993 when projects like *The Rossetti Archive* sought funding for their work, the applications failed. Then the scholarly community was not prepared to judge either the need or the adequacy of such projects. The situation in 2000 is different, for many educators now understand that our inherited archive of materials in libraries and museums will have to be re-edited with information technology (IT) tools. We see as well the kind of massive reorganization that will have to be carried out in these depositories in order to store, connect, and conveniently access their holdings. All this work is already well underway.

But also now in 2000 some are being pushed further by the inertia of the new tools being placed at our disposal. Ideas about textuality that were once taken as speculative or even imaginary now appear to be the only ones that have any practical relation to the digital environments we occupy every day. So that now all of aesthetic, literary, and humane studies appear brinked for major changes in the ways they will be studied, analyzed, and interpreted.[2]

This book tells a story of how we got to where we are now. The story describes how certain theoretical views of textuality once considered weird, impractical, and unserious discovered their moment of realization in the digital world of the late twentieth century. I first taught the works of Lautréamont, Jarry, and Roussel at the University of Chicago in the late 1960s and early 1970s in courses I then called "The Literature of Excess." Authors of their kind treated documents as scenes of *precise* imaginative possibilities. None approached their work in the spirit of a romantic hermeneutics: that is to say, under a horizon where multiple meanings are generated by readers working in and through texts imagined on an analogy with the Bible. Those kinds of text appear to us as massively authoritative and deeply mysterious, requiring devotional study to uncover their secret meanings. Reconnecting with certain performative and rhetorical traditions, however, writers like Jarry laid a groundwork for post-romantic procedural writing. They began to make clear once again the constructed character of textuality—the fact that texts and documents are fields open to decisive and rule-governed manipulations. In this view of the matter, texts and documents are not primarily understood as containers or even vehicles of meaning. Rather, they are sets of instantiated rules and algorithms for generating and controlling themselves and for constructing further sets of transmissional possibilities.[3]

How I came to write that previous paragraph constitutes the story being told in this book.

Points of Departure

In the fall of 1993 we began work on *The Rossetti Archive* and in July 2000 saw the public release of its first research installment: an online hypermedia construction of some 10,000 image and text files organized for use (and experiment) by students and scholars with many disciplinary interests. (When the archive is completed it will contain more than twice that number of files.) During those initial seven years the archive—along with the whole field of humanities computing—was swept in directions no one foresaw in 1992.

The project was consciously begun as a pragmatically-based theoretical undertaking—in fact, an experiment in Ian Hacking's sense[4]—to explore the nature of textuality: in particular, book and paper-based textualities, as well as the editorial methods for marking and interpreting these kinds of texts. The archive was built under the auspices of the University of Virginia's Institute for Advanced Technology in the Humanities (IATH), which was founded the same year as *The Rossetti Archive* was begun. The humanities computing work sponsored by IATH—a large array of research projects in texts, media, images, and information—can now be seen to mark the end of a first and distinct phase in the history of humanities computing. Our experience in building *The Rossetti Archive* is an epitome of what happened at IATH between 1993 and 1999, when humanities computing began to move in very new directions.[5]

A brief historical note here will be helpful. The use of IT in humanities disciplines began in the late 1940s with Father Roberto Busa SJ, whose work on the corpus of St. Thomas Aquinas set the terms in which humanities computing would operate successfully for more than 40 years.[6] Two lines of work dominate the period: first, the creation of databases of humanities materials—almost exclusively textual materials—for various types of automated retrieval, search, and analysis; second, the design and construction of statistical models for studying language formalities of many kinds, ranging from social and historical linguistics to the study of literary forms.

Viewed from the perspective of a humanities scholar's interests, this work has had its greatest impact on the library, which began its extraordinary digital reconstitution during this period.[7] Because the library locates the center, if not the very soul, of arts and humanities studies, this transformation carries enormous consequences for humanities students and educators. Hand catalogues have virtually disappeared and libraries everywhere are offering larger, more varied, and more integrated bodies of electronically organized and connected materials.

While everyone is directly affected by these changes in the library at the general access level, and to an increasing degree in the area of reference works of different kinds, few people, including very few humanities scholars, have been touched by more specialized work with stylometrics, cladistics, and tools for automated collation and author-attribution. This situation is especially clear in the United States, where New Criticism and its theoretical aftermath exiled nearly all kinds of statistical, editorial, and textual work to the periphery of humanities studies. Because humanities computing in its first phase was so closely linked to computational linguistics, on one hand, and to textual/editorial studies, on the other, the central lines of work in literary and cultural studies between 1950 and 1990 remained virtually untouched by developments in humanities computing. To the degree that IT attracted the attention of humanities scholars, the interest was largely theoretical, engaging the subjects of media and culture in either speculative and relatively abstract ways or journalistic treatments.

That situation has kept most humanities scholars in a state of invincible ignorance of one of the most remarkable achievements of this early phase of humanities computing: the design and development of systems for the structural description (or "marking") of textual materials. The parent of these developments is SGML (Standard Generalized Markup Language), which is a rigorously articulated logic for marking the structural parts and relations of textual documents (or bodies of material fashioned on a model of textual documents). So far as the humanities are concerned, the signal event was the development of TEI (Text Encoding Initiative). TEI is a specialized markup derivative of SGML, one designed to facilitate computer implementations of traditional humanities texts (literature, history, philosophy). By 1993, when IATH was founded, TEI was establishing itself as a professional standard for text encoding of humanities materials.[8]

These dates and events are important because of what happened in the larger world of IT between 1993 and 1994: the definitive appearance of the W3.[9] It is important to remember—not an easy thing to do at this distance—that the coming of W3 seemed to most scholars involved in humanities computing at that time as a trivial event so far as they were concerned. A hypermedia environment established on a global scale, W3 ought to have fed immediately into a number of long-standing theoretical interests in decentered and reader-oriented textualities. The scholarly meetings and journals devoted to humanities computing show with unmistakable clarity, however, that few people in those communities registered the importance of W3. Disinterest was perhaps to be expected from computational scholars, but even the hypertext community barely noticed this truly epochal event before 1995.[10] Hypertext was a playground clearly founded by the enthusiastic descendants of those earlier twentieth-century movements called New Bibliography and New Criticism. While those children played around in their hypertextual fields, "serious" humanities computing remained located in library and archival technology, on computational analyses of various kinds, and on the closely related fields of textual editing and textual markup. And meanwhile W3 arrived on its own.

The period from 1993 to 1999 gains its peculiar shape and significance largely because of the crisis W3 brought to humanities computing. Critical discussion of hypertext and hypermedia explodes throughout cultural and literary studies, with interest now fueled in practical ways by various persons, including scholars like Jay Bolter and George Landow, who launched online hypermedia constructions of many kinds. Before W3, anyone interested in building computerized humanities tools or environments would have had to learn at least elementary programming. W3 ended that situation by making HTML (Hypertext Markup Language) the language of W3 documents. Developed by Tim Berners-Lee, HTML was a brilliantly simplified subset of SGML, whose basic rules could be mastered in a few hours. As a consequence, W3 quickly burgeoned, with people throughout the world putting up terabytes of web pages and documents of all kinds. Into that expanding universe of textuality moved a small army of literary students and scholars to create an array of sites designed for various scholarly and pedagogical audiences.

Nearly all of these materials were viewed with varying degrees of skepticism or scorn by "the humanities computing community." And with good enough reason since that community had been trying for decades to develop rigorous analytic tools within a traditional milieu of work controlled by careful standards and peer review. These new materials, by contrast, usually appeared from nowhere, the brainchildren of some spontaneous overflow of powerful feeling in a particular person here or there, even a particular scholar. Idiosyncrasy ruled the World Wild West, including its humanities subset. W3 encouraged people to make and send forth digital things on their own initiative and in their own ways.

The upside of these events was the coming of a large and diverse population of new people into digital fields previously occupied by small and tightly connected groups. More significantly, they came to build things with digital tools rather than simply to reflect abstractly on the new technologies. This general situation was replicated in humanities disciplines at large. In addition, because W3 was from the beginning of its public life strongly visual rather than textual in character, humanist scholars and students brought a multidisciplinary and multimedia set of interests to the sites they were building and visiting.

Humanities Computing at the University of Virginia: 1992–1993

Insofar as humanities computing existed at the University of Virginia in 1993, it was located at the periphery—in an initiative taken by librarians at the Alderman Library to found an Electronic Text Center. Because few faculty were involved in this initiative, and none directly, it began as a speculative institutional venture—a kind of bet made by the library that the center would attract interest and use by the faculty. This center, which flourishes today, was to be an instrument for creating and disseminating electronic texts of various kinds and in many disciplines for the use of students and scholars in class and in research work. The center began its work at a minimal level, all but invisibly to the campus at large, in 1992. It is now the largest disseminator of online humanities texts in the world.

Later that same year IBM approached UVA's computer science (CS) department with an offer of $1 million in equipment for educational use over a three-year period. Two CS faculty members, Alan Batson and Bill Wulf, contacted two humanities professors, Ed Ayers and myself, to see if IBM's offer might be useful to people in the arts and sciences division of the university. A small committee was formed of these four people plus Kendon Stubbs (the Associate Librarian and chief architect of the library's Electronic Text, or E-Text, Center) and two other CS people. Out of that committee was formed what would become the Institute for Advanced Technology in the Humanities (IATH).

Because IATH came into being fortuitously, its shape and focus evolved through a randomized state of affairs. To see this let me reset the scene at UVA in late 1992:

(1)   The library's E-Text Center was begun as an independent initiative.
(2)   The grant from IBM had not been sought by the library or by anyone in humanities.
(3)   Ed Ayers and myself were only casually acquainted and neither of us knew, before the establishment of the committee that created IATH, that we each had some interests in humanities computing.
(4)   The CS faculty who initiated the committee did not have in mind any clear plan for what to do with the IBM offer, nor did they have any close (let alone working) relations with Ed Ayers or myself. When I joined the committee I knew no one on it other than Ed Ayers.
(5)   Kendon Stubbs joined the committee only after it was initially formed, and at my suggestion (because I had learned from him about the recent founding of the E-Text Center).

I give that list to emphasize the relatively atomized state of affairs when the committee was formed. That loose situation would prove an asset, for it ensured that the committee didn't begin its work in the context of a coherent institutional history or a strong set of prevenient ideas about humanities computing.

The Idea of IATH

The question to be answered by the committee was this: "What should be done with IBM's offer?" Ed Ayers and myself were invited to join the committee because the CS faculty, to whom IBM had made the offer, thought the equipment might be put to best use in the arts and sciences division rather than in the engineering school. As a result of this remarkable act of intramural collegiality (and imagination), this CS-run committee was charging itself only in relation to humanities educational needs. The object was to use the IBM offer to initiate a major change in humanities education at UVA.

The overwhelming initial answer to the central question was that the equipment should be made available as soon as possible to all arts and sciences departments for as long as possible. One person, Alan Batson, held out against that position. He argued that to move in this way would be to replicate a known history of 30 years of failure. A genuine engagement between humanities education and computer technology would not get beyond word processing if this model were adopted, Batson argued: "Throwing IT resources at people who have no special interest in them or desire to exploit them doesn't work. We know this because whenever we've done it during the past 30 years the results have been minimal at best." (Those are not exactly his words, but as Thucydides said of his *History*'s reported conversations, I'm giving the substance of what he said.)

Batson's model was different: to seek out projects with demonstrable intellectual importance for humanities scholarship and to fund those projects as completely as possible with the technical resources the projects need. His rationale: "Educational change at the level of the university is driven by the active research work of the faculty. Changes in pedagogy and classroom dynamics follow from research."

After an intense meeting in which Batson held his position against the rest of the committee, his view prevailed. Further meetings refined and modified Batson's general model. The idea of IATH thus became formulated in the following set of charges:

(1) Each year offer fellowships to UVA faculty who submit humanities research proposals to IATH. These should not be proposals for IT teaching initiatives but for scholarly research projects that use IT tools. Successful applicants become fellows of IATH for one year. They are given a one-year release from teaching plus complete technical support for their projects.

(2) Try to ensure a diverse, interdisciplinary set of research fellows (rather than a set of closely related projects).

(3) Require that the department of the successful fellowship applicants contribute materially to the fellow's work—specifically, by supplying the fellow with one or two graduate students to work on the research project and helping, if possible, with securing release time from teaching.

Two important ideas organize this plan for IATH. First of all, the plan assumes Batson's view that the educational work of a university is driven by its research activities. This idea does not imply that pedagogy is a secondary or less important university function—quite the contrary. But in a university environment students have to expect that their courses and classrooms will be organized in terms of the most up-to-date and adventurous scholarly work—work generated from research agendas that establish the standards and touchstones for a field. In the ideal university setting, a dynamic relation operates between the scholars' research work and the classrooms where it is tested, explored, and modified.

Thus one of our key expectations in founding IATH was that its research projects would become gravity centers drawing the attention of other faculty and the interest and work of students. The graduate assistants of the research fellows, it was believed, would themselves become gravity centers affecting other graduate students and undergraduates. In this way IT resources would begin to be exploited in all of the university's educational activities, in the instructional and in the research work of faculty and students alike.

Second, the plan for IATH assumed that IT tools would only be taken up by humanities faculty who had an active interest in using these tools in their primary areas of scholarly work. Simply giving equipment to faculty and offering technical support would have a minimal effect, as the dismal history of such efforts in the past has demonstrated. A steep learning curve defines the shape of one's involvement with these tools. Learning to use them is in one respect not unlike learning a new language. You may gain a certain minimal competence fairly quickly, but if your goal is more ambitious—in this case, to exploit these tools for advanced research work—a deep and long-term investment is required.

The problem with developing serious work in humanities computing is complicated by two additional factors. IT tools are in such a volatile stage of development that to use them well one has to remain vigilant about the current state of a wide range of technical resources. This takes time, real effort, and, perhaps most of all, a collective environment. Given the institutional structure of higher education, indexed by the tenure system and its measures of scholarly work, scholars—even tenured scholars—may reasonably conclude that their interests are not served by these tools. It is a fact that right now one can function most efficiently as a university scholar and teacher by working within the paper-based system we inherit. (This moment, this "now," is quickly passing away.)

In face of such a situation, IATH was founded as a resource for people who had already made a commitment to humanities computing, a commitment defined practically by an actual project with demonstrable scholarly importance. There were to be no outright gifts in the arrangement. Everyone involved in a fellow's appointment to IATH would have to make some material commitment to the work.

The hope, the goal, of this plan was a transformation of humanities education at UVA. It didn't take five years before we knew that we had succeeded far beyond what we had expected or even, speaking for myself, what we had imagined as possible. In five years the two initial research projects proliferated into more than two dozen. These included projects begun by graduate students as well as regular faculty and library staff. Faculty from more and more university departments became IATH fellows and enriched the institute's work: projects in music, art history, linguistics, architecture, urban planning, religion, archaeology, and so forth. Important work being done by scholars outside UVA gravitated to IATH because of its resources and lively intellectual scene.

The hope that the institute's research orientation would catalyze important pedagogical initiatives was also realized. After a few years IATH moved to support certain teaching-oriented initiatives that were driven by serious research agendas. In addition, the institute worked hard to help its fellows exploit the classroom potential of its research projects—a potential that extended well beyond the university to include K-12 education as well. As a consequence of all this activity, in 1995 the university established its Teaching Technology Initiative (TTI), a program organized to provide IT resources and technical help to faculty and teaching staff. Similar resources were being made available through the library's E-Text Center.

A crucial factor in UVA's involvement with humanities computing was the close liaison that was fostered from the start between IATH and the library. Nothing illustrates the depth of that liaison more than the library's decision to clear out more than 2,000 square feet of its floor space to make room for IATH's faculty and staff offices. This close working relationship expanded the university's research activities in remarkable and innovative ways. Some of the most important theoretical work in humanities scholarship is now being undertaken by faculty, graduate students, and library staff working in collaborative groups.

Finally, the remarkable success of IATH resulted in major part because its work from the outset was consciously developed in relation to W3. When John Unsworth was appointed as director in 1993, his first move was to ensure that the institute's projects were designed for web dissemination. Pursuing that direction in 1993 was to move against nearly every current in humanities computing scholarship, which was dominated by "stand-alone" ideas and technologies (epitomized in the early and short-sighted choice of CD-ROM as the venue for carrying humanities texts and hypertexts). In this situation we see once again the cultural influence of book paradigms on the new digital environments. Or, one should rather say, a certain view of books and book culture—a view defined, as I've already noted, by ideas drawn from New Bibliography and New Criticism. The convergence in 1993 of digital technology and W3 changed the shape of things, and not least the shape of humanities computing.

The Rossetti Archive and the Theory of Scholarly Editing

Under Unsworth's direction, then, the institute's work shifted in various ways from its initial conception and charges. Projects conceived by non-UVA scholars were invited to come to the institute if they brought their own funding, and certain interesting pedagogical projects were taken on board after several years. Most significantly, Unsworth invited important IT projects, especially web-based projects, to locate themselves, or instances of themselves, on the IATH server.

On the technical side, a major challenge for the institute and its fellows was to pursue long-term, large-scale humanities computing research projects with an almost ascetic rejection of the surface effects and short-term gains offered by proprietary software and proprietary data standards. In an apparently paradoxical way, IATH's W3 commitment drove its projects to make rigorous logical design a fundamental goal. This pursuit reflected a dedication to portability and the abstraction that enables it—even if it also entailed doing without good tools for creating or disseminating the scholarly work in the short run. As it happened, that commitment was to induce a profound shift in the principal focus and goals of *The Rossetti Archive*— moving it, in fact, from an editorial project per se to a machine for exploring the nature of textuality in more general and theoretical ways.

The character of the two initial IATH projects—*The Rossetti Archive* and Ayers's *Valley of the Shadow*—would exert a continuing influence on the direction of IATH's work in general. Both projects operated with large datasets of textual and visual materials. In addition, the texts in these projects were often handled both as alphanumeric data and as digital images. The image-based approach to the data was especially marked in *The Rossetti Archive* because, of course, Rossetti was not only a painter and visual artist; he was a poet who wrote under a horizon of book design and book illustration.

But what precisely was involved in *The Rossetti Archive*'s image-based approach to its materials? I can pose this question now because the hindsight of seven years has exposed how loosely and unselfconsciously we undertook our work with digital images. To unpack the import of that question is to begin exposing all the issues and problems that are the subjects of this book.

The Rossetti Archive was conceived within the context of a technological tradition that stretches across more than two millennia. I speak of the period when scroll, book, and other textual instruments were developed as tools for communication, information storage, and critical reflection. Perhaps the most sophisticated of these machines were the ones invented and refined by so-called textual scholars: text machines—the best known being the book—for preserving and studying forms of cultural memory, including texts themselves. *The Rossetti Archive* was undertaken as a practical effort to design a model for scholarly editing that would have wide applicability and that would synthesize the functions of the two chief models for such works: the critical edition (for analyzing the historical relations of a complex set of descendant texts with a view toward locating accumulated linguistic error); and the facsimile edition (a rigorously faithful reproduction of a particular text, usually a rare work, for scholarly access and study). The purpose of marrying these two kinds of scholarly instruments was based in a theory of textuality that was seriously underdeveloped 20 years ago. The theory holds two positions: first, that the apparitions of text—its paratexts, bibliographical codes, and all visual features—are as important in the text's signifying programs as the linguistic elements; second, that the social intercourse of texts—the *context* of their relations—must be conceived an essential part of the "text itself" if one means to gain an adequate critical grasp of the textual situation.[11]

That view of texts and the textual condition explains why the initial conception of *The Rossetti Archive* took shape well before we began our actual work on the project. In fact it came around 1983, when I was teaching at California Institute of Technology. That year I published *A Critique of Modern Textual Criticism,* which was the first in a series of works aimed at dislocating certain theories of textuality that dominated scholars' conceptions of their two principal disciplinary tasks: textual editing and textual interpretation. That same year I was introduced to UNIX computing systems and to hypermedia. With the convergence of these twain I knew that when circumstances were right I would undertake building a computerized hypermedia model for scholarly editing. Building the archive would articulate a powerful argument for the view of textuality I wanted to promote. The chance arrived when IATH arrived.

We spent the year from 1992 to 1993 theorizing the methodology of the project and designing its logical structure. Then in 1993 we built the first small demonstration model of *The Rossetti Archive,* which at that time I described in the following general terms:

> Like the work of Blake, Burns, and other important artists and writers, Dante Gabriel Rossetti's work is difficult to access or to edit for access. Expressive forms that work in or with visual and auditional materials do not lend themselves to the paper-based formats of traditional scholarship. Under such conditions, a more flexible medium is required.
>
> *The Rossetti Archive* has been developed in response to this situation. The scholarly models it builds have a particular applicability to artists and writers who seek to exploit and explore the expressive potential of more than one medium. We have been especially interested in developing critical tools for studying visual materials, as well as textual materials with a significant "visible" component. Concentrating on the linguistic codes of textualities, readers and even scholars regularly give scant attention to the physique of texts. But all texts deploy a more or less complex series of bibliographical codes, and page design—if not page ornament and graphic illustration—is a rich scene of textual expression.
>
> Computerized tools that deploy hypermedia networks and digitization have the means to study visual materials and the visibilities of language in ways that have not been possible before. This archive was built to harness

those capabilities, and Dante Gabriel Rossetti was chosen because the diversity of his work puts the goals of such a project to a serious test.

Rossetti's work was executed in two different media, visual and textual, and his work in each is intimately—and often explicitly—interconnected. The relations are clearest, perhaps, in those works where he made pictures for poems or other texts he had already written—like "The Blessed Damozel"—or in works where he made texts to accompany or comment upon pictures he had executed—for example, the sonnets he wrote as extensions of the meaning of his first important painting, *The Girlhood of Mary Virgin*.

That basic complexity in Rossetti's work gets deepened and elaborated because of the centrality of Rossetti's work in recovering the poetic culture of the "Early Italian Poets" of the twelfth to the fourteenth centuries. The connections between Rossetti's so-called original work, both written and pictorial, and his translations of Dante and his circle are pervasive.

Finally, Rossetti's work habits were such that these structural complexities of his art and writing get vastly extended. Rossetti was an obsessive reviser of his written work, and these revisions were carried out at every level of the writing: He worked and reworked words, phrases, passages, and he rearranged "finished" units into dizzying sets of variant organizational units. The difficulties come into sharp relief as soon as one considers any of Rossetti's works: say, the 1870 *Poems;* or "The House of Life," which was a subunit in that volume; or the introductory "Sonnet" to "The House of Life," which first appeared as part of the sonnet-sequence of "The House of Life" only in 1881. Rossetti followed the same kind of revisionary habits when he was painting and drawing.

All these features of Rossetti's work pose a complex and hitherto unsolvable editorial problem. One cannot properly study or appreciate Rossetti's work without having access to all of it. Even an introductory selection presents serious difficulties, because one needs to combine two media together and one also needs to present the materials so that the complex relations of all the parts are preserved. One easily understands why Rossetti's work has never been comprehensively edited and why the separate parts of his work are themselves available for general study only in the most limited ways. Virginia Surtees's standard catalogue of *The Paintings and Drawings of Dante Gabriel Rossetti* is excellent but quite incomplete. And to this day the "standard" edition of the writings is the 1911 *The Works of Dante Gabriel Rossetti,* edited by Rossetti's brother, William Michael. The writings have never been critically edited. As a result, their nervous structural features can only be encountered in scholarly periodicals and monographs.

A hypermedia computerized environment allows one to overleap these problems, which are a function of editing that has to be carried out in the framework of the book.

In *The Rossetti Archive* all the works are available for study in facsimiles of their original documentary forms. This means that the user has access to all his original manuscripts, printed texts, drawings, designs, and paintings. Since Rossetti designed his own books, one can appreciate the importance of reading his work in its original documentary states. And since the archive preserves these original materials in full color facsimile as necessary, one can see the great advance computerization makes in this case over Surtees's catalogue (which reproduces Rossetti's images in black and white). Furthermore, computerization allows the editor to connect all of Rossetti's documents to each other so that their relationships can be examined and better understood.

Finally, these authorial materials are embedded in a context of related documents, historical and critical, that help to illuminate the primary materials as well as their cultural context. The archive has incorporated, for example, various contemporary materials that are important for understanding Rossetti, pre-Raphaelitism, and the world in which they emerged and developed. The archive has included *The Germ,* William Michael Rossetti's early biography of his brother, as well as William Michael's 1911 edition of the works, H. C. Marillier's and Frederick Stephens's commentaries on the art, and other crucial contemporary documents (Swinburne, Buchanan, Pater, etc.). Also included is a large corpus of the photographs by which Rossetti's work was disseminated. As the archive is further developed, this body of material will be expanded. It is all marked for full electronic search and analysis. It is also supplemented by the present editor's critical essays, notes, and commentaries. The latter, of course, draw upon the considerable corpus of scholarship and criticism that has evolved over the past century on Rossetti, his circle, and their general historical milieu. (http://jefferson.village. virginia.edu/rossetti/introduction.html)

One can easily see, from this later vantage, how well that description reflects the state of humanities computing in 1993, when the TEI implementation of SGML markup was beginning to take serious hold, when hypermedia models were gaining widespread attention, and when W3 was scattering text and image constructions of many kinds across the globe.

Beginning Again

Because *The Rossetti Archive* was conceived and pursued, early on, as much as a kind of thought experiment in the theory of texts as an editorial project per se, it kept a constant focus on reflexive attention. I refer not only to the standard and highly pragmatic critical processes that regulate the design and building of any kind of tool or instrument. Of course we were constantly constructing the archive, testing what we had implemented, modifying what we had done, and then rescaling the level of implementation. Beyond those critical operations, however, the archive held our interest as a theoretical instrument for investigating the nature of textuality as such.

This inertia in the project broke out as a series of related texts. I wrote these reflexive pieces between 1993 and 2000 as expositions and critiques of our work, and all but one, the dialogue on "The Alice Fallacy," were originally published as online research reports. Writing the first set of these pieces between 1993 and 1996 brought a new level of clarity to what we were doing; and one of these, "Imagining What You Don't Know: The Theoretical Goals of The Rossetti Archive," marked a turning point in the project as a whole. It argues that to make anything is also to make a speculative foray into a concealed but wished for unknown. The thing made is not the achievement of one's desire; it is the shadow of that desire, the sign of what the poet spoke of as "something longed for, never seen." Writing that essay ushered the project of the archive to a new level of operation. It also initiated the project of this book: that is to say, the decision to draft careful written records of the critical stages in the making of the archive.

The work of those writings has been recomposed into the parts of this book, which is organized around a double vanishing point. In one perspective appears a set of related but independent explorations into the characteristics of different kinds of textualities. In another, one follows a kind of metanarrative or critical history projecting a map of future scholarly operations. We begin to explore that relatively unentered territory in the final section of the book, where the project of *The Rossetti Archive* mutates into an entirely different set of critical and scholarly demands.

These demands arise naturally—this is now clear, as it was not clear in 1993—from the way in which the project was first conceived. As a model constructed to reflect on its own process of development, the archive proved acutely sensitive in two directions at the same time: to changes taking place in the encompassing field of digital media, and to the traditional needs of humanities scholars working out of paper-based models of textuality.

Because W3 browsers had just become available, John Unsworth urged me to build the first model of the archive in HTML for web dissemination. Doing that was essentially an act of handicraft, for in 1993 we were primarily involved in discussions about how to design an SGML structure for all of *The Rossetti Archive*'s materials, visual as well as textual. The latter was to be a complex logical structure—in contrast to the HTML-marked demonstration model. One wants to hold this initial situation clearly in mind, for the contradiction between the web demo model, a simple visual interface built in HTML, and the archive itself, a set of logical relations and determinants conceived in SGML, would surface repeatedly in all our work.

Briefly, then: As we built the archive we kept encountering variations on a pair of difficulties. Both are functions of the special character of humanities materials, which are not primarily informational materials. They are made for reflective and imaginative purposes—in Rossetti's case, textual and visual works made for such purposes. Hence came our recurrent set of difficulties. First, neither the SGML markup structure nor the hypermedia design were able to integrate the textual and visual materials beyond elementary connecting, sorting, and gathering operations.[12] Second, the archive's principal objects of study—Rossetti's works—were not being interpretively exposed by the computational tools in very interesting ways. Computerization made much more information (and much more varied information) available—vast amounts of data in forms, relational as well as facsimile, that were previously unimaginable. As a tool for rethinking these materials, however, whether through structured or randomized searches of the data, the computer continually disappointed the high hopes it had raised. The archive includes a great deal of critical and reflexive materials in itself, but these materials are simply linked to the primary materials in an elementary, if also elaborate and complex, hypertext organization.

Nothing illustrates the practico-theoretical weakness of this situation more dramatically than the brave new world of hyperfiction. Armed as they are with remarkable technical resources, the works of this new genre pale in complexity before their paper ancestors: early works like *The Metamorphoses, The Arabian Nights, The Saragossa Manuscript,* or recent ones by Joyce, Riding Jackson, Borges, and of course the whole OULIPO contingent and its numerous contemporary offspring.

The example of hyperfiction may well locate a temporary condition.

We have no reason to doubt—indeed, we have every reason to expect—that remarkable imaginative works will appear in digital forms. Traditional imaginative texts developed and mutated over a long period of time and in many different environments. Hyperfiction and video games are early explorations and experiments, and if they seem primitive next to analogous works we inherit through predigital traditions, the same cannot be said of digital art, which has already developed sophisticated forms. Success in this case comes, of course, because digital imaging procedures feed upon the rich fund of electronic media that has emerged over the past hundred and more years. Traditional textualities have not been in a position to exploit ' such media until very recently.

I bring up these matters not to pass out digital merits and demerits to people working in different areas of the arts and humanities but to locate that part of the field where we have advanced hardly at all—indeed, where we have made few serious efforts to advance. More than anything else, the making of *The Rossetti Archive* has exposed the gulf that stands between digital tools and media, on one hand, and the regular practices of traditional philosophy, "theory," hermeneutics, and arts/literary/cultural criticism, on the other. Digital culture is virtually (!) an obsessional topic in all these fields, but it is a topic addressed from a distance, as a kind of fascinating and/or threatening alien form. That distance gets marked with unmistakable clarity in one way: the discursive procedures in all of these fields remain to date resolutely paper-based.

Works like *The Rossetti Archive* or *The Perseus Project* or *The Dickens Web* are fundamentally archival and editorial.[13] They gather, sort, and make things accessible, and they link these things to related things. Unlike works imagined and organized in bibliographical forms, however, these new textual environments have yet to develop operational structures that integrate their archiving and editorial mechanisms with their critical and reflective functions at the foundational level of their material form, that is, *at the digital/computational level*. Although structural coding in SGML (or XML) mitigates this deficiency to a certain degree, it is not only difficult and time-consuming to implement, but its hierarchical principles and other design characteristics set permanent and unacceptable limits on its usefulness with arts and humanities materials. Thus, however primitive hyperfiction and video games may seem, we recognize their functional relation to their underlying digital processes. In this respect they are more advanced in a practico-theoretical point of view than any of the IT-based scholarly works mentioned above. This is particularly the case with video games.

The difference implicitly traced in this discussion, between the scholar/editor, on one hand, and the critic/philosopher, on the other, was once far less sharply drawn than it is in our day. In ages and circumstances when hardly any distinction pertained between works of criticism/reflection and works of art/imagination—cultural conditions that produced the Bible, *The Book of Odes, Mahabarata,* and the works of Sophocles, Aeschylus, Lucretius, and Dante—the work of scholarship and learning was also much more integrated. Jerome, Augustine, Aquinas, Politian: All were figures of immense cultural authority. But then came the worlds of J. G. Eichhorn and G. W. F. Hegel and, later, Karl Lachmann and Friedrich Nietzsche. Two of those four names are forgotten except among circles of textual specialists; two maintain their cultural celebrity. That difference marks a notable shift in social and historical circumstances that has occurred during the past 200 years. Our digital culture is likely to reverse that difference. A hundred years from now, which of the following two names is likely to remain pertinent to traditions of critical thinking and which will seem merely quaint, if it is recalled at all outside pedantic circles: Vannevar Bush, Harold Bloom?

   For historical scholars of any kind, figures like Bloom index a serious disciplinary and cultural crisis. The digital revolution has pushed us to the brink of a great age of editorial and archival scholarship. This is plain to see—if one cares to look at all. For the past 200 years, however, the central work of cultural reflection and criticism has grown increasingly divorced from that kind of editorial scholarship. Nietzsche's critique of philology and historicist method marks the point at which the original rapprochement between what philologists called the "Lower Criticism" and the "Higher Criticism" was destroyed.

   In our day the authority of this Nietzschean break has greatly diminished. Modern computational tools are extremely apt to execute one of the two permanent functions of scholarly criticism—the editorial and archival function, the remembrance of things past. So great is their aptitude in this foundational area that we stand on the edge of a period that will see the complete editorial transformation of our inherited cultural archive. That event is neither a possibility nor a likelihood; it is a certainty. As it emerges around us, it exposes our need for critical tools of the same material and formal order that can execute our other permanent scholarly function: to imagine what we don't know in a disciplined and deliberated fashion. How can digital tools be made into prosthetic extensions of that demand for critical reflection? This is not a question to be addressed in speculative or conceptual terms. To count as adequate today, in this culture, responses to the question—most especially theoretical responses—require the deployment of computational instruments. Paper-based forms like this book can now, I think, only come to assist in a process of exploration and study that will henceforth be determined by digital forms. The next generation of literary and aesthetic theorists who will most matter are people who will be at least as involved with *making* things as with writing text.

These kinds of issues won't be usefully engaged without reconsidering certain fundamental problems of texts and textuality. The critical possibilities of digital environments require that we revisit what we know, or what we think we know, about the formal and material properties of the codex. We shall see that the advent of digital tools promotes this kind of critical reflection and leads to a view of books and of language itself that breaks with many common and widely held ideas. We shall see how, in a pragmatic as well as a theoretical perspective, the normative form of language is most usefully approached not as informational and expository but as poetic and polyvalent. Though informational and expository models of language have been taken as normative for more than three centuries, they are in fact specialized models, sophisticated derivatives. They were installed to facilitate certain instrumental tasks. We shall also see how texts deploy complex visible codes—how printed pages function both in semantical and imagistic ways—and how the executable codes (algorithms) of computational devices have much to tell us about the functioning structures of traditional textual devices. Finally, we shall trace in these investigations the discovery of a graduated series of critical moves that were generating unapparent consequences. These mutate under different topical conditions and then get reinvested as new critical opportunities.

The completed form of this essentially stochastic critical process comes in the final section of this book. At that point we lay out a model for a procedure of critical thinking that calls for digital implementation. This model appears in "The Ivanhoe Game," whose origins lie in the concealed pressures that drive and sustain the more immediate reflexive goals of this book's purely textual investigations. The game, which is procedural and structured for random turns of event, will be formally described, its prehistory will be documented, and its digital existence forecast.

Part I

Hideous Progeny,
Rough Beasts: 1993–1995

Attempting to be more than Man we become less said Luvah
As he arose from the bright feast drunk with the wine of ages.
                                        —*William Blake,* The Four Zoas

Haud ignara loquor; these are nugae, quarum
Pars parva fui, but still art and part.

                                        —*Byron,* Don Juan

1993: The year of the emergence of W3 involved a crucial moment of intersection with my own work, although at the time I was scarcely aware of the connections. Those points of relation are central to the arguments of this book.

That year saw the publication of the last volume of my critical edition of Byron, a project I had been working on for 22 years. Also published that year was *The Textual Condition,* the last of a series of six books I wrote and published during the previous ten years, beginning with *A Critique of Modern Textual Criticism* (1983). These were written to establish a broad foundation for a materialist program of sociohistorical hermeneutics and textual criticism. Pursued as highly organized and even systematic projects, both the Byron edition and the project in theory of texts inevitably had their fault lines exposed during the course of their development. Consequently, in the five years before 1993 I began to feel a need to turn critically on these projects and rethink them from the historical perspective that evolved during their development. This critical process centered in a series of dialogues that were written between 1988 and 1993. The last of those dialogues is the first chapter of this section of the book.

My argument begins, therefore, with a performative definition of the state of my thinking in 1993, just before I undertook *The Rossetti Archive,* about problems of scholarly method and aesthetic interpretation. Like its companion dialogues, "The Alice Fallacy" is an open-ended inquiry into current ideas about textuality, on one hand, and interpretive method, on the other. It is the most elaborately "performative" of those dialogues and was specifically written for dramatic presentation. (It had a theatrical performance at the University of North Carolina and two dramatic readings, one at the University of Virginia and the other at Stanford.)

In scholarly discourse, the dialogue form has several distinct virtues: It allows self-consciousness and self-criticism to be advanced as enactments rather than idea(l)s; and it opens its topics of discussion, as well as its treatment of those topics, to a playful and even a ludic treatment. The critical procedure has much in common with what Rossetti called an art of "the inner standing point," whereby an artist deliberately seeks a presentational form that assumes no privileges for itself. Nearly all aesthetic theory up to (and including) Marx argues that "art is not among the ideologies." Rossetti's view, which perhaps receives its most eloquent statement a half-century later in the work of Laura Riding Jackson, is very different and, from a critical perspective, very useful.

Even more than artistic practice, scholarship and philosophy pursue objectivity, so-called, and privileged discourse. If we would not devalue those commitments, neither should we imagine them as anything but useful heuristic procedures and strategies of persuasion. Objectively considered, objectivity is impossible. It is also undesirable if it stands in the way of another necessary commitment of scholarship and philosophy: self-conscious subjectivity.

Although unapparent at the time, this dialogue cast a shadow of futurity over the whole of this book's ideas, not least of all the ideas being pursued in "The Ivanhoe Game," the ongoing scholarly project discussed in the final section of the book. The importance of the dialogue got set aside almost immediately, however, when the chance came—fortuitously, as I've already noted—to build *The Rossetti Archive.* The latter brought the possibility of demonstrating the practical "truth" of the theoretical arguments about the nature of texts that I had been mounting since 1983. The demonstration would be the archive itself.

Aside from *The Rossetti Archive's* online descriptions and instructions for its users written between 1993 and 1995, chapter 2, "The Rationale of Hypertext" provides a first accounting of the general theoretical and methodological goals of the Rossetti project. It was deliberately written to solicit inquiry about the relation of paper-based critical forms—in particular the editorial forms that such criticism has taken—and the new digital forms. Even in 1993 one could see that designing a general purpose computerized model for critical editing was as much a theoretical undertaking—a thought experiment, in fact—as a concrete project to implement the design goals of the archive in a practical form. Nonetheless, building the archive significantly clarified some of its crucial theoretical assumptions and procedures. Not the least was the understanding that the praxis of editing—that is, being required to execute one's ideas in a determinate procedural (rather than merely conceptual) form—would alter the very ground and "theory" of theory.

"The Rationale of Hypertext" thus initiates this book's broad discussion of the theoretical relation of paper-based and digital semiotic environments. The degree to which paper-based textual models inform their digital instantiations has to be a regular object of critical attention if the aptitudes of digital instruments are to be exploited. Such attention is also useful for gaining greater insight into the functional structure of paper-based technologies.

Furthermore, the concluding discussion of "the decentred text" in chapter 2 contrasts the "open" structure of digital hypertexts with systems of textual closure built into most traditional paper-based scholarly editions. The immediate focus of that argument was the debate among editorial theorists about the possibility of creating, in scholarly form, the "social text"—that is, a critical edition that would not privilege the authority of one particular text or document. This debate erupted after the publication of my *A Critique of Modern Textual Criticism,* in which positivist approaches to editorial method were called into question. A persistent critique of the *Critique* argued that its "social theory of text," as it has come to be known, was unrealizable in practice. *The Rossetti Archive* was developed in major part to demonstrate the practical feasibility of the *Critique's* alternative approach to textuality and editing theory.

"The Rationale of Hypertext" is thus a coda to the *Critique.* It argues that textuality *as such* operates as a radiant and decentered structure. Hypertext theorists and creators of hyperficton began pursuing the idea (and practice) of decentered textuality in the late 1980s. One consequence of that important work—perhaps an unintended consequence—was to promote the view that digital forms were "open and interactive" whereas traditional textual forms were "static and linear." The library as model for a dynamic and decentralized system—indeed, as the model underlying the invention of the Internet—resists that way of distinguishing digital and paper-based textualities.

Thus, if in 1993 this essay was "a coda to the *Critique,*" it set the stage for further investigations into the functional structure of all forms of textuality and semiosis—investigations, in fact, that comprise the last five chapters of this book. This result ensued because "The Rationale of Hypertext" aspired to lay down a set of textual rules and ideas of the most comprehensive kind. The title of the original essay—preserved here—fairly declares its hubris. It alludes to and plays with the title of one of the foundational theoretical essays of modern textual criticism, W. W. Greg's classic "The Rationale of Copy Text."

"Editing as a Theoretical Pursuit" was the dialectical offspring of "The Rationale of Hypertext." In a chronological sense, it is the pivotal chapter of this book. It was written and rewritten over an extended period, beginning in 1995, when we were being forced through a series of difficult modifications in the design of the archive. These modifications generated a set of ongoing discussions, some formally organized but many occasional, about the theoretical goals of the project. Those discussions led in turn to a number of talks and papers I gave from 1996 to 1999 on the progress and problems of the archive as it was undergoing its development.

The paradigm of the situation, not discussed in this essay or elsewhere in the book, centers in our involvement with a university press from 1995 through 1999. This is a key story for several reasons, although I shall only give the briefest account of it here. First, it epitomizes a dominant theme of chapter 3—the last chapter of this first series—and of the book as a whole. John Unsworth has called this theme "The Importance of Failure." The story of our failure with the university press illuminates the scale of the issues that are always being engaged—whether one is conscious of the engagement or not—in projects of this kind. It proved an enlightening story for everyone at IATH since it showed so clearly how in experimental circumstances, difficulties and impasses arrive that are beyond everyone's imagining, good will, and control.

In 1994 we entered into an agreement with the university press to publish *The Rossetti Archive* online. This move was made because it served our research interests as well as the press's desire to develop its online publishing capacities. Publishing a large and complex project like *The Rossetti Archive* would be a useful practical testbed for the press. On our end, the relationship opened up a research area we would not have explored had we followed our original plan to publish the archive ourselves using the resources of IATH. That is to say, we saw the institutional aspect of the archive as an essential component of its research program. Because traditional scholarly books are published through a long-standing and well-developed set of institutional structures, the influence of those structures on the works produced is almost never examined in the works themselves. The structures are handled as if they were transparent, as if the works did not reflect their presence and influence.

The radical changes introduced into the publishing scene by digital technology removes that transparency. All aspects of a work's production are suddenly forced into sharp critical view, from issues of copyright to questions of publishing procedure and book design, logical as well as material, at every level. Just as we wanted to use the development of the archive as a practico-theoretical instrument for investigating the nature of texts and textuality, we saw our arrangement with the press as an opportunity for extending those investigations into the social and institutional aspects of the work.

As it turned out, after four years working together we were forced to break off our relationship. In January 2000 we set about our original plan to publish the archive ourselves, and seven months later we were able to bring out the first of our four planned installments.

It was a dismaying turn of events on all sides—a failure in fact—not least because our publication schedule was set back by a year and a half. Nevertheless, the failure brought with it important new understandings about what we were doing and trying to do. Working with the press for those four years we were caught up in yet another process of imagining what we didn't know. Online publishing, scholarly as well as commercial, is as certain as tomorrow's sunrise, but it won't come until it has been imagined into existence. The discipline of failure is essential to such an imagining.

Chapter 1

The Alice Fallacy; or,
Only God Can Make a Tree

A Dialogue of Pleasure and Instruction

Did you ever read one of her Poems backward, because the plunge from the front overturned you? I sometimes (often have, many times) have—A something overtakes the Mind—

—*Emily Dickinson,* "Prose Fragment 30"

[SCENE. The Faculty Club of a university. INSTRUCTION enters looking downcast, puts his papers on the bar and throws himself into a chair next to PLEASURE, who is reading. PLEASURE looks up from her book and smiles with cool amusement at her friend. Across the room is a bar at which two figures stand very erectly. They resemble waiters; they are FOOTNOTE and PRINTER'S DEVIL, respectively. A Brechtian sign stands over the bar and reads in large letters: INTERSPACE, which is the play space for the dialogues between FOOTNOTE and PRINTER'S DEVIL.]

INSTRUCTION. I need a drink. (Calling toward the bar.) Two vodkas, please.
[FOOTNOTE and PRINTER'S DEVIL bring the drinks and return to their places.]
PLEASURE. Another enjoyable and informative faculty meeting?
INSTRUCTION. "Pleasure and Instruction"—isn't that our *business?* Isn't it what poetry's supposed to deliver?
PLEASURE. We schoolmasters keep saying so, but who believes *us?* We're teachers after all, not players.

INSTRUCTION. How true. A little teaching is a dangerous thing. A lot is a disaster. Take me to the river. Drop me in the water.

PLEASURE. As bad as that, hm?

INSTRUCTION. Same as it ever was—a kind of moral sickness unto death, one more Great Awakening to righteousness and virtue.

PLEASURE. And what an odd symmetry at the moral extremes! Political or religious correctness, left or right, either will do. What *is* this need for a Codex Prohibitorum? We've got to get over it.

INSTRUCTION. How?

PLEASURE. We could go back to 1966, back to Susan Sontag. *Against Interpretation*.

INSTRUCTION. Her "erotics of reading," is that what you mean?

PLEASURE. One could do worse, one could have more Legions of Decency. Yes, an erotics of reading. "I'll call the work 'Longinus o'er a bottle,' / Or, Every [Critic] his *own* Aristotle" [Byron, *Don Juan*]. And we won't neglect instruction either.

INSTRUCTION. That's thoughtful.

PLEASURE. We'll have lots of commandments and "fallacies" and that sort of thing.

[INTERSPACE 1]

PRINTER'S DEVIL. What's this about fallacies and commandments? Is Pleasure serious? She seems to be contradicting herself.

FOOTNOTE. Maybe this is what it means to be beyond the pleasure principle. Not that Pleasure has much to do with principles. I guess she's just being silly. She's remembering that epidemic of 50 years ago when professors and critics started cranking out all kinds of literary "fallacies" as they called them—the intentional, the affective, the fallacy of imitative form. And there were "primers of modern heresy" and "defenses of reason" and all that sort of thing.

PLEASURE (resuming). It'll begin with a commandment forbidding students (and anybody else) to talk about ideas in literature until they show they can sight-read 50 lines of verse without sending everyone howling from the room.

I mean just think about what our classes have turned into! The "teacher" comes in and talks about (and about and about) some wonderful poem, say *The Rape of the Lock* or "Goblin Market." He (or she) burrows into the "text" and comes away with all those ideas and meanings it's been concealing from us—meanings it either contains (new critically) or locates (with cultural studiousness).

Or the teacher *doesn't* teach, he (or she) comes in and starts a ("Socratic") "discussion" by proposing some question, or by directing the class to talk about some passage or other that "problematizes" what we might think about the poem's "meaning." Then the class is encouraged to talk about it and we get a free-wheeling "discussion" of what the poem means, which is to say what everybody is thinking it means or it might mean. And the livelier the discussion the better the class seems to be, and when it's over everybody once again realizes how complex and rich poetry is, and how clever or how serious one has to be to read it.

About seven years ago the wickedness of all this suddenly "rose from [my] mind's abyss, like an unfather'd vapour"—as the poet once said. We were in fact discussing that very poet, Wordsworth, and that very passage in the *Prelude*. The class was talking in such animated ways about what it might mean that I began to feel they were losing hold of the poem's words as they raised up and tracked through great thickets of ideas. So I called a halt and asked a bright student to help clear the air. "George, read the passage for the class."

It was appalling. He stumbled across that splendid set of lines like "one that hath been stunn'd / And is of sense forlorn"—wrecking the phonemes, the phrasings, the entire play of the metrical scheme in its unfolding grammatical order. He couldn't *read the poem*. He could "read off" the poem and generate all sorts of ideas. But the oral delivery? It was a total crack-up.

Quel giorno piu non vi spiegammo avante. We just went around the class and everybody took turns reading or trying to read. It was an amusingly painful experience.

For the rest of that term we spent much of our classtime simply reading and rereading the printed texts and talking about these different performances. Everybody got better at reading, and not just because they were forced to practice recitation. They began deliberately to look at the words, paying attention to their parts as well as to the many kinds of physical relations that different passages of poetry built between the words.

An erotics of reading. Or call it interpretation through the performance of language—something like the way musicians interpret a piece of music by rendering the score. I'm bringing it into all my classes. The rule is that no one will raise questions of meaning unless he or she is prepared to perform the work. And if we're not ready for that, we spend our time reciting until we are ready.

INSTRUCTION. I like it. It makes me think of Blake's program for cleansing the doors of perception: "For man has clos'd himself up till he sees all things through the narrow chinks of his cavern" [Blake, *The Marriage of Heaven and Hell* plate]. That's to say, through embrained organs of attention and awareness. Recitation as a route back to the body in the mind, back through "the chief inlets of soul in this age," "the senses." PLEASURE. Sometimes I think it's best to work from poems that aspire to the condition of music—poems that work to collapse the distinction between the physique of their language and the content of their ideas: poems committed to what Shelley called "Intellectual Beauty." Poems like Shelley's own, "Which walk upon the sea, and chant melodiously":

> Life of Life! thy lips enkindle
> With their love the breath between them;
> And thy smiles before they dwindle
> Make the cold air fire; then screen them
> In those looks, where whoso gazes
> Faints, entangled in their mazes.
>
> Child of Light! thy limbs are burning
> Through the vest which seems to hide them;
> As the radiant lines of morning
> Through the clouds ere they divide them;
> And this atmosphere divinest
> Shrouds thee wheresoe'er thou shinest.
>
> [Shelley, *Prometheus Unbound*]

That's on Mondays, Wednesdays, and Fridays. On Tuesdays, Thursdays, and Saturdays I think we're better off reading Pope or Byron than Shelley or Christina Rossetti—poems where the thought seems so clear we can easily neglect its articulate energies:

> Ovid's a rake, as half his verses show him,
> Anacreon's morals are a still worse sample,
> Catullus scarcely has a decent poem,
> I don't think Sappho's Ode a good example,
> Although Longinus tells us there is no hymn
> Where the sublime soars forth on wings more ample;
> But Virgil's songs are pure, except that horrid one
> Beginning with "*Formosum Pastor Corydon.*"
>
> [*Don Juan* I st. 42]

The schools are far too preoccupied with what young people should or shouldn't be thinking. Let's get back to the words, to the language—to the bodies of our thinking. I'm "against interpretation," I'm *for* recitation. And for memorizing. I want my students to memorize and recite. If they can do those things well, it's enough for me. For the time being at any rate.
INSTRUCTION. It's not enough, though I admit it makes a good start. It's not even *erotic* enough. Your "erotics of reading" stays too close to the shore of the physical senses. It makes for a charming and delicious ride, I grant you, but it won't satisfy an adult, full-fledged eroticism. We want more from our reading experiences. Let's head out to sea.

Go back to the classroom and think about it again. The worst that goes on there isn't what you're complaining about. The worst is the hypocrisy of it, the pretense to freedom of thought. Everybody knows that the thinking in these "discussions" is controlled by the agenda—maybe even the ideology—of the teachers. The best one can hope for is that the agenda be made explicit—so the students understand from the start that they're being taught to think in certain ways.

And the longest lesson of all is the old Platonic one—that poetry will be justified when it becomes useful to society. If it occurs to someone that "society" always seems to have very different opinions about itself, then what? Well, you "teach the conflicts."[1] But nothing has really changed, then, has it? We keep trying to make teaching and literature socially productive—the usual "war of the many with one." And so students keep turning into what their teachers have become—

[INTERSPACE 2]

PRINTER'S DEVIL. I don't get it. If you don't teach an agenda and you don't "teach the conflicts" of the different agendas, what's left to teach?
FOOTNOTE (rummaging around in some papers). These are Instruction's classnotes and syllabi. What a mess! It's a miracle if anybody learned anything from him. Instruction's all over the place, he can't even make up a common syllabus. There are no conflicts to "teach," no one's even reading the same books. There's just difference, going this way and going that.
PRINTER'S DEVIL. Maybe Instruction wants to stop teaching altogether.
FOOTNOTE. Maybe he *should* stop. He can't be doing a very good job.
PRINTER'S DEVIL. I think his classes are very popular.
FOOTNOTE. Right. And so students keep turning into what their teachers have become.

✦　✦　✦

INSTRUCTION (resuming). . . . moralists and utilitarians.

You were awakened one day when you realized how many of your students, how many of their teachers, couldn't *read*. Well here's the story of my awakening.

I was teaching Keats's "Ode on a Grecian Urn." I was running a Socratic discussion (so-called) and we were all having a splendid time. We were gradually unfolding the poem's delicate ironies, and I was leading them as well into the brave world of new historicist revelation.

[VIRTUAL REALITY appears. This is the audience. Jennifer, Christopher, Margaret, and Geoffrey are seated toward the front. INSTRUCTION turns and begins speaking, as if he were talking to his class.]

"And notice the word 'legend'; I mean in the line: 'What leaf-fringed legend haunts about thy shape.' Does the poem answer that question? Christopher, what do you think about that?"

"Well Sir, I'm not sure. I hadn't really thought about it."

"What *is* a 'leaf-fringed legend' anyhow, do you think? Margaret, can you tell us?"

"It's a strange phrase, Sir. To me a legend is a kind of fabulous but traditional story that people tell and retell. So I guess Keats is thinking back through the phrase 'sylvan historian,' as if to say that the Grecian Urn retells for us an old story or set of stories."

"Like the stories implied by the images on the urn, the images Keats redescribes for us in his poem?"

"Right."

"Yes, I think so too. But do you know about any other meanings for the word 'legend'?"

[Long silence]

"Geoffrey, how about you? Do you know any other meanings?"

"Uh, I can't think of any."

"Do you want to say something, Jennifer?"

"Well, when we were studying Shelley I read a passage I loved so much I copied it out. It's short, just a couple of lines: 'Like a child's legend on the tideless sand / Which the first foam erases half, and half / Leaves legible' ["Fragments from an Unfinished Drama," lines 152–154]. Now in that passage 'legend' means something like 'inscription,' doesn't it? And I think I'm right in remembering that people talk about 'legends' on coins and graves and things."

"Yes, that's exactly right. But does that meaning have anything to do with this poem?"

[Long silence]

"Well, what about the famous conclusion to the ode? 'Beauty is Truth, Truth Beauty. That is all / Ye know on earth, and all ye need to know.' Notice it's in quotation marks."

"You said yesterday that there are different possible placements for those quotation marks."

"Right, Chris. But what does that have to do with the problem we're talking about now?"

[Silence]

"Well, let's bracket out the question of the alternative punctuations of the passage, for the moment anyhow. Let's just think about the fact that some part of the text is being set off here as if it were a quotation."

"Like an inscription or something?"

"Exactly, Chris. Does that make sense for the poem?"

"Well, do you mean that we're supposed to think of the quotation as the 'legend' mentioned earlier?"

"What do *you* think?"

[INTERSPACE 3]

PRINTER'S DEVIL. How I hate that classic classroom move! That wide-eyed teacher's hypocrisy, talking as if he wanted his students to think for themselves. He's got his lively "discussion" in good train and he knows how to keep it going where it's supposed to go.

FOOTNOTE (checking through a pile of papers). I don't find any documentary evidence of that at all. What makes you think he's manipulating his class? Margaret's free to say what she wants. He can't know what she's going to say.

PRINTER'S DEVIL. He knows the class is trying to figure out a good answer, the *best* answer. He knows the class thinks he knows what that is, or knows at any rate the range of the best answers (ahead of time), or knows how to tell if an answer is a good one or not. So they're thinking on his terms and grounds.

FOOTNOTE. The discussion does run along in pretty predictable ways.

PRINTER'S DEVIL. It can't be a good sign that Instruction comes in with his telling questions at crucial points.

FOOTNOTE. But isn't he supposed to know the answers?

PRINTER'S DEVIL. What answers? Even Instruction knows you don't read poetry to get answers. That's the whole *point* of his coy question. He's pretending they're having a conversation and that it's free and open. He's pretending he isn't what he clearly is, a pompous know-it-all. So he asks his contemptible leading question—"What do *you* think?"

INSTRUCTION (resuming). "Margaret, you want to say something?"

"Suddenly it came to me. I mean, what *is* a Grecian Urn? It's like one of those amphora I saw when I was visiting the Getty Museum with my parents. And I remember some of them had *inscriptions* on them, and these inscriptions sometimes circled the neck of the urn, and often they would be decorated with ornamental leaves and things like that."

"Right."

"And so I think I know the answer to your earlier question, about whether the poem has an answer to *its* question about the 'leaf-fringed legend.' The answer is 'Yes'—in fact, the answer is literally that 'inscription' given to us as the poem's sententious conclusion about truth and beauty. It's wonderful."

We were all quite pleased with ourselves during this "discussion," as you may imagine. In fact, so far as I was concerned all we had left to do was mop up the details. That's when it happened.

"Well, does anyone have any other questions?"

[Pause]

"Sir, what's an 'Attic shape'?"

"Does anybody want to answer that question for Christopher? Geoffrey?"

"Well here it must be some kind of ghostlike thing, some old piece of memorabilia or whatever?"

[I smiling] "Why do you say that? I don't really understand."

"It's an *attic* shape, it's some kind of thing from an attic. I mean, it goes back to that line we began with: 'What leaf-fringed legend *haunts* about thy shape.' Keats is imagining some kind of moldy apparition whose features aren't too clear—something slightly ghoulish from the dead past, 'with brede / Of marble men and maidens overwrought.' I love those lines. This ghost is Keats's cobwebbed version of Mozart's stone guest, or Roger Bacon's Brazen Head, something like that. I love the puns on "brede" and "overwrought." Keats's 'Attic shape' is a pretty lively stone guest after all. And when Keats lets the ghost speak at the end—well, it's a kick! He must have loved making that final comic move, sending the whole thing up and over the top at the end."

[I smiling more deeply] "But Geoffrey, 'Attic' here doesn't *mean* what you're thinking. Keats's word means something like 'classical'; 'Attic' refers to Attica, in Greece.

"Oh. I thought Keats was thinking of an attic, like at the top of a house, under the roof."

"I know." [Smiling in an understanding way]

"Well it made sense that way to me. I mean, the poem is about old legends and haunting shapes. And where would you find an urn like the one in the poem? In a museum maybe, or buried somewhere, or left forgotten in some storeroom or attic. They didn't have garages in Keats's day, did they Sir?"

"No Geoffrey, they didn't. And while I do see the way you're thinking about the poem, it's just not possible. Keats is using the word in a specific way, it means 'classical.' Look at the text. Keats capitalizes the word to emphasize its particular reference to 'Attica' and ancient Greek civilization."

"Sir, couldn't it mean what Geoffrey says? I mean historically speaking."

"Well, Jennifer, yes it could—that is, technically. 'Attic' had both of those meanings, as well as some others, when Keats wrote his poem."

"Then what's wrong with Geoffrey's reading? It makes sense in the poem. And it even adds a whole new way of thinking about it. I like what it does to the poem, it makes it richer, wilder. Or it helps to explain that peculiar way Keats loads and even overloads his poems with figural effects: 'to set budding more, / And still more, later flowers for the bees.' Here the text is 'overwrought' not only because of that strange pun (and the equally strange one on "brede"). The word 'overwrought' works so well exactly because, in *one* sense, it appears to make so little sense in this poem. The style of the verse is cool and controlled. If I imagine the 'bold lover' 'overwrought' with his passion, the poem toys easily with this thought. It wants to play a game of passion 'far above' 'breathing human passion.' So it constructs images made not only of sounds ('Attic'/'attitude'; 'ear'/'endeared'), but of 'unheard' sounds and melodies. In this world the lover appears as it were unimaginably 'overwrought,' a verbal figure everywhere conjured in unexpected forms and antitheses ('Cold Pastoral').

"Look at that completely arbitrary juxtaposition of 'Attic' and 'attitude.' Sounds pull the words together, but their horizons of meaning never quite connect. And the verse doesn't stay to let the reader stabilize their surprising relations. Even stranger verbal creatures immediately appear ('brede,' 'overwrought'). The effect is finally uncanny, as if one had entered a purely magical space—a vitalist and metamorphic world. It's all apples and oranges. It's a garden that 'breeding flowers, will never breed the same.' In

Keats's gardens words miseginate ('brede'). Their relations and their offspring seem a kind of 'wild surmise' of a new world—a world far more
wondrous than the America that set Keats voyaging in his sonnet on Chapman's Homer."

"Well that's a remarkable set of imaginations, Jennifer. And I'm more
than a little surprised that Geoffrey's mistake about the meaning of the
word 'Attic' should have triggered those thoughts. Because so much of
what you say makes sense for anyone wanting to read Keats's poetry. I don't
know what to make of that. All I *do* know is that Geoffrey's meaning for
'Attic' is out of the question."

[INTERSPACE 4]

PRINTER'S DEVIL. So much for our instructor's pretense of catholicity.
What his talking head *can't* do, at any rate, is stop making sense. That's out
of the question.

INSTRUCTION (resuming). "Keats clearly intended it to mean 'classical.'
[Smiling at a happy thought] After all, if we go along with Geoffrey we'll
have to set up the Humpty Dumpty School of Criticism."

[Puzzled laughter] "What's that, Sir?"

"Don't you remember *Alice in Wonderland?* When Humpty Dumpty
tries to assign purely arbitrary meanings to certain words, Alice challenges
him about 'whether you *can* make words mean so many different things'?"

"But didn't Humpty Dumpty have an answer? Didn't he reply: 'The
question is . . . who is to be master—that's all.' It seems to me that Lewis
Carroll didn't take a position on the problem. Humpty Dumpty isn't talking foolishness. So why can't we go with Geoffrey's reading?"

"Well of course poetry wants to multiply meanings, but only within the
limits that are permitted by the poem."

[INTERSPACE 5]

FOOTNOTE. I wonder what he means by "the limits of the poem"?
PRINTER'S DEVIL. Not much. He's forgotten to think about that
thought, hasn't he? He throws it out, as if it were self-transparent. What
"limits," what "poem"? It's not as if Keats or anyone else had the authority to declare what they or it might be. When Blake and Shelley decided it
would be a good idea to take Satan as the hero of *Paradise Lost,* they

exploded those limits for good. But there never were any such limits. That's what upset Plato about poetry in the first place. That's why he wanted to throw the poets out.

FOOTNOTE. It's interesting that Instruction talks as if the poem were a person, as if it could give and take permissions. As if it laid down a law that it comprehended, or maybe embodied.

PRINTER'S DEVIL. He talks as if he were Jesus Christ himself, "like one having authority." He talks, he always talks, when he should be paying attention to the text of the Ode and to what his students are saying. He should be listening within the limits that are permitted by the poem.

INSTRUCTION (resuming). "And here 'Attic' in Geoffrey's meaning just doesn't make sense."

"Yes it does. It made sense to Geoffrey. And when he explained it, it made sense to me too. And it made more sense of the poem, and it made sense for Keats's poetry in general."

"It made *nonsense* of the poem! It's a travesty."

"Well then maybe nonsense is sometimes more sense. I thought poetry was *supposed* to open up doors of perception. Isn't that what you're always telling us, Sir? This reading opens up the poem in lots of new and interesting ways."

[Silence from the front of the room]

"She's right, Sir, it's as if Keats were playing with his subject, making sure it didn't kill itself with its own seriousness and classicism."

"Well, . . ."

"Actually, I like that reference Jennifer made to Keats's sonnet on Chapman's Homer. It made me think again about the mistake Keats made—confusing Cortez and Balboa. The mistake turns out to be a happy one—what's that phrase you like to use, Sir?—a kind of 'felix culpa.' I like Keats a lot more than Wordsworth and Byron just because his poems are so unguarded, so—full of surprises. You walk into a Keats poem and suddenly all things become possible. But Wordsworth seems so worried about losses and disruptions that he can't help making sure everything is organized. And Byron's deliberateness is positively fanatical. That's why his great hero is Lucifer, immortalized in his dark, unchanging splendour. Keats is always so fresh."

[As Jennifer is about to speak] "My goodness how late it's gotten! The period will be over in five minutes so why don't we stop now. I'm sure we can take up these subjects another time. —Next class, remember, we move on to Shelley. Read his 'Defence of Poetry' and Peacock's 'Four Ages of Poetry.' Make sure you check the notes in our text. These essays are difficult to understand."

"But Sir, what do you think—I mean about what we've just been saying?"

"Well, it's very interesting. I'll have to think more about it."

[VIRTUAL REALITY recedes; INSTRUCTION resumes his conversation with PLEASURE.]

PLEASURE. A pretty embarrassing experience.

INSTRUCTION. I was mortified. I still am. The only thing that kept me going for the next few days was remembering Whitman: "He most honors my style who learns under it to destroy the teacher" [*Song of Myself*]. And Jesus: "He who would save his life must lose it."

PLEASURE. So what did you do?

INSTRUCTION. I started trying to imagine new kinds of critical thinking. Remember Emily Dickinson's suggestion about reading poems backwards? It seemed like a good place to start. So I began reciting poems in reverse—just the words, just pronouncing the texts."

PLEASURE. An excellent thought.

INSTRUCTION. And then I started other kinds of exercises. I'd go to famous passages randomly. Say, *Macbeth*: "Be innocent of the knowledge, dearest chuck, / Till thou applaud the deed" [III:2]. Or Wordsworth (again): "To me the meanest flower that blows can give / Thoughts that do often lie to deep for tears" ["Ode. Intimations of Immortality . . ."]. Then I'd propose an arbitrary task—say, "Give a homoerotic reading of that text." The results were surprising—truly the Humpty Dumpty School of Criticism. The *Macbeth* passage turned out to be a wonderful Shakespearean joke, a Brechtian moment when the actors slyly reveal that Lady Macbeth is being played by a boy. And the "Intimations Ode" passage! It will never be the same for me, indeed the whole poem is "changed, changed utterly."

PLEASURE. By giving the Ode a kind of Platonic blow.

INSTRUCTION. Well that's the least of it, really. Let's say we just keep it from turning into an Ode to Duty. These kinds of critical moves free poetry from its obligations to the state and the state's representatives, the teachers: everyone who is presumed to know. Truly now one can begin to imagine "voyaging through strange seas of thought, alone"—or not alone. With others. Like all games, such readings work best when people play at them together.

And then after I worked hard at these kinds of exercises, I decided to try a full dress effort with something unlikely—

[INTERSPACE 6]

PRINTER'S DEVIL. There's something wicked happening here. Suddenly Alice has become Humpty Dumpty.
FOOTNOTE. Right. Those interpretive exercises Instruction talks about—they can't be serious. Do you think they were actual class exercises?
PRINTER'S DEVIL. They're jokes, of course. They're the exercises of his sick brain.
FOOTNOTE. Bad jokes.
PRINTER'S DEVIL. Deliberately bad, that's what makes the whole thing so irresponsible. Don't you see, he's manipulating those ridiculous signs to play out a play. Through this looking glass Alice undergoes a sex change. She becomes Humpty Dumpty—truly a full dress effort at something unlikely.

INSTRUCTION (resuming)—something important partly because it would seem so unlikely. I meant to set my sights high. I wanted a reading that could make a real difference in the way we go about our intercourse with poetry. And I didn't want something smartass and deconstructive, some gloomy "exposure" or negation of a canonical text, or whatever.

It took a while but one day I realized what I wanted. I wanted to read a poem that would help us begin reading poetry all over again. I wanted to go back to the beginning—or to some place that seems like a beginning. For me that meant one thing: Brooks and Warren's school anthology *Understanding Poetry*. I had to go back there and start all over again—back to the road not taken by the schools.

Frost says it makes a great difference when you decide between roads. He also suggests that once you make a decision and travel along, you can't go back again. And Frost was the darling of New Critical reading, as one can see from his dominant presence in *Understanding Poetry*.

But maybe that idea is just part of what comes with having taken a frostbound road in the first place. Maybe along another road one can go backwards or forwards or any old way one wants.

So back I went to *Understanding Poetry*. And I set off from the book's most crucial moment, the moment when it began to issue its Everlasting

Nay. I wanted to plant roses where Brooks and Warren's thorns had begun to grow. I wanted to redeem their time.

[VOICEOVER intones Joyce Kilmer's "Trees" while INSTRUCTION mouths the words.]

Trees
(For Mrs. Henry Mills Alden)

I think that I shall never see
A poem lovely as a tree.

A tree whose hungry mouth is prest
Against the sweet earth's flowing breast;

A tree that looks at God all day,
And lifts her leafy arms to pray;

A tree that may in Summer wear
A nest of robins in her hair;

Upon whose bosom snow has lain;
Who intimately lives with rain.

Poems are made by fools like me,
But only God can make a tree.

Now before I give my comments on this poem I want you to look at the essay that inspired me. You will recognize it I'm sure. Few of the critical pieces in Brooks and Warren's *Understanding Poetry* were more famous than their commentary on Kilmer's "Trees."

[INTERSPACE 7]

FOOTNOTE (handing a manuscript to PRINTER'S DEVIL). Here's the actual original. We can check it against what we're about to hear. I don't trust any of this anymore. I mean *really*. Joyce Kilmer's "Trees"!?

(INSTRUCTION begins reading from the manuscript)

"This poem has been very greatly deplored by a large number of people. But it is a good poem."

[INTERSPACE 8]

FOOTNOTE. Why go on, it's just a travesty, isn't it? The actual "original of the essay" begins: "This poem has been very greatly admired by a large number of people. But it is a bad poem." The game is to read black where Brooks and Warren read white.

PRINTER'S DEVIL. And so not a "positive image to a negative" but a negative to a positive. As you say, a travesty of Brooks and Warren.

FOOTNOTE. I suppose it all depends on where you stand. That's part of the point of Instruction's joke, isn't it—to turn Brooks and Warren's debunking "negative" reading of "Trees" into a positive act of appreciation. To develop the picture they took of Kilmer's poem and make a positive (re)print from it.

PRINTER'S DEVIL. Clever. But *is* it a good poem?

(INSTRUCTION resumes reading) "First, let us look at it merely on the technical side, especially in regard to the use Kilmer makes of his imagery. Now the poet, in a poem of twelve lines, makes only one fundamental comparison on which the other comparisons are based; this is the same method used by Housman in 'To an Athlete Dying Young.' In 'Trees' this fundamental comparison is not definitely stated but is constantly implied. The comparison is that of a tree to a woman. If the tree is compared to a woman—literary tradition weighs heavily here, as it does for so much modernist writing—the reader can't expect a consistent use to be made of the aspects of the woman which appear in the poem. . . ."

[PLEASURE. My God, what a sexist remark! Did Brooks and Warren actually write that?

INSTRUCTION. Hold your questions till I get to the end of this. We don't want to spoil the coherence of the argument with interruptions.

"Look at stanza two. [VOICEOVER intones stanza 2; INSTRUC-TION mouths the words.] Here the tree is metaphorically treated as a sucking babe and the earth, therefore, as the mother—an excellent comparison that has been made for centuries—the earth as the 'great mother,' the 'giver of life,' and so on.

"But the third stanza introduces a confusion [VOICEOVER intones stanza 3; INSTRUCTION mouths the words.] Here the tree is no longer a sucking babe, but, without warning, is old enough to indulge in religious devotions. But that isn't the best part of this confusion. Remember that the tree is a woman and that in the first stanza the *mouth* of that woman was the *root* of the tree. So now, if the branches are 'leafy arms,' the tree has metamorphosed in a very strange way. The poem's woman begins to appear an uncanny, a wholly imaginative creature.

"The fourth and fifth stanzas maintain the same anatomical arrangement for the tree as does the third, but they make other unexpected changes: the tree that wears a 'nest of robins in her hair' must be grown up, perhaps bejewelled; yet the tree with snow on her bosom is also a chaste and pure girl, or so the *associations* of snow with purity and chastity tell the reader; and then the tree that 'intimately lives with rain,' who is she? A chaste and pure girl? A woman vain enough to wear jewels? Our difficulties at this point have grown extreme. For this girl/woman, though living in an intimate relationship with someone ('rain'), also appears withdrawn from the complications of human relationships and might be said to be nunlike, an implication consonant with the religious tone of the poem.

"Now it would be quite pedestrian for the poet to use only one of these thoughts about the tree (1. the tree as a babe nursed by mother earth, 2. the tree as a nun praying all day, 3. the tree as a girl with jewels in her hair, or 4. the tree as a woman involved in an ambiguous sexual relationship) and to limit himself to a single metaphoric structure. The poem's success comes because the poet has tried to convey all of these features in terms of his single basic comparison to a woman. As a result, he presents a poetical image that has all the confused and metamorphic power so typical of modernist works of art and poetry.

"For a moment it may seem possible to attack the poem by pointing out its absurd romantic title, 'Trees,' with its implicit appeal to the consistencies of an organic approach to art: one tree is like the babe nursing at its mother's breast; another tree is a girl lifting her arms to pray, and so on. But this line of attack would damage itself more than the poem it seeks to denigrate: for 'Trees' is not consistent and romantic, it is modern and grotesque, and as such it refuses to provide any real or natural basis for seeing one tree as a babe and another as a devout young woman—and least of all for establishing a 'natural' consistency between those figures and the complex sexual being who emerges toward the climax of the poem."

PLEASURE. The essay is strangely familiar—like something often thought but never so well expressed.
INSTRUCTION. It ought to be required reading in our introduction to

poetry classes. I especially like the tact of its historical awareness. The authors don't belabor the point, but they lead us to see how important historical context must be for "understanding poetry."

[INTERSPACE 9]

PRINTER'S DEVIL. Clever. But is it a good poem?
FOOTNOTE. Maybe that's not the point at issue—I mean, whether "the poem itself" is good or bad.[2]
PRINTER'S DEVIL. What's the point then?
FOOTNOTE. I suppose Instruction wants to show up the fragile authority of even the most authoritative critical moves. Alter a few words and this famous foundational essay of twentieth century criticism changes from a duck to a rabbit. The arguments and evidence brought forward support antithetical readings.
PRINTER'S DEVIL. So Instruction wants to "teach the conflicts" after all!
FOOTNOTE. More than that, surely. He wants to generate the conflicts. Play the gadfly.
PRINTER'S DEVIL. As I say, "teach the conflicts."
FOOTNOTE. No, it's more aggressive, more like "teaching conflict" than "teaching the conflicts." Look carefully at those last remarks about "required reading" and "the tact of its historical awareness." They're corroded with an ironical attitude toward "introduction to poetry classes" and the modern founding fathers of those classes. And as for those founding fathers, well, Brooks and Warren made their reputations by a wholesale assault on historical awareness. Instruction isn't *sincere*. He has nothing but contempt for teaching and for understanding poetry.

INSTRUCTION (resuming). Not once do they tell us that Kilmer was editor of *The Dial,* for example, or that the poem comes out of the same period and place—New York in the teens of this century—that produced Stevens's *Harmonium.* Yet how obvious the connection must now seem to us! One thinks immediately of Stein's early cubist poetry, and we may even remember that *Tender Buttons* was published at exactly the same time as Kilmer's book.

But "Trees" has more in common, I think, with more traditional kinds of Modernist experimental writing. Surely the similarity of Kilmer's poem to Stevens's "Thirteen Ways of Looking at a Blackbird" is obvious! It isn't just the physical shape of the two works that recall each other, though that's very striking. Think of Stevens's disorienting and revelatory shifts of focus. These dominate Kilmer's poem as well, and the regularity of Kilmer's rhyme only makes the shifts more shocking. Besides, in Stevens's charming poem the romantic commitment to a specular order of attention is hardly violated, so that his poem has more than a trace of that "consistency" (properly) deplored in Brooks and Warren's hypothetical critique of "Trees." But in "Trees" the order of things is fractal and chaotic—an effect heightened exactly by the poem's seductive apparition of consistency.

Not that Brooks and Warren's essay has given the last word on Kilmer's poem. On the contrary, their reading's preoccupation with "technical" matters has caused it to misrepresent a key feature of the work and to miss altogether the literal meaning of the final two lines' climactic and defining moment.

PLEASURE. What do you mean?

INSTRUCTION. I'll explain by making a confession about the text of the essay I gave you. The truth is that I slightly altered what Brooks and Warren originally wrote. I did so to highlight something important that's missing from their reading.

PLEASURE. Go on.

INSTRUCTION. In the essay I gave you, whenever Brooks and Warren wrote "human being," I substituted the word "woman."

PLEASURE. Is *that* all?

INSTRUCTION. No, but it's important. Now I did this because "human being" is completely untrue to the meaning of the poem. "Trees" is not only written *to* a woman, its running human analogy is gendered female at every point. The subject of the poem is what Robert Graves would soon name "The White Goddess." So the title is apt—"Trees," not "Tree" or "The Tree."

PLEASURE. But the women in the poem appear so *un*mythic—despite what Brooks and Warren say about "the earth mother" and all that. So quotidian and, in one case—the baby girl I mean—so completely nonsexual. Think of Keats's La Belle Dame. *There's* the White Goddess! Kilmer's Trees are hardly pagan at all; they're too correct—too American and Irish-Catholic.

INSTRUCTION. You're deceived by one level of the poem's appearances. Think again. Think, for example, about the dedication to Mrs. Henry Mills Alden.

[INTERSPACE 10]

FOOTNOTE. That dedication line, incidentally, isn't reproduced in the text of *Understanding Poetry*. Brooks and Warren took it out, I guess, because they thought it wasn't part of "the poem itself."
PRINTER'S DEVIL. Is it?
FOOTNOTE. Of course, just as much as the title. But Brooks and Warren want to uncouple poems from their explicit historical connections. Removing this actual woman rarifies the poem. And these losses of textual reference tend to affect all the more concrete aspects of poetic language—for example, the signs themselves. The poem's signs slip loose from their physicalities—from their phonemic and rhythmic structure—and readers begin to treat poetic language as "a text," a conceptual organization, a play of Saussurean signifieds. It's important to see the particular woman standing among Kilmer's trees—Mrs. Henry Mills Alden.

PLEASURE. Who is she?
INSTRUCTION. Kilmer's mother-in-law, a woman who for years had moved at the center of the New York literary world. A poet herself, she married Henry Mills Alden—the editor of *Harper's*—when she was a young, aspiring writer and after a whirlwind three-month courtship. Their love sprang up when Mrs. Alden, then Mrs. Kenton Murray, submitted some poems to *Harper's*.
PLEASURE. So?
INSTRUCTION. You're so ignorant, all you care about are the surfaces of things! Read between the lines, behind the words! Mrs. Alden's obituary notice in the *Virginia Pilot and Norfolk Leader* (14 April 1936) describes her as "a woman of high intellectual attainments, of courageous spirit, and of marked personal charm." The significance of this language in that newspaper becomes clear when one recalls that her first husband had been editor of the Norfolk *Landmark*.

Furthermore, although married to Alden she continued to publish her poetry under the name Ada Foster Murray. (She was born Ada Foster and grew up near Huntington, Virginia—now West Virginia.)

In short, the words "Mrs. Henry Mills Alden" release the poem under the sign of a woman and a poet. More significantly, this person would be seen—we are looking from Kilmer's point of view—as a volatile and complex being. Brooks and Warren's remarks on the poem's inconsistencies are subtle glosses on the name standing at the head of the text. Look again at the text of the verse! Kilmer's Trees are populated by evanescent Ovidian figures. "Moving about in worlds not realized"—moving about the poem's forest of strange symbols—are "light winged dryads" whose presences we glimpse by oblique suggestion—as we glimpse them in Heine and Baudelaire, and in so many poet/painters of modern life: "Gods float in the azure air / bright gods and Tuscan" [Ezra Pound, *Cantos*]. From Poe to Pound, even North America did not free itself of that world. Mrs. Henry Mills Alden, upright and respectable, comes from that world.

The first sections of Kilmer's verse text are full of deliberate deceptions; so we only glimpse, by various stylistic plays of confusion and indirection, the poem's disturbing and erotic presences. In the end, however, they are presences that are not to be put by.

> Upon whose bosom snow has lain;
> Who intimately lives with rain.
>
> Poems are made by fools like me,
> But only God can make a tree.

All further commentary proves unnecessary as soon as we realize the startling sexual wordplay in the word "make." Kilmer descends to this kind of vulgarity only once in the poem. But it is a descent that must be made, a descent to coarse pagan earth. The descent is telling and overthrows the whole fabric. What did you say about Dickinson reading poems backwards? This word "make" unmakes the text, forcing us to read it all backwards: back over again, back against the deceptive inertia put in forward motion at the outset of the work.

But we are ready for this backward overthrow because—despite its appearances—the poem has never settled into its rectitudes. As Brooks and Warren were the first to notice, it is far too inconsistent and "confused" for that.

PLEASURE. But then the poem is some grotesque male joke—is that what you're saying?

INSTRUCTION. Not at all. As in "La Belle Dame Sans Merci" and so many similar poems, "Trees" is written out of a certain kind of male eroticism. After all, what else *is* the so-called myth of the White Goddess? But if this were all the poem had to offer—serving up another coarse of that myth—it would have scarcely arrived at the level of Keats's traumatic fantasy. What distinguishes Kilmer's poem is the fact that it is *God* who makes the tree. This literal (religious) fact can barely tolerate the extreme "opposite and discordant" suggestion introduced by the wordplay. In forcing that extremity upon us, the text leaps to an unspeakable imaginative level. The achievement recalls nothing so much as certain analogous moments in Lautréamont's *Les Chants de Maldoror*—for example, the great scene in Canto III when Maldoror narrates the story of God and his desolate strand of hair. I think Nietzsche wrote the moral for Kilmer's poem before Kilmer ever wrote the poem: "It is with people as it is with trees. The more they aspire to the height and light, the more strongly do their roots strive earthward, downward, into the dark, the deep—into evil" [*The Gay Science*, sec. 371].

This is a thought fully realized in Kilmer's shocking last couplet, where we come upon something far worse than a simple religious blasphemy. The coarse final wordplay doubles back upon the penultimate line, undoing the idea of *poiesis* itself. From the original sin committed among the trees of his little garden, Kilmer has imagined the adamic fall of the poem itself.

[*INTERSPACE* 11]

PRINTER'S DEVIL. How right you were about Instruction's insincerity. This is all an outrageous act of cleverness and self-display. Instruction tells a greater (and a worse) truth than he realizes when he turns Kilmer's wretched little verses into an allegory about "the adamic fall of the poem itself." His cynical games with poetry will be the death of poetry.

FOOTNOTE. Did you catch the sly allusion in that phrase? "The poem itself" is one of those word plays Instruction seems incapable of resisting. He's recalling another famous book from the period of New Criticism's hegemony, Stanley Burnshaw's *The Poem Itself*.

PRINTER'S DEVIL. So?

FOOTNOTE. I guess his reading wants to imagine "the fall" of a certain kind of "poem" or idea about poetry. In this sense his "allegory," as you call it, would be a historical allegory, not a transcendental one. Which makes sense, given his critical view of Brooks and Warren's (*un*historical) way of "understanding poetry."

PRINTER'S DEVIL. And what's Instruction's "way" of "understanding poetry"? It's to invade the texts and force them to turn nonsensical. Every critic his own Aristotle indeed!

FOOTNOTE. Satan as the hero of *Paradise Lost* is a nonsensical idea. But you gave it your good housekeeping seal.

PRINTER'S DEVIL. Yes, because its nonsense is useful. It helps to expose the contradictions that run through Milton's Christian mythology. In doing that, it helps to expose the structure of poetical discourse in general.

FOOTNOTE. As nonsensical?

PRINTER'S DEVIL. As incommensurable. What did Wilde say? "A truth in art is that whose contradictory is also true."

FOOTNOTE. I think your ideas have more in common with Instruction's than you realize, or admit. You have highbrow ideas so you want highbrow examples. That appeal of yours to Blake could have been made by our Instructor.

PRINTER'S DEVIL. Yes, but in his mouth it would have been a rhetorical *jeu,* a sign that poetical authority rests with him, with the meanings he sets in play. If I'm highbrow, he's just a vulgarian. Besides, the incommensurability of poetic discourse is for me one of its key *objective* features. That's a crucial difference between us. Another—it's even more crucial— relates to the fundamental unseriousness of Instruction's critical methods. And in truth how *could* he take himself or his ideas seriously! They're grounded in nothing beyond his own fancies—mere airy nothings, as fragile as himself, as all subjective criticism will always be.

FOOTNOTE. Or as Shakespeare?!

PRINTER'S DEVIL. What?

FOOTNOTE. I was just reflecting on your allusion to Shakespeare and *his* airy nothings, his poetry and his ideas about poetry. Maybe you shouldn't be quoting Shakespeare, or appealing to Oscar Wilde. You don't help your case.

PRINTER'S DEVIL. What are you thinking?

FOOTNOTE. I'm thinking about Instruction's "unseriousness," as you (rightly) call it. About how studied it is.

PRINTER'S DEVIL. Right. That mannered style is what stamps his thinking as irredeemably trivial. It doesn't even take itself seriously.

FOOTNOTE. But what if that's the point? What if the question isn't "*how* could he take himself or his ideas seriously" but "why *should* he take himself or his ideas seriously"?

PRINTER'S DEVIL. Explain please.

FOOTNOTE. Why do you, why does anyone, privilege "objective" values? Because they're imagined to have weight and substance, something more solid than mere personal ideas and subjective whimsies. When Instruction flaunts the fancifulness of his critical ideas, when he—in effect—turns them over to his friend Pleasure, he puts them in that "unsubstantial faery place / That is [their] fit home" [Wordsworth, "To the Cuckoo," lines 31–32].

In this sense, the deliberateness of his unseriousness would thus not be a "cynical" gesture, at least not in the usual sense we give that term. It would be a move to label the fundamentally subjective character of his criticism, and perhaps to suggest as well that all criticism—even criticism, like Johnson's, committed to objective standards—operates subjectively.

PRINTER'S DEVIL. So what else is new!

FOOTNOTE. Two things, perhaps. First, Instruction's game-playing assumes a formidable (double) standard for critical acts: a demand for a high level of reflective self-awareness, on one hand, and for a matching style and practice, on the other—for a sound that would be the echo of its sense. His triviality is significant exactly because it's so cultivated. He is labeling his proposals "modest."

PRINTER'S DEVIL. Or "indecent."

FOOTNOTE. Yes, modest and indecent both. It's Pleasure's ideal of an erotics of reading, a move "against interpretation." And the move is important because of the implicit challenge he's laying down. His criticism of "Trees" emphasizes the *rhetoric* of interpretation, so his studied triviality signals that he appreciates the difficulty of the reciprocal demand his challenge puts on us. He comes forward not as a master but as just another player. Or if he seems a master, his behavior emphasizes the mortal limits of mastery.

Second, the dialogue argues that meaning comes as acts of thinking (which may get reified into sets of ideas), and thinking comes as exchange of thought. All sorts of uncommon critical possibilities might flow from that view of things.

PRINTER'S DEVIL. Including the slaughter of criticism's innocence.

FOOTNOTE. A prophetic sign announcing a new day, perhaps, when we may repeat, in a finer tone, "the adamic fall of 'the poem itself.'"

INSTRUCTION (resuming). So a modest and even genteel irony turns corrosive. Aspiring to the height and light, Kilmer's poem discovers its damnation.

PLEASURE. If this is how one finds meaning in poems you could almost persuade me back to interpretation.

INSTRUCTION. Sometimes you do read your texts too simply. "Against interpretation," for instance. It's clear that you've let your enthusiasm carry you away. For the phrase has, I think, graces beyond the reach of the art you have in mind. You read the word "against" as a mere prepositional call to arms. And that's fine, I like that reading—even if it is pretty commonplace.

PLEASURE. Novelty isn't everything, my friend. What is it Byron says? "I care not for new pleasures, as the old / Are quite enough for me—so they but hold" [*Don Juan*].

INSTRUCTION. Well, what I like about that Byron remark—about Byron in general—is the cool, self-conscious way he approaches the pursuit, and the question, of pleasure. What did he say in *Childe Harold's Pilgrimage* about thought? Didn't he call it "our last and only place of refuge"?

Don't just *run* with that phrase "against interpretation," *think* about it. *Imagine* what you know. Suppose "against" were an adjective instead of a preposition.

PLEASURE. The Everlasting Nay becomes the Everlasting Yea!

INSTRUCTION. Ever the enthusiast. Suppose it were an adjective *and* a preposition.

PLEASURE. Then you would have invented what Xerxes wanted, a new pleasure.

INSTRUCTION. Or a new thought.

Chapter 2

The Rationale of Hypertext

To see a world in a grain of sand
And a heaven in a wild flower,
Hold infinity in the palm of your hand
And eternity in an hour.
              —*William Blake,* "Auguries of Innocence"

Or if it indeed be so, that this other Space is really Thoughtland, then take me to that blessed region where I in Thought shall see the insides of all solid things. . . . *In that blessed region of Four Dimensions, shall we linger on the threshold of the Fifth, and not enter therein? Ah, no! Let us rather resolve that our ambition shall soar with our corporal ascent.*
              —*E. A. Abbott,* Flatland. A Romance of Many Dimensions

Lofty reflections on the cultural significance of information technology are commonplace now. Tedious as they can be, they serve an important social function. Some distribute general knowledge to society at large, some send it to particular groups whose professional history makes information about information an important and perhaps problematic issue.[1]

Literary scholars comprise just this kind of group. If certain features of the new information technologies have overtaken us—for instance, the recent and massive turn to word processing—more advanced developments generate suspicion. When one speaks to colleagues about the emergence of the electronic library, information networks, or about the need and usefulness of making scholarly journals electronic, brows grow dark and troubled. And yet it is clear to anyone who has looked carefully at our postmodern condition that no real resistance to such developments is possible, even if it were desirable.

In this chapter I focus primarily on a particular feature of literary works—their physical character, whether audial or visible. I shall be pointing out why these features are important in a literary point of view and also sketching certain practical means for elucidating these textual features. This last matter is also the most difficult. The methodology I shall be discussing requires the scholar to learn to use a new set of scholarly tools.

One final introductory comment. My remarks here apply only to textual works that are instruments of scientific knowledge. The poet's view of text is necessarily very different. To the imagination the materialities of text (oral, written, printed, electronic) are incarnational, not vehicular, forms. But for the scientist and scholar, the media of expression are primarily conceptual utilities, means rather than ends. Scholars often seek to evade or supercede an expressive form to the extent that it hinders the conceptual goal (whether it be theoretical or practical). But good poets do not quarrel with their tools in this way, even when they are developing technical innovations. As William Morris famously observed, "You can't have art without resistance in the materials."

Here I shall work entirely within the terms of this distinction between a scholarly/scientific and an artistic/aesthetic point of view. Establishing the usefulness of the distinction is important, of course, for the purposes of this chapter's argument. But the same move will prove equally important in the later chapters of the book, in which I shall be working to explore the fault lines in this same distinction. As we shall see, efforts toward "rethinking textuality"—traditional as well as digital—are impeded by the uncritical assumption of the authority of this same distinction. We will come at a later point to see how this distinction functions and under what circumstances one might want either to assume it or to set it aside.

The Book as a Machine of Knowledge

Let us begin with the question "why": *Why* take up these new digital tools or seek new editing methods, especially when both tasks make such demands upon us? At this point most scholars know about the increased speed and analytic power that computerization gives and about the "information highway" and its scholarly possibilities. Major changes in the forms of knowledge and information are taking place. From a literary person's point of view, however, the relevance of these changes can appear to be purely marginal: for whatever happens in the future, whatever new electronic poetry or fiction gets produced, the literature we inherit (to this date) is and will always be bookish.

Which is true—although that truth underscores what is crucial in all these events from the *scholar*'s point of view: We no longer have to use books to analyze and study other books or texts. That simple fact carries immense, even catastrophic, significance. Until now the book or codex form has been one of our most powerful tools for developing, storing, and disseminating information. In literary studies, the book has evolved (over many centuries) a set of scientific engines—specific kinds of books and discursive genres—of great power and complexity. Critical and other scholarly editions of our cultural inheritance are among the most distinguished achievements of our profession.

When we use books to study books, or hard copy texts to analyze other hard copy texts, the scale of the tools seriously limits the possible results. In studying the physical world, for example, it makes a great difference if the level of the analysis is experiential (direct) or mathematical (abstract). In a similar way, electronic tools in literary studies don't simply provide a new point of view on the materials, they lift one's general level of attention to a higher order. The difference between the codex and the electronic *Oxford English Dictionary* provides a simple but eloquent illustration of this. The electronic *OED* is a metabook, that is, it has consumed everything that the codex *OED* provides and reorganized it at a higher level. It is a research tool with greater powers of consciousness. As a result, the electronic *OED* can be read as a book or it can be used electronically. In the latter case it will generate readerly views of its information that cannot be had in the codex *OED* without unacceptable expenditures of time and labor.

Scholarly editions comprise the most fundamental tools in literary studies. Their development came in response to the complexity of literary works, especially those that had evolved through a long historical process (as one sees in the Bible, Homer, the plays of Shakespeare). To deal with these works, scholars invented an array of ingenious tools: facsimile editions, critical editions, editions with elaborate notes and contextual materials for clarifying a work's meaning. The limits of the book determined the development of the structural forms of these different mechanisms; those limits also necessitated the periodic recreation of new editions as relevant materials appeared or disappeared, or as new interests arose.

So far as editing and textual studies are concerned, codex tools present serious difficulties. To make a new edition one has to duplicate the entire productive process and then add to or modify the work as necessary. Furthermore, the historical process of documentary descent generates an increasingly complex textual network (the word "text" derives from a word that means "weaving"). Critical editions were developed to deal with exactly these situations. A magnificent array of textual machinery evolved over many centuries.

Brilliantly conceived, these works are nonetheless infamously difficult to read and use. Their problems arise because they deploy a book form to study another book form. This symmetry between the tool and its subject forces the scholar to invent analytic mechanisms that must be displayed and engaged at the primary reading level—for example, apparatus structures, descriptive bibliographies, calculi of variants, shorthand reference forms, and so forth. The critical edition's apparatus, for example, exists only because no single book or manageable set of books can incorporate for analysis all of the relevant documents. In standard critical editions, the primary materials come before the reader in abbreviated and coded forms.

The problems grow more acute when readers want or need something beyond the semantic content of the primary textual materials—when one wants to hear the performance of a song or ballad, see a play, or look at the physical features of texts. Facsimile editions answer to some of these requirements, but once again the book form proves a stumbling block in many cases. Because the facsimile edition stands in a one-to-one relation to its original, it has minimal analytic power—in sharp contrast to the critical edition. Facsimile editions are most useful not as analytic engines, but as tools for increasing access to rare works.

Editing in codex forms generates an archive of books and related materials. This archive then develops its own metastructures—indexing and other study mechanisms—to facilitate navigation and analysis of the archive. Because the entire system develops through the codex form, however, duplicate, near-duplicate, or differential archives appear in different places. The crucial problem here is simple: The logical structures of the "critical edition" function at the same level as the material being analyzed. As a result, the full power of the logical structures is checked and constrained by being compelled to operate in a bookish format. If the coming of the book vastly increased the spread of knowledge and information, history has slowly revealed the formal limits of all hardcopy's informational and critical powers. The archives are sinking in a white sea of paper.

Computerization allows us to read "hardcopy" documents in a nonreal or, as we now say, a "virtual" space-time environment. This consequence follows whether the hardcopy is being marked up for electronic search and analysis, or whether it is being organized hypertextually. When a book is translated into electronic form, the book's (heretofore distributed) semantic and visual features can be made simultaneously present to each other. A book thus translated need not be read within the time-and-space frames established by the material characteristics of the book. If the hardcopy to be translated comprises a large set of books and documents, the power of the translational work appears even more dramatically, since all those separate books and documents can also be made simultaneously present to each other, as well as all the parts of the documents.

Of course, the electronic text will be "read" in normal space-time, even by its programmers: the mind that made (or that uses) both codex and computer is "embodied." This means that, from the user's point of view, computerization organizes (as it were) sequential engagements with non-sequential forms of knowledge and experience—immediate encounters with abstract or complexly mediated forms. If the limits of experience remain thus untranscended through computerization's virtual enginery, however, the new tools offer a much clearer and more capacious view of one particular class or "order of things"—in this case, the order of those things we call texts, books, documents.

Hyperediting and Hypermedia

The electronic environment of hyperediting frees one to a considerable extent from these codex-based limits. Indeed, computerization for the first time releases the logical categories of traditional critical editing to function at more optimal levels. But "editing" text through word processors is not, in the view being taken here, "hyperediting" because word processing engines are structured only for expressive purposes. On the other hand, the deployment of "hypertext" software should not be judged a necessity of hyperediting. The electronic *OED* does not use hypertext but it is certainly a hyperediting project. So too is the work initiated by Peter Robinson and the COLLATE program he has developed. To function in a "hyper" mode, an editing project must use computerization as a means to secure freedom from the analytic limits of hardcopy text.[2]

Nonetheless, hypertext programs provide the clearest model for hyperediting. Hypertexts allow one to navigate through large masses of documents and to connect these documents, or parts of the documents, in complex ways. The relationships can be predefined (as in George Landow's various "webs," like *The Dickens Web*) or they can be developed and pursued "on the fly" (through the relationships created in the SGML mark-up of a work). They are called hypermedia programs when they have the power to include audial and/or visual documents in the system. These documentary networks may or may not be interactively organized (for input by the reader/user). They can be distributed in self-contained forms (for example, on CD-ROM disks, like *The Perseus Project*) or they can be structured for transmission through the network. In this last case, the basic hypertext structure is raised to a higher power (but not to a higher level): a networked structure (say, W3) of local hypertexts opens out into a network of networks.

I rehearse these matters, which are familiar enough to increasing numbers of scholars, to remind us that the different purposes of different scholars determine the choice of an actual hyperediting procedure. The range of options also indicates that hyperediting should be seen as a nested series of operational possibilities (and problems). In my own view, for example, a fully networked hypermedia archive would be an optimal goal. Because such an archive of archives is not yet a practical achievement, however, one must make present design decisions in a future perfect tense. What that means in practice is the following: (1) that the hyperediting design for a specific project be imagined in terms of the largest and most ambitious goals of the project (rather than in terms of immediate hardware or software options); and (2) that the design be structured in the most modular and flexible way, so that inevitable and fast-breaking changes in hardware and software will have a minimal effect on the work as it is being built. In practice, then, one would not lock into a front-end hypertext system prematurely or choose computer platforms or hardware because of current accessibility. Similarly, one wants to store data in the most complete forms possible (both as logically marked-up e-text and as high-resolution digitized images).

Obviously this paper cannot deal with all these matters in any extended way. One topic will be paramount: the importance, as I see it, of organizing a hyperediting project in hypermedia form. Hypereditions built of electronic text alone are easier to construct, of course, but they can only manipulate the semantic level of the original work. Hypermedia editions that incorporate audial and/or visual elements are preferable since literary works are themselves always more or less elaborate multimedia forms. When Pound spoke of the three expressive functions of poetry—phanopoeia, melopoeia, and logopoeia—he defined the optimal expressive levels that all textual works possess by their nature as texts. Texts are language visible, auditional, and intellectual (gesture and [type]script, voice and instrumentation, syntax and usage).

The Necessity of Hypermedia

The most direct way to show this need is through a set of examples. In these illustrations I shall move from a straightforward presentation of the elementary material demands raised by texts, to the more complex interpretive issues that those demands create.

Example A

First, then, think about songs and ballads—think in particular about Robert Burns's ballad "Tam Glen." For a text we might turn to what is now widely regarded as the definitive (so-called) edition of Burns, the Kinsley/Clarendon Press edition, where the ballad is printed from a manuscript text sent by Burns to James Johnson, who first published it in his collection the *Scots Musical Museum* in 1790. Kinsley's (like Burns's and Johnson's) is a text for the eyes, and because the text of this essay is also typographical, I could easily reproduce it here.[3]

Yet the ballad interested Burns exactly because it was an auditional text. Under different circumstances I could give a reasonable reproduction of that ballad. I could play for you an audio version of, say, Jean Redpath singing the ballad to a score imitating the ballad as Burns might have heard it sung. Or I could play for you Andy Stewart's "version" of the ballad, or others as well.

The words of "Tam Glen" were in fact written by Burns, though the air for it is traditional. Many of the texts in Kinsley's edition of Burns, however, are hybrid works fashioned by Burns from Scots songs he collected and then modified, more or less drastically.[4] Burns did not hesitate to make his own changes in these works because in collecting his Scots songs he heard many versions. The ones he himself published, and the texts that come down to us through an edition like Kinsley's, do not represent the kinds of variety Burns would have known.

Besides, contemporary performances probably stand far removed from what Burns must have originally heard. In this sense, the Kinsley/Clarendon Press printed text is perhaps truer to its (printed) textual tradition than contemporary performances could be to their oral traditions. Nonetheless, if our primary care is toward preserving the original materials in a living way, could anyone prefer a paper text of such a work to an audial text?

"But that question compares apples and oranges," you will say. "The tape is the equivalent of a popular, a modernized, an 'uncritical' text. It is good for what it does, of course, but it cannot be imagined as a model for replacing what one gets in a complete critical edition like Kinsley/Clarendon."

Then let us go further: Would anyone who had it to choose prefer the Kinsley/Clarendon edition of Burns's complete works to an equivalent edition based primarily on audial texts?

Burns's work is grounded in an oral and song tradition. Paper editions are incompetent to render that most basic feature of his verse. (The same might be said, incidentally, of much of the work of Thomas Moore—a lesser writer than Burns altogether, of course, but a central romantic figure nonetheless, and one who has suffered badly from the inability of scholarship to preserve the memory of his work in living forms.)

The point is not to denigrate the Kinsley/Clarendon edition, which is in fact a model of scholarship. It gives us not only good reading texts, it supplies us with an apparatus, a glossary, excellent notes, and—a very nice feature—a few bars of sheet music for each text, so that we can hum up in our minds the memory of the original tunes. And all this in three volumes.

"Yes. And to have the equivalent in an oral form would take many tapes or disks. Besides, those musical documents wouldn't be able to organize and interrelate the audial materials the way the Kinsley/Clarendon edition has done with its textual materials—the way any good critical edition will do."

But what if one could do that? What if one could have a critical edition of Burns's work in audial forms that allowed one to engage the songs in the same kind of scholarly environment that we know and value in works like the Kinsley/Clarendon edition? An environment allowing one to navigate between versions, to compare variants, an environment able to supply the central documents with a thick network of related critical and contextual information that helps to elucidate the works?

What if one could do that? The point is, we can.

Example B

When I was asked to edit the *New Oxford Book of Romantic Period Verse* I wanted to print texts that stayed as close to the original ones as possible. I also wanted to print a good deal of the most characteristic and popular work of the period, as well as work (for example, Blake's) that only came into prominence at a much later time.

So I wanted color facsimiles of Blake and color facsimiles of a poem like William Roscoe's "The Butterfly's Ball and the Grasshopper's Feast." And I wanted to print one of the most popular and important satires of the day, William Hone's "The Political House that Jack Built," with the original (and closely integrated) Cruickshank illustrations. And I had other similar ideas. As it turned out, various commercial and institutional circumstances shot down most of these plans. All that remains of them is a facsimile of the wonderful Hone/Cruickshank satire.

The *New Oxford Book* is a reader's edition, not a critical edition. Nonetheless, it is a reader's edition sieved through a scholarly conscience. To give adequate reading texts of Blake, then, it ought to have given us color facsimiles. The edition doesn't do that, and it is less than I had hoped as a result. Of course the edition does many other things, and does them (I hope) well. Its unusual organization is something not every press would have permitted, especially in such a well-established series. But in the matter of visual materials, the edition's limits are clear.

I give this example partly to foreground the technical, commercial, and institutional realities that determine what scholars can do in book forms. We have already glimpsed such determinants in the example from Burns. The present example reminds us how poetical texts frequently use the visual features of their media as part of their imaginative field. Just as Burns's poetry almost always exploits the language's auditional forms and materials, Blake's almost always exploits the print medium for expressive effects. A text of Blake's *Songs,* for example—whether critical or otherwise—that does not at a minimum give us a color facsimile, is simply an inadequate text.

These two examples may stand as paradigms for a whole range of textual materials that scholarly editing to this point in time has not dealt with very well. We have had many fine editions of ballads and songs since the late eighteenth century, but none has been able to accommodate, except in minimal ways, the auditional features of the texts. Similarly, expressive typography and other visually significant features of book design have been handled to date in facsimile editions, which rarely—and never adequately—incorporate critical and scholarly apparatuses into their structure. The failure to meet the latter needs is especially apparent in the work produced during the periods I have been most involved with. The renaissance of printing that took place in the late nineteenth century utterly transformed the way poetry was conceived and written. In England, William Morris and D. G. Rossetti stand at the beginning of a poetical history that to this day shows no signs of abatement. The evolution of the modernist movement could (and at some point should) be written as a history of book production and text design.

These developments in England and America trace themselves back to William Blake, whose work was put into circulation and made historically significant largely through the efforts of the pre-Raphaelites, especially Rossetti. Blake's work thus forecasts the massive opening of the textual field that took place in the nineteenth century, when image and word began to discover new and significant bibliographical relations. Technological breakthroughs like lithography and steel engraving are more than causes accelerating these events. They are the signs of a culture-wide effort for the technical means to raise the expressive power of the book through visual design.

An adequate critical representation of such work has to this point been seriously hampered by the limits of the book as a critical tool. To date, for example, it has been impossible to produce a true critical edition of the works of Blake. Because Blake's texts operate simultaneously in two media, an adequate critical edition would have to marry a complete facsimile edition of all copies of Blake within the structure of a critical edition. One needs in such a case not a critical edition of Blake's work but a critical archive. This archive, moreover, must be able to accommodate the collation of pictures and the parts of pictures with each other as well as with all kinds of purely textual materials. Hypermedia structures for the first time make this kind of archive possible; indeed, work toward the development of such a Blake archive is now underway.

The problem of editing Blake's work in a thoroughly critical way is not peculiar to Blake's idiosyncratic genius, however; it is symptomatic and widespread. To show how and why this is the case I offer three further examples, all from the nineteenth century. The first and third involve authors as famous as Blake, Emily Dickinson, and William Wordsworth. The second will also be brought forward under an authorial sign, the once-celebrated poet Laetitia Elizabeth Landon. The examples of Dickinson and Landon will show the structure and extent of the editing problems already glimpsed through the example of Blake's work. We conclude with a discussion of the historical significance of the most recent critical editions of Wordsworth.

Example C

It has taken 100 years for scholars to realize that a typographical edition of Dickinson's writings—whether of her poetry or even her letters—fundamentally misrepresents her literary work. A wholesale editorial revaluation of Dickinson is now well under way. A particularly telling example appeared recently in an article by Jeanne Holland on the Dickinson poem "Alone and in a Circumstance." Holland's facsimile reprint of the poem shows a work structured in a close, even a dialectical, relation to its physical materials.[5]

Dickinson set up a kind of gravitational field for her writing when she fixed an uncanceled three-cent stamp (with a locomotive design) to a sheet of paper and then wrote her poem in the space she had thus imaginatively created. Whatever this poem "means," the meaning has been visually designed—more in the manner of a painter or a graphic artist than in the manner of writers who are thinking of their language in semantic or— more generously—linguistic terms.

One could easily multiply instances of this kind of text construction in Dickinson's work. As we know, she refused what she called "the auction" of print publication. All of her poetry—including those few things put into print during her lifetime without her permission—was produced as handicraft work. This means that her textual medium is treated in the writing process as an end in itself—ultimately, as part of the aesthetic field of the writing. Again and again in Dickinson's work we observe her using the physique of the page and her scripts as expressive vehicles of art. In an age of print publication, manuscripts of writers tend to stand in medias res, for they anticipate a final translation into that "better world" conceived as the printed word. In Dickinson's case, however, the genres that determine the aspirations of her work are scriptural rather than bibliographical: commonplace book writing, on one hand, and letter writing, on the other.

To edit her work adequately, then, one needs to integrate the mechanisms of critical editing into a facsimile edition—which is precisely the kind of thing that codex-based editing finds exceedingly difficult to do.

Example D

Here I shall turn to another kind of text—apparitionally very different, but finally closely related to Dickinson's work. Before we look at it, however, some preliminary comments may be useful.

The nineteenth century is famously the age of the novel. Quantities of verse continued to be written and read, of course, and the period has more than its share of poets who were either very important or very successful or both. Nonetheless, it is a commonplace that the period approximately defined by the deaths of Byron on one end and Tennyson on the other was a great age of fictional prose.

This decline in the cultural fortunes of poetry, if in fact such occurred, has often been connected to the explosion of late romantic sentimental verse, a kind of writing typically associated with women or a feminized imagination. Dickinson, we know, became a great poet by exploiting and modifying the sentimental tradition that so evidently supports her work. In the version of this tale told by the ideologues of modernism, Dickinson did not simply exploit and modify the tradition, she exploded it altogether and escaped thereby into greatness.

Like most such tales, this last inscribes a highly moralized fiction on a body of evident fact. For example, probably the most important venue for nineteenth-century poetry were the gift books and annuals that began to appear in the early 1820s and that dominated the market until late in the century. Scores of these works were produced, though now we remember them, if at all, in terms of a very few: *The Keepsake, Bijou, Forget-Me-Not*. Literary history pigeonholed them years ago. They became a synonym for bad and sentimental writing and to this day remain—properly too—an index to the feminization of culture.[6]

An equivalent textual condition develops in the world of nineteenth-century fiction. The genre of the novel underwent a great transformation as a consequence of new methods of producing and distributing these works. This story is now well-known. Suffice it to say here that serialization (in its many forms) and the triple-decker format had a decisive impact on the character of fiction writing. These and other new transmissional mechanisms not only gave authors fresh opportunities to change and revise their works, they complicated the fictional options in other ways as well. The illustrated novels of Dickens and Thackeray are simply the most outstanding examples of the generic changes being brought about through new methods of book production.

Out of this cultural context emerged one of the most distinctive minor genres of the period: the poem on the subject of a painting or picture. The form would be elaborated in remarkable ways by the pre-Raphaelites, and in particular by Rossetti, but it began much earlier. Good examples can be found throughout the early nineteenth century, but it was not extensively developed until the advent of the period of gift books and annuals. At that point the form undergoes a distinct mutation, as one can see by comparing (say) a poem like Wordsworth's "Peele Castle" elegy with the picture-poems of Laetitia Elizabeth Landon. In Landon's work, Wordsworth's psychologically dynamic form passes beyond (perhaps also through) the Keatsian and Shelleyan process of aestheticization so brilliantly analyzed in Arthur Hallam's essay on Tennyson's early poetry.[7] What is dynamic and psychological in Wordsworth becomes formal and literal in Landon and, after Landon, in Tennyson, whose early poetry is clearly written out of the same kind of sensibility.

The queen of the annuals, Landon was obliged to write a great many poems for pictures, and her work nicely illustrates the two dominant stylistic procedures encouraged by the genre. First is the poem that tries to render, more or less faithfully, the details of the picture's imagery. To this is added, or interwoven with it, an interpretive element. Some of Landon's best known works are of this kind: for example, "A Child Screening a Dove from a Hawk," after Stewardson, and "The Enchanted Island," after Danby.

Both of these poems are from Landon's 1825 series "Poetical Sketches for Modern Pictures" (published in the volume *The Troubador, and Other Poems*). Because the texts were originally printed without accompanying engravings, we might think that a scholarly edition now could suitably forego reproducing their related pictures. The opposite, it seems to me, is true. Wordsworth's Peele Castle poem, for instance, does not absolutely need its picture, is not integrated into its visual materials the way Landon's poems are. For her part, Landon has not just written poems after pictures that have moved her, she has written picture poems for an audience whom she expects to be familiar with the pictures. In each case we are dealing with something very different from Wordsworth's "picture of the mind" ("Tintern Abbey" 61). Wordsworth takes his picture from an imagination of the individual person—ultimately, from the figure Wordsworth made of himself in his verse. By contrast, Landon's individual—her figure of herself—is everywhere represented in her work as a function of social codes and attitudes. In this respect her work recalls Burns's: Though many of his songs were printed without (sheet) music, they nonetheless bear their music in their heart, like the original solitary reaper, and they expect their audience to be familiar with that music. (On the other hand, Burns stands closer to Wordsworth to the extent that his audience has forgotten or lost touch with those songs.)

Many—perhaps even most—of Landon's picture-poems were printed with engravings of the pictures. This happens because of the generic character of the gift book, which was primarily organized around its visual materials. Texts, both prose and verse, were written in relation to pictures rather than (as in illustrated editions of Scott or Dickens) the other way round. A typical example comes in *The Keepsake* for 1829: Landon's untitled piece written after Landseer's portrait of *Georgiana, the Duchess of Bedford* ("Lady, thy face is very beautiful").

As with much of Landon's best work, these lines evolve a kind of antipoem that self-consciously exploits its own factitiousness. Much could be said about its mannered poeticality, the work's false elegancies that startle and disturb the reader from the outset—as the word "very" in the first line emphasizes. But I leave such readings for another more appropriate time. Here it is sufficient to see, and to say, that the poem properly exists in the closest kind of relation with the actual picture, as Landon's socioeconomic treatment of her subject emphasizes. Furthermore, in this case art's relation to the economics of class, so central to Landseer's original painting, receives a full bourgeois reinscription.

The textual situation here is subtle and complex. Proceeding from the semantic wordplay in the line "But thou art of the Present," we begin to observe the relationship that this work is fashioning, in every sense, between text and picture. For instance, at the semantic level the poem simultaneously reflects upon its nominal subject, the duchess, and addresses its real subject, the "art of the Present." For Landon's poem is not written on the duchess or painting so much as on the relation of the two. As such, the most important subject of all is neither duchess nor painting, it is *The Keepsake* itself and its (reproduced) engraving.

Here one wants to recall the fact that Landseer's fame as an artist was largely secured through the engravings that broadcast his work rather than through the original oils. *Georgiana, the Duchess of Bedford* is "of the Present" in several senses, all of which are important to Landon. But most important are the contemporary artistic representations of the duchess— the painting, the engraving, and now Landon's poem, the last two being framed and represented in *The Keepsake for MDCCCXXIX,* which is how the title page reads. Signifiers of Beauty come forward here in a self-conscious, perhaps even a shameless, state of artistic exhaustion. Completely integrated, the engraving, the poem, and the book correspond precisely to what Marx would shortly call "the soul of the commodity."

The picture-poem was a characteristic form in gift books and annuals, which often constructed themselves around sets or groups of pictures rather than collections of texts. Contributors were asked to write poems *to* specific pictures, just as novelists of the period were asked to write novels in three volumes, or in a sequence of episodes of a certain number and size. Under such circumstances, the poets all but completely abandoned the usual romantic conventions of sincerity. If the conventions appear at all, as they often do in Landon, they tend to come like ghosts, conscious of their afterlife. Tennyson's *In Memoriam* is the epic of all such writing.

In this example from Landon I have allowed myself to range beyond bibliographical issues into interpretive commentary. I have done this because literary history has long invisibilized Landon and the gift book traditions she used. And yet it is a historical fact that for 50 years and more that tradition was a dominating influence on imaginative writing that exploited relatively brief forms (like lyric and short story). Indeed, it could easily be argued that Landon wrote in and through the single most important (and institutionally based) poetic genre of the period. Even more interesting, this genre was not a conceptual form (like epic, sonnet, or the novel) but a material one: the gift book and literary annual. As we know, "serious" people long ago stopped reading writers like Landon and Felicia Hemans. But their work will perforce become difficult to understand if we do not receive it in forms that at least approximate its original imaginative condition. In Landon's case, the pictorial and ornamental context of gift book production can be torn away from her work only at the cost of its destruction.

The example of Landon therefore culminates my answer to the question of "why" one would want to exploit hypermedia environments in scholarly work. I submit that no edition aspiring to represent the kinds of textual situation we have been examining would be happy with the removal of any of the materials, or—what often happens—with the translation of concrete textual features into those thin, abstract presences: a bibliographical notation or a scholar's narrativized description. I submit further that every critical and scholarly edition will be—has been—forced into such abstractions when it aspires, *within the physical constraints of a traditional book format,* to a comprehensive treatment of its materials. The more complex the materials, the more abstract and/or cumbersome the edition becomes.

Example E

In this case I ask you to recall the Cornell Wordsworth, in particular the three volumes devoted to *The Prelude:* Stephen Parrish's edition of the "Two Book" *Prelude* (1977), W. J. B. Owen's edition of the "Fourteen Book" *Prelude* (1985), and Mark Reed's edition of the "Thirteen Book" *Prelude* (1993). All three are models of their kind, meticulous and thorough. Nonetheless, in their heroic efforts to represent that original complex and unstable scene of writing, these editions—*coming at just the historical moment that they do*—have put a period to codex-based scholarly editing.

Here is a true story that may help to explain my meaning. Several years ago I wrote to Mark Reed to ask who was going to edit the "Five Book" *Prelude.* He wrote back and said there would be no such edition since (a) that particular form of the work only attained a fleeting existence, and (b) the *Prelude* project was already dauntingly large and, from the publisher's point of view, textually repetitive. Instead, his edition would provide a narrative description and textual history of the "Five Book" *Prelude.* He sent me a copy of this narrative, which eventually appeared as part of his edition.

Mark Reed narrativized the "Five Book" *Prelude* for one reason only: The book format (including the commercial factors governing that format) did not lend itself to printing yet another *Prelude* volume in the Cornell series. Too much of the material was viewable in the other volumes. Indeed, the limits of the codex imposed all kinds of constraints on the editors of Wordsworth's great uncompleted work, so that one will find it difficult to use: on one hand full of scholar's codes, on the other cumbersome when one wishes to compare different documents and texts.

As I have already pointed out, these problems inhere in the codex form itself, which constrains the user of the critical edition to manipulate difficult systems of abbreviation and to read texts that have (typically) transformed the original documents in radical ways. In an electronic edition, however, both of these hindrances can be removed. Precisely because an electronic edition is not itself a book, it is able to establish itself in a theoretical position that supervenes the (textual and bookish) materials it wishes to study. The operations carried out by the traditional book-based abbreviation systems continue to be performed in the electronic edition, of course, for they are central to the whole idea of the scholar's critical edition. In the computerized edition, however, the reader does not have to learn or even encounter the codes in order to execute critical operations (e.g., moving back and forth across different parts of books or separate volumes, carrying out analytic searches and comparisons). These operations are performed on command but out of sight. In addition, of course, the computerized structure allows the reader to undertake searches and analyses of the material that would have been impossible, even unimaginable, in a codex environment.

Conclusion: The Rossetti Hypermedia Archive

Hyperediting is what scholars will be doing for a long time. Many difficult problems will have to be dealt with, of course, including major problems hardly touched on here: questions of copyright, for instance, or the whole array of problems posed by the emergence of the vast electronic information network that is even now coming into being. In the immediate context, multimedia hyperediting poses its own special difficulties.

For instance, hypermedia projects (like *The Perseus Project,* for instance) are notably constrained by a structural feature of the digitized images they employ. When these images are introduced into a hypermedia structure, they have had to serve as simple illustrations; for the (bitmapped) information in the digitized image cannot be searched and analyzed as electronic texts can be.

How to incorporate digitized images into the computational field is not simply a problem that hyperediting must *solve;* it is a problem created by the very arrival of the possibilities of hyperediting. In my own case, the Rossetti hypermedia archive was begun exactly because the project forced an engagement with this problem. Those of us who were involved with *The Rossetti Archive* from the beginning spent virtually the entire first year working at this problem. In the end we arrived at a double approach: first, to design a structure of SGML markup tags for the physical features of all the types of documents contained in *The Rossetti Archive* (textual as well as pictorial); and second, to develop an image tool that permits one to attach anchors to specific features of digitized images. Both of these tools effectively open visual (and potentially audial) materials to the full computational power of the hyperediting environment. At this writing the DTDs (Document Type Definitions) for all textual materials, including digitized materials, are fully operational. The image tool is currently in its first release.

It is important to realize that the Rossetti project is an archive rather than an edition. When a book is produced it literally closes its covers on itself. If its work is continued, a new edition, or other related books, have to be (similarly) produced. A work like the Rossetti hypermedia archive has escaped that bibliographical limitation. It has been built so that its contents and its webwork of relations (both internal and external) can be indefinitely expanded and developed.

The "hyper" organization has also permitted the archive to escape another bookish horizon that has profoundly affected editorial theory and textual scholarship. A major aspect of this scholarship has been the investigation of ancient texts—in particular, the scholarly reconstruction of such works from textual remains that have been seriously broken over time. Such work encouraged scholars to focus on a single text, the ideal goal of their reconstructive operations.

In more modern periods, however, the textual remains are often very numerous. The history of the texts of Wordsworth and Blake and Dickinson is not seriously fractured. Indeed, the scholarly problem in such cases is how to sort out the relations of the documents and put all those relationships on display. However, the goals of classical scholarship and the material formalities of the book encouraged scholars to imagine and produce single-focus works—editions that organized themselves around what used to be called a "definitive" text, the source and end and test of all the others.

Whatever the virtues of this kind of focus—there are many—one would like to be free to choose it or not, as one needs. In most cases scholars confront a vast, even a bewildering, array of documents. Determining a single focus can be analytically useful, even imperative for certain purposes. On the other hand, one can easily imagine situations where a single determining focus hinders critical study. Besides, in many other cases one would like the possibility to make ad hoc or provisional choices among the full array of textual alternatives—to shift the point of focus at will and need. One cannot perform such operations within the horizon of the book. A hypermedia project like *The Rossetti Archive* offers just these kinds of possibilities, for the data in the archive is not organized hierarchically. It resembles more that fabulous circle whose center is everywhere and whose circumference is nowhere.

The change from paper-based text to electronic text is one of those elementary shifts—like the change from manuscript to print—that is so revolutionary we can only glimpse at this point what it entails. Nonetheless, certain essential things are clear even now. The computerized edition can store vastly greater quantities of documentary materials, and it can be built to organize, access, and analyze those materials not only more quickly and easily, but at depths no paper-based edition could hope to achieve. At the moment these works cannot be made as cheaply or as easily as books. But very soon, I am talking about a few years, these electronic tools will not only be far cheaper, they will also be commonplace. Already scholars are creating electronic editions in many fields and languages and are thereby establishing the conventions for the practice of hyperediting. *The Rossetti Archive* is one project of this kind.

Coda. *A Note on the Decentered Text*

Editors and textual theorists interested in computerized texts appear to differ on a significant point: whether or not hyperediting requires (even if it be at some deep and invisible level) a central "text" for organizing the hypertext of documents. My judgment is that it doesn't.

The question here can and often does get quite muddled. Enthusiasts for hypertext sometimes make extravagant philosophical claims, and skeptics are then drawn toward sardonic reactions. Hypertext is no more a sign of the Last Days than was moveable type five centuries ago.

To say that a hypertext is not centrally organized does not mean—at least does not mean to me—that the hypertext structure has no governing order(s), even at a theoretical level. Clearly such a structure has many ordered parts and sections, and the entirety of the structure is organized for directed searches and analytic operations. In these respects the hypertext is always structured according to some initial set of design plans that are keyed to the specific materials in the hypertext and to the imagined needs of the users of those materials.

Two matters are crucial to remember here, however. First, the specific material design of a hypertext is theoretically open to alterations of its contents and its organizational elements at all points and at any time. Unlike a traditional book or set of books, the hypertext need never be "complete"—though of course one could choose to shut the structure down if one wanted, close its covers as it were. But the hypertextual order contains an inertia that moves against such a shutdown. So, for example, if one were to create a hypertext of (say) *King Lear,* the "edition" *as it is a hypertext* can pass forward in time indefinitely. Someone will have to manage it, but if it remains hypertextual it will incorporate and then go beyond its initial design and management. It will evolve and change over time, it will gather new bodies of material, and its organizational substructures will get modified, perhaps quite drastically.

The second point goes to the matter of the conceptual form of hypertext as such (as opposed to the specific implementation of that form for certain materials and purposes). Unlike a traditional edition, a hypertext is not organized to focus attention on one particular text or set of texts. It is ordered to disperse attention as broadly as possible. Of course it is true that every *particular* hypertext at any particular point in time will have established preferred sets of arrangements and orderings, and these could be less, or more, decentralized. The point is that the hypertext, unlike the book, encourages greater decentralization of design. Hypertext provides the means for establishing an indefinite number of "centers" and for expanding their number as well as altering their relationships. One is encouraged not so much to find as to make order—and then to make it again and again, as established orderings expose their limits.

An important historical fact might be usefully recalled: that the Internet, which is an archive of archives, was originally designed precisely as a decentered, nonhierarchical structure. The point was to have an information network that could be destroyed or cut at any point, at any number of points, and still remain intact as a structured informational network. The theory of hypertext flows directly from this way of imagining a noncentralized structure of complex relationships. With hypertext, as with the Net, the separate parts of the ensemble (nodes on the Net, files in a hypertext) are independently structured units. That kind of organization ensures that relationships and connections can be established and developed in arbitrary and stochastic patterns.

This kind of organizational form resembles our oldest extant hypertextual structure, the library, which is also an archive (or in many cases an archive of archives). As with the Internet and hypertext, a library is organized for indefinite expansion. Its logical organization (for example, the Library of Congress [LC] system) can be accommodated to any kind of physical environment, and it is neutral with respect to user demands and navigation. Moreover, the library is logically "complete" no matter how many volumes it contains—no matter how many are lost or added.

The noncentralized character of such an ordering scheme is very clear if one reflects even briefly on the experience of library browsing. You are interested in, say, Dante Gabriel Rossetti's writings. So you move to that LC location in the library (any library). You stand before a set of books and other documents, which may be more or less extensive. *Nothing in that body of materials tells you where to begin or what volume to pull down. It is up to you to make such a decision.*

You can only find your way to that point in the library if you can negotiate its logical structure; and further browsing (or directed research) requires an even greater self-conscious understanding of the organization. Neophite library users are often intimidated by a library precisely because they can't immediately tell how to use it. Guides to a library will explain its logical structure as well as the physical implementation of that structure. Even so, they are conceived in the same spirit as the Internet and hypertext.

Subnets (or substructures) of these kinds of organization may be more or less hierarchically organized than other substructures. In a library, for example, historical orderings of various kinds appear everywhere. Nevertheless, these local basins of order are arbitrary with respect to the total archive. This result is obtained because each unit of the organization (each document and also each set of documents), like each node on the Internet, is logically defined as an independent item.

In a hypertext, each document (or part of a document) can therefore be connected to every other document (or document part) in any way one chooses to define a connection. Relationships do not have to be organized in terms of a measure or standard (though subgroups of organization can be arbitrarily defined as nonarbitrary forms). From a scholarly editor's point of view, this structure means that every text or even every portion of a text (i.e., every logical unit in the hypertext) has an absolute value within the structure as a whole unless its absolute character is specifically modified.

The Rossetti Archive imagines an organization of its texts, pictures, and other documents in this kind of noncentralized form. So when one goes to read a poetical work, no documentary state of the work is privileged over the others. All options are presented for the reader's choice. Among those options are arbitrary constraints that can be placed on the choices available. These constraints, which can be defined at any level of the organization, can be invoked or revoked at will. The point is that the structure preserves the independence of every document because the organization, like the Net, is "divided into packets, [with] each packet separately addressed." Since each of these packets has "its own authority to originate, pass, and receive messages," each is free to "wind its way through the [archive] on an individual basis."[8] Of course that is a metaphoric way of putting the matter: Files in a hypertext, like documents in a library, are not active agents. It is the user who moves through the hypertext. Nevertheless, the ordering of the hypertext materials is, by default, arbitrary and discrete. If the archive contains any more centralized or hierarchical structures, these have to be (arbitrarily) introduced. Furthermore, if they are introduced, the extent of their authority over the user has to be (arbitrarily) defined as well.

The problem here returns us once again to the fundamental issue of the relation of (hard copy) text to (electronic) hypertext. The decentralized forms of hypertextual archives clearly possess logical structure. That structure is designed to facilitate navigation through the archived materials irrespective of the purposes of the navigation.[9] When the hypertext is used to manage study of and navigation through complex bodies of (hardcopy) documentary materials—the kinds that traditional scholarly editors deal with—a special type of "decentralism" appears. The exigencies of the book form forced editorial scholars to develop fixed points of relation—the "definitive text," "copy text," "ideal text," "Ur text," "standard text," and so forth—in order to conduct a book-bound navigation (by coded forms) through large bodies of documentary materials. Such fixed points no longer have to govern the ordering of the documents. As with the nodes on the Internet, every documentary moment in the hypertext is absolute with respect to the archive as a whole, or with respect to any subarchive that may have been (arbitrarily) defined within the archive. In this sense, computerized environments have established the new "rationale of hypertext."[10]

But we have to add one word more on this matter because this discussion of the decentered text has left out of account the actual implementation of the theoretical design. It has left out of the account the *user interface* that organizes and delivers the logical design of the archive to specific persons. The interface one encounters in the actual Rossetti archive is, in fact, anything but decentered. In this respect it is quite like every other scholarly and educational hypertext work known to me—*The Perseus Project,* say, or any of George Landow's "webs." All are quite "centered" and even quite nondynamical in their presentational structure. We want to be aware of this since a major part of our future work with these new electronic environments will be the search for ways to implement, at the interface level, the full dynamic—and decentering—capabilities of these new tools.

Chapter 3

Editing as a Theoretical Pursuit

In darkness by day we must press on,
giddy at the tilt of a negative crystal.
The toy is childish, almost below speech
lip-read by swaying lamps. It is not
So hard to know as it is to do.

—*J. H. Prynne,* The Oval Window

In a trenchant metatheoretical essay, Lee Patterson investigates what he calls "The Kane-Donaldson *Piers Plowman*," that is to say, the 1975 Athlone Press edition of the poem's so-called B Text. I say "metatheoretical" because the edition itself constitutes the primary theoretical event. Patterson's essay elucidates the theory of that extraordinary work of scholarship.

According to Kane and Donaldson, their edition is "a theoretical structure, a complex hypothesis designed to account for a body of phenomena in the light of knowledge about the circumstances which generated them" (212). Needless to say, this "body of phenomena" is problematic to a degree. Patterson studies the evolution of Kane and Donaldson's "complex hypothesis" about these phenomena as the hypothesis gets systematically defined in the edition itself. These are his conclusions:

> As a system, this edition validates each individual reading in terms of every other reading, which means that if some of these readings are correct, then—unless the editorial principles have been in an individual instance misapplied—they must all be correct. This is not to say that the edition is invulnerable, only that criticism at the level of counterexample . . . is

inconsequential. . . . Indeed, the only way [criticism] could be effective would be if [it] were part of a sustained effort to provide a contrary hypothesis by which to explain the phenomena—to provide, in other words, another edition. (69)

Patterson's startling last judgment—deliberately outrageous—is not simply a rhetorical flourish. He is aware of the intractable character of the *Piers Plowman* materials. But he admires, justifiably, the comprehensiveness and the rigor of the Kane-Donaldson work. Even more, he admires its visionary boldness. In thinking about Kane and Donaldson's project, was Patterson also thinking of Blake? "I must Create a System, or be enslav'd by another Mans / I will not Reason & Compare, my business is to Create" (*Jerusalem* 10: 20–21). If he wasn't, he could have been; perhaps he should have been. For Patterson's essay is acute to see what is so special about the Kane-Donaldson edition: not merely that it is based upon a clearly imagined theory of itself but that the theory has been given full realization. "Counterexample" will not dislodge the "truth" of the Kane-Donaldson edition. Indeed—Patterson himself does not say this, though it is implicit in his argument—even a different "theory" of the *Piers Plowman* materials will necessarily lack critical force against the *theoretical* achievement represented in the Kane-Donaldson edition. Only another theory of the work *that instantiates itself as a comprehensive edition* could supplant the authoritative truth of the Kane-Donaldson text.

Why this requirement should be the case is one part of my subject. The other part, which is related, concerns procedures of theoretical undertaking as such. In this last respect we will be focusing on electronic textuality.

Let's take the first issue, then. In an important sense, the Kane-Donaldson project is a gage laid down, a challenge to scholars to imagine what they know or think they know about certain complex materials and disciplinary procedures. The edition begs to be differed with, but only at the highest level—only at an equivalent theoretical level, in another edition. In this respect it differs from other editions that have seen themselves as theoretical pursuits. Here I would instance Fredson Bowers's *The Dramatic Works of Thomas Dekker* (1962) or almost any of the editions of American authors that were engaged under the aegis of the so-called Greg-Bowers theory of editing. These works do not go looking for trouble, as the Kane-Donaldson project did (so successfully). They imagine themselves quite differently, as is readily apparent from the scholarly term they aspired to merit: "definitive." In this line of work the scholar proceeding with rigor and comprehensiveness may imagine a de facto achievement of critical completeness. Not that other editions might not be executed, for different reasons and purposes. But the "theoretical structure" of the so-called critical edition, in this line of thought, implicitly (and sometimes explicitly) argues that such undertakings would be carried out within the horizon of the "definitive" critical edition.

In the past 20 years or so scholars have all but abandoned the theory of the "definitive edition," although the term still appears from time to time. The Kane-Donaldson theoretical view, that a critical edition is a hypothesis "designed to account for a body of phenomena in the light of" our given historical knowledge, must be judged to have gained considerable authority during this period. As Patterson's essay suggests, theirs is fundamentally a dialectical and dynamic theory of critical editing. Not of course that a Greg-Bowers approach need fail to appreciate the indeterminacy of particular editing tasks and problems. On the contrary. But the general theoretical approach is different. Bowers, for example, inclines to technical rather than rational solutions to problematic issues, as his famous insistence on collating multiple copies of a printed work clearly demonstrates. This is a procedure that flows from a disciplined theoretical position. But it differs from the theoretical posture adopted by Kane and Donaldson, who take a much more skeptical view of the authority of positive data.

Over against these two theoretical approaches to editing stands that great tradition of what Randy McLeod would call (I think) "un-editing": that is, the scholarly reproduction of text in documentary forms that reproduce more or less adequate replicas of the originary materials. Until recently this approach has scarcely been seen as "theoretical" at all. But McLeod and others have been able to show the great advantages to be gained by theoretically sophisticated forms of documentary procedures. Many doors of perception have been cleansed by R. W. Franklin's *The Manuscript Books of Emily Dickinson* (1981), by Michael Warren's *The Parallel King Lear* (1989), and by the astonishing genetic texts that have come to us from Europe, like D. E. Sattler's *Friedrich Hölderlin. Sämtliche Werke* (1984).

Let us remind ourselves about what is at stake in these kinds of work. In another day—say, in the late nineteenth century—an edition like Warren's would have emerged from the influence of institutions such as the Early English Text Society. To that extent it would be seen as an archival work meant primarily to preserve and make accessible certain rare documents. But of course Warren's edition is very different; it is an investigation into the character and status of documents and their relationships (intra- as well as extratextual). Like Sattler's edition, it instantiates a self-conscious and theoretical argument. Moreover, Warren's immediate subject, *King Lear,* is implicitly offered as a strong argument for rethinking the textuality of the Shakespeare corpus as a whole. The play isn't taken precisely as *representative* because the case—which is to say, the documentary material—is too idiosyncratic. This unusual documentary survival, however, is used to encourage and license new acts of attention toward the whole of the Shakespeare canon, as well as to analogous texts beyond.

The scholarship of the past 30 years generically designated "theory" operates very differently from works like Warren's and Sattler's. Having emerged from the genre of the scholarly essay and monograph, speculative theory tends to move an argument through processes of (as it were) natural selection. Paul De Man was a careful builder of the absences he presented, sieving his materials with great discrimination. In textual and editorial works, by contrast, the whole of each phyla as they have ever been known—every material instance of all the known lines—lays claim to preservation and display. Everyone comes to judgment: strong and weak, hale and halt, the ideal and the monstrous.

Even the living and the dead, the existent and the nonexistent. They come, moreover, *in propria persona,* and to that extent they come on their own terms. Franklin's edition of Dickinson points to the theoretical advantage that flows from this method of proceeding. His fidelity to the original manuscripts was so resolute that the documents would eventually be called to witness against him—or rather, against certain of Franklin's less significant ideas about Dickinson's texts. Franklin's work exploded our understanding of Dickinson's use of the physical page as an expressive vehicle. We now see very clearly that she often designed her textual works in the manner of a visual or graphic artist. These unmistakable cases have come to function something like the case of *King Lear*—strange survivals helping to elucidate surfaces that might otherwise seem commonplace and unremarkable.

Franklin himself has resisted and even deplored many of the critical moves that his own work made possible. His edition did not set out to demonstrate some of its most important ideas: that Dickinson used her manuscript venue as a device for rethinking the status of the poetic line in relation to conventions of print display, for example; or that the execution of the (private) fascicles and the (public) letters together comprise a "theory" of verse freedom every bit as innovative as Whitman's; or that fragmentary scripts might possess an integrity that develops through a dynamic engagement between a text and its vehicular (material) form. These ways of thinking about texts are real if unintended consequences of Franklin's work. The edition itself, however, was clearly undertaken through a different set of ideas. Most apparent, it was a kind of preliminary move toward producing a new print edition of the poems, this time organized by fascicle rather than by hypothetical chronology or topical areas (the two previously dominant ordering systems). Franklin has now completed that print edition. And while it may have considerable success—Dickinson is one of our central American myths—it is unlikely to match the theoretical achievement of *The Manuscript Books.*

Why? Because Franklin's editions have emerged under a digital horizon and they prophecy an electronic existence for themselves. Each of the remarkable scholarly books we've been examining, because they come to us in codex form, comprise our age's incunabula, books in winding sheets rather than swaddling clothes. At once very beautiful and very ugly, fascinating and tedious, these books drive the resources of the codex to its limits and beyond. Think of the Cornell Wordsworth volumes, a splendid example of a postmodern incunable. Grotesque systems of notation are developed in order to facilitate negotiation through labyrinthine textual scenes. To say that such editions are difficult to use is to speak in vast understatement. But their intellectual intensity is so apparent and so great that they bring new levels of attention to their scholarly objects. Deliberate randomness attends every feature of these works, which are as well read as postmodern imaginative constructions as scholarly tools. This result comes about because their enginery of scholarship is often as obdurate and nontransparent as the material being analyzed. Think (again) about Hans Gabler's celebrated edition of Joyce's *Ulysses.*

Theoretical Embodiments

Most scholarly editions follow a path of what we call "normal science." We want them to be learned, dependable, meticulous. We expect them to adhere to standards that have evolved through a long series of testing replications carried out by authoritative persons. Hundreds, even thousands, of years oversee these standards and procedures. Other editions and editorial projects are different. Lachmann's *Lucretius,* Bowers's *Dekker,* the Kane-Donaldson *Piers Plowman,* and so forth—these works "prey upon high adventure," as Byron said of Napoleon. Like all editorial undertakings, they are called to meet the foundational standards of accuracy and thoroughness. But they also seek discoveries that stand beyond the purposes of customary scholarly practices.

So projects like these illustrate what the phrase "editing as a theoretical pursuit" can mean. To encounter them is to have one's imagination fronted with a Thoreauvian dawn. A large and interlocking set of conceptions—foundational ideas about the nature of texts and their negotiability—orbit *The Dramatic Works of Thomas Dekker* or *Piers Plowman: The B Version*. They are polemical works bearing within themselves complex and far-reaching arguments, some explicit, many not.

Most important, their arguments are not made abstractly, nor even through a set of illustrative examples. They are instantiated arguments—what William Carlos Williams called "The Embodiment of Knowledge"—and they call attention to the theoretical opportunities involved in making an edition. The totalized factive commitments and obligations of an editorial project open into a theoretical privilege unavailable to the speculative or interpretive essay or monograph. For what these kinds of works know (and don't know) will be carried to the limit of their capabilities and beyond—"beyond" because they are forced by their obligation to documentary completeness to expose their own fault lines.

I had access to none of those judgments and understandings before I undertook the editing of *Lord Byron. The Complete Poetical Works* in 1970. The edition was begun with no programmatic goals or textual theories; it was to be a work of "normal science," an edition in the long-established Oxford English Texts (OET) series published by the Clarendon Press imprint of Oxford University Press. But the event itself—the need to produce the seven volumes of the edition—lifted every conceptual issue to a new level of attention. The traditional distinction between documentary and critical editing, for instance, emerged again and again as a vexing and finally an insoluble problem. It began early. I thought it would be helpful to choose one difficult case as a model for testing my editorial procedures and then scale up from that model. I chose *The Giaour* because of its complex textual evolution between 1812 and 1815. As it turned out, I found no way to "edit" this poem in the OET format without seriously misrepresenting—or obscuring—its original textual condition. The work had too many documentary incarnations, all of them authoritative in different ways. And while it would have been possible to translate many (but not all) of these documentary states into the abbreviated codes of my critical edition, the process of translation itself would regularly be preventing access to the true character of the original materials.

The Byron edition thus brought home the degree to which our scholarly instruments and institutions establish a horizon of critical possibilities. Editing in paper-based formats, for example, literally creates the set of contradictions that mark the differences between documentary and critical approaches to editing. More than that, the "hypothesis" represented by an editorial undertaking is very different from the hypothesis of a theoretical or interpretive book or essay. In the latter we can qualify arguments if necessary, or—more commonly—can shape and specialize the material in more or less drastic ways. (That is to say, we can misrepresent the truth and be happy, even celebrated, in the event.) More broadly registered factive obligations confront a person setting out to edit a body of texts. Those obligations—often comprised in the dictum to "put all one's cards on the table"—force editors into impossible positions. Hungry and random clouds swag on our editorial deeps, leading us to imaginations of un-editing and un-editions, because editions assume an obligation to completion and completeness. When these obligations are fulfilled—that is simply to say, when the printed volumes appear—the failure of the edition, which is equally the fulfillment of its obligations, appears.

The publication of the first volumes of the Byron edition in 1980 was therefore an equivocal event for me. But as the later volumes emerged I was already far gone into thinking about the theoretical function of editing in a different light. It is a way of thinking first glimpsed in studying editions like the Kane-Donaldson *Piers* project during the 1970s. Introduced to digital textuality in 1981 and 1982, I began to see how the practical task of making an edition might be imagined (and executed) as a theoretical pursuit feeding upon and developing from its own blindnesses and incapacities. As a theoretical pursuit, an edition need not only seek to illustrate and argue for a certain set of ideas, which is what we see in a project like *The Dramatic Works of Thomas Dekker*. An edition is conceivable that might undertake as an essential part of its work a regular and disciplined analysis and critique of itself. In a certain sense all editions end up doing that. Shakespeare and the Bible and our entire archive of textual works undergo repeated re-editing because we respond to the inadequacies and limits of previous editions. But electronic texts have a special virtue that paper-based texts do not have: They can be designed for complex interactive transformations.

Thus, the general theoretical significance of editorial projects—once scarcely regarded—grows more clear than ever when they are drawn into the orbit of an encompassing innovation: digital textuality. In that context, the aspiration of works like the Kane-Donaldson edition seems more challenging than ever. They become stimulants to the pursuit of new—now imaginably more adequate—editorial tools. These would be tools with far greater powers of critical reflection and analysis because they would be capable of integrating documentary corpora that were larger and more diverse than one had ever thought possible.

The history of *The Rossetti Archive* traces one such pursuit. It is a history in which we were to discover the unexpected rewards of failure.

Horizons of Failure

The theoretical stage of the project began with the decision to design and build a critical edition in electronic, and in particular hypermedia, form. In describing it then, I said that its aim was to integrate for the first time the procedures of documentary and critical editing.

But this initial purpose was governed by received understandings of these two approaches. Formed through a long history of scholarship grounded and organized in codex forms, these two editorial models would have their imaginative limits searched and exposed in the practical work of designing and executing *The Rossetti Archive*. This result was inevitable. Although *The Rossetti Archive* was not initially conceived as a tool for studying the theoretical structure of paper-based textual forms, it would quickly prove very apt in that regard. Translating paper-based texts into electronic forms entirely alters one's view of the original materials. So in the first two years of the archive's development we were forced to study a fundamental limit of the scholarly edition in codex form that we had not been aware of. Using books to study books constrains the analysis to the same conceptual level as the materials to be studied.

The continued development of *The Rossetti Archive* brought new alterations to the work's original conception and purposes. Or perhaps they were not so much alterations as supplements. For the project "to integrate the procedures of documentary and critical editing" kept turning to worlds unrealized. *The Rossetti Archive* seemed more and more an instrument for imagining what we didn't know. The event of its construction, for example, gradually exposed the consequences of a crucial fact we had not at first adequately understood: that the tool had included itself in its own first imagining. We began our work of building the archive under an illusion or misconception—in any case, a transparent contradiction: that we could know what was involved in trying to imagine what we didn't know. Four years of work brought a series of chastening interdictions, stops, revisions, compromises.

In the end, not despite but because of these events, one grows to realize how to imagine what you don't know. You can build *The Rossetti Archive,* which is just such an imagining, and fashion it to reveal its various (and reciprocal) processes of knowing and unknowing. Designed as a textual environment open to continuous transformation and development, its projected content might be not only the edition (or archive) of Rossetti's works; it might also involve a process of critical reflection on those transformations.

The process as a whole illustrates what I would call the pragmatics of theory, and the sharp difference between theory, on one hand, and hypothesis or speculation, on the other. In humanities discourse this distinction is rarely maintained, and the term "theory" is characteristically applied to speculative projects—conceptual undertakings (gnosis) rather than specific constructions (poiesis). In terms of that ancient distinction, *The Rossetti Archive* is a poiesis, although modern disciplinary conventions would see it as a kind of engineering project—instrument or machine-making. Patterson's discussion of the Kane-Donaldson edition of *Piers Plowman* implicitly affirms the same kind of distinction, where "theory" operates through concrete acts of imagining.

The close relation it bears to artistic work is important because poiesis-as-theory makes possible the imagination of what you don't know. Theory in the other sense—for instance, Heideggerian dialectic—is a procedure for revealing what you *do* know but are unaware of. Both are intellectual imperatives, but in humanities disciplines the appreciation for poiesis-as-theory has grown attenuated, despite some remarkable practitioners (like Poe, Wilde, Derrida). The need to accommodate electronic textualities to humanities disciplines, which are fundamentally document- and text-based, is bringing a radical change in perspective on these matters.

The force of these circumstances has registered on nearly every aspect of *The Rossetti Archive,* sometimes within its logical structure, sometimes in a spin-off set of other papers and projects. What I didn't comprehend—I might have known better—was the degree to which the implementation of our theoretical designs would generate a "logical structure" comprised in part of impasses, contradictions, and strange diagonal wanderings.

The appendix to this chapter supplies a narrative of this bullet-ridden "logical structure" of *The Rossetti Archive.* It supplies a decent (if by no means comprehensive) account of what John Unsworth has discussed as "The Importance of Failure."[1] Imagining what you don't know cannot take place without the logic, so to speak, of failure. But that logic doesn't comprehend the entirety of such an imaginative horizon, and I want to conclude this chapter by turning to another part of that horizon. This is a place where we glimpse the intellectual authority of chance and randomness, those swerves from orderliness that order itself demands—as Lucretius argued so long ago.

The commitment of *The Rossetti Archive* to elucidating digital images kept generating one of its most important series of logical impasses and failures (for more on this, see the appendix). The problem—images recalcitrance to analytic treatment—meant that we were continually kvetching over the matter, which in turn meant that I would often find myself engaging the problem in undisciplined ways and circumstances.

On one such occasion—visiting an artist friend in D.C.—I showed my friend the archive and some of its images. We pulled up the image of Rossetti's famous painting *The Blessed Damozel* in Adobe Photoshop and began filtering it in a series of playful and random ways. At a certain point we generated an image that startled me. The arbitrary distortion had suddenly clarified a chromatic organization I had never noticed in the picture, familiar as it was.[2]

The rhetorical power of Rossetti's art is such that its intellectual beauties, which are always primary concerns for him, get thrown out of relief (as it were) when we encounter them in their natural (so to speak) condition. That is to say, Rossetti works hard to ensure that his arguments will register as primary apparitions rather than as abstract ideas. He works this way programmatically—indeed, much of his importance as an artist depends upon the way he explores the liminal moment between the conventions of pictorial illusionism, on one hand, and modernist abstraction on the other.[3] One may well recall here his famous dictum on the relation of spiritual and material presences, ideas, and phenomena: "Thy soul I know not from thy body, nor / Thee from myself, neither our love from God" ("Heart's Hope," 7–8).

The formal relations between the flesh of the damozel, the stars in her crown, her symbolic flowers, and the glimpsed world behind the heaven of embracing lovers is exposed in these distorted images: in one case through the patterns of blue/green, in the other through their gold equivalents. Those patterns help to explain how Rossetti manages to evoke, in this voluptuous Venetian exercise, the presence of a transnatural or divine order of reality. He has concealed within the painting's decorative opulence a subtle allusion to a commonplace feature of primitive religious pictorialism. We glimpsed the allusion in our two initial deformations, but it leapt to attention when the original image was passed through a black and white emboss filter. In this deformation we realized that an iconic gold ground is being subtly evoked in the broken, sinuous line of interstitial moments near the emparadised lovers, and that the line explicitly relates to her crown of stars and to the central triangle of her face, her hands, and the lilies she is holding.

Our image distortions exposed another key feature of the painting: the composition by rhyming circular forms, with the damozel as the central form (circling clockwise) and the embracing lovers as repetitions (circling counterclockwise). The exposure of this structure in turn revealed another: that 6 of the 11 pairs of lovers are arranged in an ellipse echoing the damozel's crown of stars.

These images call attention to important elements in Rossetti's picture. They recall those developed by art historians to demonstrate pictorial formalities—for example, when full-color paintings are analytically recast in black and white with edges or other forms highlighted in bold. What is important—and new—about our electronic deformations, however, is their arbitrary character. They come to us like what Blake called the "dictations" of "Eternity." We register the formal exposures they execute because we possess an a priori understanding of formal relationships. Nevertheless, because aesthetic forms like *The Blessed Damozel* always pursue orders of appearance, their intellectual beauties are wrapped in veils, as Shelley might have put the matter. Art works lead us to respond equally to the veils and to their informing ideas. The deformed images suggest that computerized art editing programs can be used to raise our perceptual grasp of aesthetic objects.

There are critical opportunities to be exploited in the random use of these kinds of deformation. For instance: take a given set of paintings and run them through a series of deformations—let us say, a set of Rossetti's paintings, or a set of works chosen from a known corpus of pre-Raphaelite, aesthetic, and symbolist art. Every time an altered image is generated that is judged interesting or revealing in some way, save the settings by which the image was produced. Then use those settings randomly on all the pictures in the chosen set and compare the results. The operation might well lead us to some new views of the intellectual organization or stylistic conventions of symbolist art. Artists are of course already using these digital tools in analogous ways. Critics and scholars are perhaps less imaginative beings, but even we needn't commit ourselves only to imagining what we already know.

One of our deformations proved especially stimulating. This image arrived when we were simply playing around with the image editor so as to twist and distort the original completely. Most people take immediate delight in this image and talk volubly about what they see. Their meanings range from suggestive redescriptions to abstract discussions of critical methodology. Some doubt that the image has any interpretive relation to Rossetti's original picture, but many see the matter very differently. My own response, at first, was that this type of distortion, while charming,

lacked the critical function I saw in the images discussed above. In the latter, one could readily appreciate how the filtered forms clarified important
aspects of Rossetti's famous painting. They typically revealed not what we
didn't know but what we didn't know we knew. I think it's also true that
the filterings delivered some things we didn't know at all, or at any rate that
I didn't know. I didn't know, for example, that the spaces separating the
background of kissing lovers had been chromatically organized so that the
spaces would relate simultaneously to two different, and in other respects
two contradictory, forms of pictorial order. This startling fact about the
picture only emerged when two of the distorted images were set beside
each other. But that revelation was unusual, and it seemed clear to me that
the deformations largely functioned in a pedagogical way. Insofar as these
images brought an imagination of the unknown, they were pointing to the
image editor as a critical and interpretive tool.

One is impressed to realize that random manipulations of an indeterminate set of filter settings can perform useful critical operations. Conversations with students, however, continually returned to the last deformed
image, and I have come to think very differently about it. The critical force
of the Photoshop deformations develops from their ability to expose matters that will be generally recognized, once they are seen. We might differ
on how we evaluate the formalities exposed through the Adobe filterings,
but not about the structures and forms as such. What arrests us in the final
image is its idiosyncrasy. This image generates what we would elsewhere
and otherwise call "subjective" interpretations.

We don't as yet have a vocabulary for talking about this process of
developing unknown images in relation to familiar aesthetic images. If the
'pataphysical and OULIPian programs were brought into more regular
critical use, such a vocabulary and set of methods might begin to develop.
The process I've been describing invites us to reconsider the critical
authority of so-called subjective aesthetic engagement and to see that a
"science of imaginary solutions" is no mere witticism.[4] Strange images
evoke our interest exactly because they don't pretend to supply us with a
generic response to the picture—a response viewers would agree to share
as a general truth about the picture (which is what we are offered in icono-
graphical and formal redescriptions). They are exceptional and, in that very
fact, they acquire critical edge and force.

The distortions arrest our attention, moreover, only because we already
know the original, which comes back to us through them as if from an
unimaginable world or point of view. Distortion and original stand in

immediately dialectical relation to each other. As a form of interpretive action, the images recall Galvano della Volpe's idea that interpretation develops a "quid" against which the unique qualities of an art work can be measured. The "quid" is critically useful not insofar as it mirrors its object but insofar as it fails to do so—or perhaps, rather, insofar as it dramatizes the fact that an art work abides no equivalences even as it seems poised to generate the shapes of equivalence forever. In this respect the distortions suggest the usefulness of thinking about art—at any rate, certain art works—as if they were informed by an idea, or an inertia, that has not been exhausted in the executed fact of the work we think we have and we think we know. This is an ancient way of engaging art that was revived in symbolist and surrealist practice. Not suprisingly, it is a view that Rossetti shared.

Appendix to Chapter 3

The following examples emerge from a praxis of theory we are familiar with, though perhaps not so much in a humanities context: the process of imagining what you know, testing it, scaling it up, modifying it, and then reimagining it; and then the process of repeating that process in an indefinite series of iterations and modifying your work as a consequence.

Current work in electronic text and data management fall into two broad categories that correspond to a pair of imaginative protocols. On one hand we have hypertext and hypermedia projects—information databases organized for browsing via a network of complex linkages. These characteristically deploy a mix of textual and image materials that can be accessed and traversed by means of a presentational markup language like HTML. On the other hand are databases of textual materials organized not so much for browsing and linking/navigational moves as for in-depth and structured search and analysis of the data. These projects, by contrast, require a more rigorous markup in SGML. If they deploy digital images, the images are not incorporated into the analytic structure. They will be simple illustrations, to be accessed—perhaps even browsed in a hypertext— for reference purposes.

One kind of project is presentational, designed for the mind's eye (or the eyes' mind); the other is analytic, a logical structure that can free the conceptual imagination of its inevitable codex-based limits. The former tend to be image-oriented, the latter incline to be text-based.

Not without reason do hypertext theorists regularly imagine their world in terms of spatial and mapping metaphors. Not without reason did the greatest current hypertext project (W3) decide to code its data in HTML (it could have supported a more rigorous DTD for its materials), or make the accessing of images (rather than the analysis of their information) a key feature of its work. W3's success derives from its humane— indeed, its humanistic—interface. Of course W3, like all hypermedia engines, is grotesquely pinned down by the limits of the color monitor. Still, though limited by the monitor (whether in two or three dimensions), hypertexts like W3 can simulate fairly well the eye-organized environment we are so used to.

By contrast, SGML-type projects need take little notice of the eye's authority. They are splendid conceptual machines, as we see when we reflect on the relative unimportance of sophisticated monitor equipment to text-based SGML projects. The appearance of text and data is less crucial than their logical organization and functional flexibility.

The computerized imagination is riven by this elementary split, as everyone knows. It replicates the gulf separating a Unix from a Mac world. It also represents the division upon which *The Rossetti Archive* was consciously built. That is to say, from the outset we held the project responsible to the demands of hypermedia networks, on one hand, and to text-oriented logical structures, on the other. This double allegiance is fraught with difficulties and even with contradictions, as would be regularly shown during the first period of the archive's development (1993–1995). Nevertheless, we determined to preserve both commitments because each addressed a textual ideal that seemed basic and impossible to forego. We knew that we did not have the practical means for reconciling the two demands—perhaps they can never be reconciled—but even proprietary products like Dynatext, imperfect as they were (and are), held out a promise of greater adequacy that spurred us forward. Besides, the tension fostered and exacerbated by this double allegiance might prove a kind of *felix culpa* for the project, a helpful necessity to mother greater invention. This was my initial belief, and events have only strengthened that faith.

So our idea was to build the archive along a kind of double helix. On one hand we would develop a markup of the text data in SGML for a structured search and analysis of the archive's materials. On the other we would design a hypertext environment for the presentation of the primary documents—Rossetti's books, manuscripts, proofs, paintings, drawings, and other designs—in their facsimile (i.e., digital) forms. A key problem from the outset, then, was how to integrate these different organizational forms. We arrived at two schemes for achieving what we wanted. One involved a piece of original software we would develop, now called Inote. The other plan was to develop an SGML markup design that would extend well beyond the conceptual framework of TEI, the widely-accepted text markup scheme that had spun off from SGML. TEI has become the standard protocol for organizing the markup of electronic textual projects in humanities.

But the hierarchical and linguistic orientation of TEI did not suit our documentary demands. The overlapping structures of literary works and their graphical design features are not easily addressed by TEI markup. But those textual elements are primary concerns of the literary scholar. We had chosen Rossetti as our model exactly because his work forced us to design an approach to text markup that took into account the visibilities of his expressive media. What we wanted was a text-markup scheme that could deal with the whole of the textual field, not simply its linguistic elements. So in 1993 we began the effort to design an SGML-based documentary markup for structured search and analysis of all the work of Dante Gabriel Rossetti.

That decision meant we had to confront the problem of the hierarchical structure of SGML/TEI encoding procedures. SGML markup organizes its fields as a series of discrete textual units. Each unit can comprise embedded subseries of the same logical form, and further subseries can be developed indefinitely. But SGML processors have a poor aptitude for markup of textual features that are concurrent but logically distinct. A simple instance would be trying to permit a simultaneous markup of a book of poems by page unit and by poem. In SGML you are led to choose one or the other as the logical basis of the markup design. TEI scholars proposed that the problem could be solved by deploying either a CONCUR element or a system of parallel DTD processing, but neither procedure would be practically implemented for various reasons.

At that point we had two options: to abandon SGML and look for a markup language that could process concurrent structures; or to try to modify SGML to accommodate the needs of *The Rossetti Archive.* In choosing the latter option, as we did, we were consciously committing ourselves to an inevitable set of unforeseeable problems. For the truth is that all textualizations—but pre-eminently imaginative textualities—are organized through concurrent structures. Texts have bibliographical and linguistic structures, and those are riven by other concurrencies: rhetorical structures, grammatical, metrical, sonic, referential. The more complex the structure the more concurrencies are set in play.

We made our choice for SGML largely because we could find no system for dealing with concurrencies that possesses the analytic depth or rigor of SGML, and because the project was not to design a new markup language for imaginative discourse. True, building a general model for computerized scholarly editing depends on an adequate logical conception of the primary materials, and it does not bode well to begin with a logic one knows to be inadequate. On the other hand, what were the choices? If natural languages defeat the prospect of complete logical description, an artistic deployment of language is even more intractable. In such cases adequacy is out of the question. Besides, SGML is a standard system. We are aware of its limitations because the system is broadly used and discussed. As Hamlet suggested, we seemed better off bearing the ills we had than flying to others we knew nothing of. And there was one other important consideration: the basic concurrency of physical unit versus conceptual unit might be addressed and perhaps even accommodated through other parts of the design structure of the archive—through the markup of images, through software for analyzing image information, and through the hypermedia design.

So in 1993 we began building *The Rossetti Archive* with what we knew were less than perfect tools and under clearly volatile conditions. Our plan was to use the construction process as a mechanism for imagining what we didn't know about the project. In one respect we were engaged in a classic form of model-building whereby a theoretical structure is designed, built, and tested, then scaled up in size and tested at each succeeding juncture. The testing exposes the design flaws that lead to modifications of the original design. That process of development can be illustrated by looking at one of our SGML markup protocols—the DTD for marking up every Rossetti archive document (or RAD). This DTD is used for all textual (as opposed to pictorial) documents of Rossetti's work, as well as for important related primary materials (like the pre-Raphaelite periodical *The Germ*). It defines the terms within which structured searches and analyses of the documents will be carried out. My interest here is not in the SGML design as such but in the record of modifications to the design. That record appears as the list of dated entries at the top of the document.

Before discussing some of these entries let me point out two matters of importance. First, note that the date of the first entry is "6 Oct 94." That date is just about one year after we completed the first design iterations for the Rossetti archive DTDs. A great many modifications to the initial design were made during that year, but we did not at first think to keep a systematic record of the changes. So there is a prehistory of changes held now only in volatile memory: that is, the personal recollections of the individuals involved, and in paper files that contain incomplete records of what happened in that period.

Second, the record does not indicate certain decisive moments when the archive was discovering features of itself it was unaware of. In these cases no actual changes were made to the DTDs. For example, we regularly discovered that different persons implementing the markup schemes were liable to interpret the intent of the system in different ways. We tried to obviate this by supplying clear definitions for all the terms in use, as well as a handbook and guide for markup procedures. But it turned out—surprise, surprise—that these tools were themselves sometimes ambiguous. The archive is regularly reshaped, usually in minor ways, when we discover such indeterminacies.

External factors have also had a significant impact on the form and content of the archive, and we found ourselves driven into unimagined directions. One of the most interesting shifts came about because of our problems with permissions and copyrights. The cost of these exploded as the archive was being developed, and in certain cases we were simply refused access to materials. This problem grew so acute—the date was 1994—that I decided on a completely new approach to the issue of facsimile reproduction of pictures and paintings. Rather than construct the first installment of the archive around digital facsimiles made from fresh full-color images (slides, transparencies, photographs), I determined to exploit a vast contemporary resource: the photographs made of Rossetti's works during and shortly after his lifetime, many done by friends and other early pioneers in photography. Rossetti is one of the first modern artists to take a serious interest in photography—the photographs he made of Jane Morris and Fanny Cornforth with J. R. Parsons are themselves masterpieces of the art.

This shift to early photographic resources—the materials date from the mid-1860s to about 1920—has two great advantages, one both scholarly and practical, the other scholarly. The move allows us to temporize on the extremely vexed issue of copyright. We use whatever fresh full-color digital images we can afford and work toward developing standards for the scholarly use of all such materials. These procedural advantages bring a number of significant scholarly gains as well. On one hand we now comprehensively represent Rossetti's visual work in the medium that was probably its major early disseminating vehicle. On another, we create a digital archive of great general significance for studying both the history of photography and the history of painting.

Whether extramural or intramural, however, these changes to *The Rossetti Archive* are, first, the realized imaginings of what we didn't know; and second, clear instances of a theoretical power beyond the range of strictly speculative activities. Let's look again for a moment at some intramural examples coded in the historical log of the RAD DTD. The recorded alterations in that DTD design were made as we scaled up the project from its initial development model (which involved only a small subset of Rossetti documents). This is a record of a process of imagining what we didn't know. The imagining comes through a series of performative moves that create a double imaginative result: the discovery of a design inadequacy and a clarification of what we had wanted but were at first unable to conceive.

Some of the modifications are relatively trivial—for example, this one:

```
<!— div1 ornLb added to titlePage 11–20–96 A.S. —>
```

The change permits the markup of an ornamental line break on title pages. Small as it is, the change reflects one of the most important general demands laid down by our initial conceptions: to treat all the physical aspects of the documents as expressive features.

A more obviously significant change is the following:

<!— revised: 9 Mar 95 to add r attr to l, lg and lv (seg) —>

This calls for the introduction of the attribute "r" (standing for "reference line") to all line, line group, and variant line values in the archive. The small change defines the moment when we were able to work out a line refer-encing system for the archive that permits automatic identification of equivalent units of text in different documents. We of course knew we wanted such a system from the outset, but we were unable to feel confi-dent about how the system should be organized until we had three years of experience with many different types of textual material.

Working out this scheme for collating Rossetti's texts revealed an inter-esting general fact about electronic collating tools: that we do not yet have any good program for collating units of prose texts. The poetic line is a useful reference unit. In prose, the textual situation is far more fluid and does not lend itself to convenient division into discrete units. The problem is especially apparent when you try to mark up working manuscripts for collation with printed texts. The person who discovers a reasonably simple solution to this problem will have made a signal contribution not just to electronic scholarship but to the theoretical understanding of prose textu-ality in general.

But let us return to the history of RAD revisions. Look at the notation for 14 June 1995:

<!— revised: 14 Jun 95 to add group option to rad for serials —>

A large-scale change in our conception of the archive's documentary struc-ture is concealed in this small entry. The line calls for the use of the "group" tag in the markup structure for the serials to be included in the archive (like *The Germ*). Behind that call, however, lies a difficult process that extended over several years. The problem involved documents with multiple kinds of materials (like periodicals). The most problematic of these were not the periodicals, however, but a series of primary Rossettian documents—most importantly, composite manuscripts and composite sets of proofs. In these materials the problems of concurrency became so extreme that we began to consider the possibility of abandoning SGML altogether—which would have meant beginning the whole project from scratch.

As it turned out, we found a way to manipulate the SGML structure so as to permit a reasonably full presentation of the structure of these complex documents. That practical result, however, was not nearly so interesting as the insights we gained into general problems of concurrency and into the limitations of SGML software.

Consider the following situation. Rossetti typically wrote his verse and prose in notebooks of a distinctive kind. Two of these survive intact to this day, but the fragments of many others are scattered everywhere. Many are loose sheets or groups of sheets, many others come down to us as part of second-order confederations of material that Rossetti put together, or that were put together by others (during his lifetime or after his death) as other second or even third-order arrangements. Problem: devise a markup scheme that will reconstruct on-the-fly the initial, but later deconstructed, orderings. Or—since in many cases we can't identify for certain which pages go with which notebook phylum—devise a markup scheme that constructs on-the-fly the various possibilities. Or: Devise a system that lays out an analytic history of the reorderings, including a description of the possible or likely lines by which the distributed documents arrived at their current archival states.

An instrument that could perform any or all of these operations would have wide applicability for textual scholars of all kinds and periods. I am sure it could be developed, perhaps even within SGML. It is an instrument that was imagined into thought by building *The Rossetti Archive*. We saw it as we were trying to devise markup systems that would accommodate the composite proofs and manuscripts that are so characteristic of Rossetti's extant textual materials. It is an instrument that we would like to develop ourselves—except that everyone is far too busy with other basic problems and demands.

Another example—this one coming from the history of the development of a piece of software mentioned earlier, Inote (formerly called the Image Tool). More than an exemplum of theory-as-poiesis, the story indicates, I believe, the "strange days" that lie ahead for humanities scholars as we register the authority of these new electronic textualities.

Inote was originally an idea for computing via images rather than with text or the data represented in text. Because information in bit-mapped images cannot be coded for analysis, our technical people were asked if it would be possible to lay an electronic transparency (as it were) over the digital image and then use that overlay as the vehicle for carrying computable marked-up data and hypertext links. The idea was to treat the overlay as a kind of see-through page on which one would write text that elucidated or annotated the imaged material "seen through" the overlay. (The idea originates in scholarly editions that utilize onionskin or other transparent pages to create an editorial palimpsest for complex textual situations.)

As with virtually all work undertaken at IATH, this tool's design was influenced by many people who came to have an interest in it. Consequently, because I was initially most preoccupied with designing *The Rossetti Archive*'s markup structure, my interest in the development of Inote hung fire. My own early thought had been that such a tool might enable *The Rossetti Archive* to incorporate images into its analytic text structure and thus establish a basis for direct searches across the whole of the archive at the image level. As I worked more and more closely with SGML markup, however, I began to suspect that the same result might be achieved through the design of a DTD for images. That idea, plus the technical difficulties in building Inote, drew my attention away from the tool's development.

Inote thus began to evolve in ways I (at any rate) had not anticipated. As others looked for features that would answer their interests, Inote emerged as a device for editing images with multiple-style overlays that, if clicked, would generate a text file carrying various annotations to the image. These annotations would be saved as part of the total archive structure and hence could be imbedded with hypertext links to other images or archival documents.

At that point—the date was early 1995—my practical interest in the tool was revived. This happened because my work on the DTDs for the archive, nearing completion, began to expose certain limitations in the overall design structure. It was growing very clear that the archive's two parallel universes continued discontinuous in fundamental and (in this case, I thought) unhelpful ways. Inote had become a device with two primary functions: (1) it allowed one to build a random set of image points or areas to which one could attach text materials of varying kinds; (2) it allowed one to imbed hypertext links to those materials. So while the tool created navigational paths from text to image and vice versa, thus connecting the two basic (and different) kinds of objects in the archive, and while it drew these image-related texts (and hence the images as well) into the full computational structure, it did not organize these materials *within a logical structure readable in the archive*. Any searches of the materials would have to be in effect string searches. (Inote in its first iteration, for example, could not

function in close cooperation with the indexable fields of information as
established through the archive's DTDs).

This limitation in the tool recalled my attention to the archive's basic
contradiction and double allegiance. The full evolution of the markup
structure—the building of the DTDs for all text and image documents—
had not been matched by a corresponding development in Inote, at least
for those who would want—as I did—a tool that could function within the
SGML marked database (with texts as well as pictures). This discrepancy
arises because the first version of Inote, unlike the DTDs, was not mapped
to the logical (DTD) structure of the files in the archive. It would be formally integrated with the SGML marked database only when it could summon its materials within pre-established indexable categories. Furthermore,
an adequate integration would require some kind of mappable relation
between those indexable forms and the SGML marked database.

To address these problems I suggested that we limit our consideration,
at least initially, to textual images—that is, images of manuscripts, proofs,
and printed documents—since these are far simpler than pictorial images.
We began by posing the question "what is the formal structure of a text
page?"

This initial query rises through a pair of presuppositions implicit in *The
Rossetti Archive*. The first reflects the archive's practical delivery of its
images, which the archive manipulates as units of either single pages or single page openings (that is, a pair of facing pages). That procedure flows
from a second assumption about texts in general. We assume that a "text"
is a rhetorical sequence organized by units of page, with each page centrally structured in terms of a sequence of lines commonly running from
top to bottom, left to right, and within some set of margins (which may
be reduced to nil [practically] on any side).

In marking up the formal structure of the text image, these general
conventions defining the shape of the page will govern the markup. Consequently, I proposed the following: that the page be formally conceived as
a structure of different spatial areas. I initially proposed four marginal areas
(left and right margins plus header and footer) and a central text area
stacked into four equal horizontal sections. This design was found to be
more complex than necessary, and we eventually settled on a page design
of three stacked horizontal areas with no mapping at the margins.

The essential point of this structure is to permit SGML marked textual
materials to be mapped directly to digitized images. An indexable code is
supplied to digital materials so that a formal relation can be established
between the two conceptual states of every text (i.e., texts conceived as lin-

guistic fields and texts conceived as bibliographical fields). SGML marked texts have nothing to say about the physical status of marked materials because the markup is not conceived in terms of spatial relations. Even if a set of SGML fields were to be defined for bibliographical features of text, no formal structure would exist to connect the digital images to the SGML marked texts—because the latter have not been conceptually defined in relation to the former. In the case of textual materials, this formalized representation of the bibliographical field would serve primarily to facilitate the study of documents with "irregular" textual conditions (e.g., documents with many additions, corrections, and erasures; or documents with nonlinguistic elements, such as Blake's illuminated texts). At least that was the initial imagination for the scheme.

Inote has now been developed along these lines and its functions have been applied and adapted by the editors of *The Blake Archive*. The results can be seen in *The Blake Archive*'s recent release of its first installment, an edition and study tool for *The Book of Thel*.

But not all the results. The practice of the theory of Inote revealed some interesting ideas about computerizing textual materials in relation to a database of images. For instance, it is apparent that in such cases one should define the basic textual unit as the page (as is done in *The Blake Archive*) rather than the work (as is done in SGML and—alas—in *The Rossetti Archive*). Only if the basic unit is the page (or the page opening) can the lineation in the digital image be logically mapped to the SGML markup structure. Of course if SGML software were able to handle concurrent structures, this consequence would not necessarily follow.

The Blake Archive's work conforms to the original thought about Inote that it be shaped to integrate the metadata in an SGML-marked text to the direct study of the digital images that constitute that metadata. As the tool was being adapted by *The Blake Archive* editors, however, their work exposed more severely than ever the problem of analyzing the data of digital images. Blake's work lent itself to the idea of Inote because that idea was fundamentally a textual one; and while Blake's works are profoundly iconological, they are also, at bottom, texts, not pictures.

We still do not have means for carrying out on-the-fly analyses of the iconological information in pictures (let alone pictures that are aesthetically organized). Our work with Inote shows how far one might go—and it is pretty far, after all—to integrate an SGML approach to picture markup and analysis. But the limitations of such an approach are also painfully clear.

Part II

Imagining What You Don't Know: 1995–1999

These two chapters represent a second-order critical turn upon the problems and "failures" that emerged through our work with *The Rossetti Archive*. The title of the section is taken from an essay written during the same period by Lisa Samuels, "Poetry and the Problem of Beauty." That essay spun off our work together on what would eventually become "Deformance and Interpretation," chapter 4 in this section of the book. Samuels's essay inquires into "non-conceptual way[s] of knowing" and the *critical* importance of aesthetic work for what Laura Riding used to call "the knowledge professions." For Samuels (a poet), the resistance that aesthetic form raises against a "translation back to knowledge" is not cognitively "useless . . . private and incommunicative," as knowledge professions from at least the time of Plato have commonly assumed or argued. On the contrary, "knowledge is also—perhaps most importantly—what we do not yet know." Beauty's resistance to knowledge—if not truth—"is therefore endlessly talk-inspiring, predictive rather than descriptive, dynamic rather than settled, infinitely serious and useful" (1–2).

"Deformance and Interpretation" is an attempt to develop an elaborate practical and theoretical demonstration of those ideas. I've been told that a better title for the chapter would be "Transformation and Interpretation" since "deformance" can suggest that aesthetic work rests in an originary or final integrity, a kind of unfallen condition that gets subsequently interfered with by later critical responses. All forms are transforms, however, including aesthetic forms. But while that is the case, one also wants to bear in mind the illusion of translational transparency that threatens critical work—not least of all the immensely self-conscious critical work of our own day. For all its usefulness, twentieth-century theory of the sign has helped to perpetuate an uncritical understanding of the illusion of transcendental form. If we reflect on the materiality of the sign, however, semiosis emerges to our view as a system of deliberated transformations with no untransformed origin or end. The transcendental sign is a signifying transformation mapped on the discourse of formalization, where it serves an important heuristic function for both reflective and procedural thinking. Philosophers and engineers alike have their Platonists, as they should and must.

Galvano della Volpe's important insight was to see interpretation as an interface for organizing and generating critical thinking. An interpretation so-called makes a record of a particular act of critical reflection and analysis. This record is at the same time an algorithm for generating further reflection and analysis, starting with the record itself. In this respect the record is less clearly understood as a meaning or even a form than as a program, in the computational sense of the term.

As originally conceived (and named), "Deformance and Interpretation" offered itself as an explicit program for this altered view of the act of interpretation. The critical history it narrates is a program script and so are its examples, developed by Lisa Samuels, of textual deformance. The script's emphasis was placed on de- rather than transformance in order to sharpen the difference between a performative and a hermeneutical approach to meaning production. The object of critical reflection is not ultimately directed to the sign as such but to the rhetorical scene and its functional (social) operators, not least of all the person(s) engaged in the acts of deformance we commonly locate in a file headed "Interpretation."

Samuels undertook her work immediately after seeing some of the deformations of Rossetti's pictures that I was doing in Adobe Photoshop. These experiments would later expand and develop into the "Metalogics of the Book" projects of 1999 to 2000 (see Part III of this book) and, ultimately, into "The Ivanhoe Game." The impetus for those studies came in 1999 as I was preparing for that year's joint annual meeting of the ACH/ALLC (Association for Computers and Humanities and Association for Literary and Linguistic Computing).

Certain events and conversations at the convention forced our work with *The Rossetti Archive* to a new critical focus. I decided two subjects had to be addressed at a level I had not yet tried to reach. Both followed upon the unsettling critical ideas that were generated by our "deformance" experiments. The first subject called for a clear response to the question "What is Text?" The second raised a fundamental problem of humanities computing: Why work in such a field at all? What do these simple on/off machines have to contribute to our understanding of such complex and nuanced phenomena as poetry, works of art, music?

The very existence of *The Rossetti Archive* implicitly argues that these two questions are closely connected. Articulating a clear sense of that relation is difficult. On one hand, we are still only beginning to explore the possibilities of digital tools; on the other, texts (so called) comprise a complex variety of powerful phenomena.

Susan Hockey organized an important occasion for addressing the first question, "What is Text?" A shrewd observer of the controversies growing around the SGML/TEI approach to textuality since the early 1990s, Hockey chaired an open meeting on the question at the 1999 ACH/ALLC meetings and asked Allen Renear and myself to speak to the matter. My critical reflections on that panel, written shortly afterwards, come here as the appendix to chapter 6. Writing that piece proved important for revisiting in a fresh way the persistent failure of computers to make important appointments with humanities scholarship (and vice versa). Relations developed only at what most humanities scholars, particularly in the United States, I grieve to say, regard as the margins of humanities disciplines—that is, among editors, archivists, bibliographers. This situation appeared all the more frustrating since artists in every medium were adopting computerized technologies with ease and notable success. What were the constraints keeping the vast majority of "scholars of the book" from serious practical engagements with this new medium of textuality?

That problem, along with the disfunctions and anomalies it involves, urged one to "rethink" the question of textuality beyond the context explicitly framed by the ACH/ALLC meetings. "Whereas we thrive in a world of analogues and fuzzy logic, computers exploit a different type of precision." What if the point were not to try to bridge that gap but to feed off and develop it? Meditating *that* question is the recurrent object of this book's last five chapters. All move in pursuit of a new ground on which to build computerized tools that generate and enhance critical reflection. It turns out to be a ground of cultivated differences rather than failed equivalences: *What Computers Can't Do* names a place where we will want to meet the machines and lay out some cooperative plans. That place, it also turns out, is where we have always been when we try to reflect critically on works of imagination. Electronic or not, our tools are prostheses for acting at a distance. It is exactly that distance that makes reflection possible.

Chapter 4

Deformance and Interpretation
(with Lisa Samuels)

With nothing can one approach a work of art so little as with critical words: they always come down to more or less happy misunderstandings.
　　　　　　　　　—Rainer Maria Rilke, Letters to a Young Poet

I have often noticed that we are inclined to endow our friends with the stability of type that literary characters acquire in the reader's mind. No matter how many times we reopen King Lear, *never shall we find the good king banging his tankard in high revelry, all woes forgotten, at a jolly reunion with all three daughters and their lapdogs. Never will Emma rally, revived by the sympathetic salts in Flaubert's father's timely tear. Whatever revolution this or that popular character has gone through between the book covers, his fate is fixed in our minds, and, similarly, we expect our friends to follow this or that logical and conventional pattern we have fixed for them. Thus X will never compose the immortal music that would clash with the second-rate symphonies he has accustomed us to. Y will never commit murder. Under no circumstances can Z ever betray us. We have it all arranged in our minds, and the less often we see a particular person the more satisfying it is to check how obediently he conforms to our notion of him every time we hear of him. Any deviation in the fates we have ordained would strike us as not only anomalous but unethical.*
　　　　　　　　　　　　　　　—Vladimir Nabokov, Lolita

A Question of Interpretation

Works of imagination encourage interpreters, who respond in diverse and inventive ways. The variety of critical practices—indeed, the number of differing interpretations directed at the same works—can obscure the theoretical commonality that holds those practices together. We can draw an immediate distinction, however, between critical practices that do or do not aim to be interpretive: bibliographical studies and prosodic analysis, for example, typically discount their interpretive moves, if any are explicitly engaged.

The usual object of interpretation is "meaning," or some set of ideas that can be cast in thematic form. These meanings are sought in different ways: as though resident *in* the work, or evoked through "reader-response," or deconstructable through a process that would reinstall a structure of intelligibility at a higher, more critical level. The contemporary terminology will not obscure the long-standing character of such practices, which can be mixed in various ways. In all these cases, however, an essential relation is preserved between an artistic work and some structure of ideas, that is, some conceptual form that gets more or less fully articulated *for* the work. To understand a work of art, interpreters try to close with a structure of thought that represents its essential idea(s).

This chapter proposes—or recalls—another way of engaging imaginative work. Perhaps as ancient as our currently more normative practices, this way has been less in vogue for some time. Its alternative does not stand opposed to interpretive procedures as such, nor to the elaboration of conceptual equivalents for imaginative work. But it does try to set these modes of exegesis on a new footing. The alternative moves to break beyond conceptual analysis into the kinds of knowledge involved in performative operations—a practice of everyday imaginative life. We will argue that concept-based interpretation, reading along thematic lines, is itself best understood as a particular type of performative and rhetorical operation.

Reading Backward

In an undated fragment on a leaf of stationery, Emily Dickinson wrote what appears to be one of her "letters to the world": "Did you ever read one of her Poems backward, because the plunge from the front overturned you? I sometimes (often have, many times) have—a Something overtakes the Mind—" (Prose Fragment 30) In the light of recent promotions of "antithetical" reading models, we might find Dickinson's idea a compatible one. But the physical and performative character of her proposal sets it in a tradition of reading and criticism far different from those we have cultivated in the twentieth century. This difference is exactly why we should listen to what she is saying.

Most antithetical reading models operate in the same orbit as the critical practices they seek to revise: When critics and scholars offer to "read," or reread, a poem, they hold out the promise of an interpretation. The model for this time-honored procedure is well illustrated in a work like Dante's *Convivio*, which has been so influential for later critical and academic procedures. Dante explains four of his canzoni according to his well-known scheme of fourfold and leveled interpretation. These explanations implicitly represent what he elsewhere and frequently calls the poem's *ragionamento*—its thematic content, which can be explicated apart from the ornamental and rhetorical forms comprising the other aspect of poetical making.

But the *Convivio* is not only a model of thematized interpretation: When we recall its rhetorical context we see a very different dynamic at work. That context exposes the *Convivio* as one of our best and earliest examples of reading "backward" within an interpretive tradition (as opposed to Dickinson's performative tradition). Book II of Dante's prose work supplies a reading of his canzone "Voi ch' intendendo il terzo ciel movete." Part of that reading involves an interpretation of another of Dante's poems, the canzone "Gentil pensero che parla di vui," which formed part of *La Vita Nuova*'s narrative ten years before the *Convivio*. In his early programmatic autobiography the canzone seems to deal with a personal crisis involving Dante and various real people. The *Convivio* brings forward a different view of the canzone, however, and of *La Vita Nuova* in general. The poem, Dante tells us in the *Convivio*, is not what *La Vita Nuova* makes it appear to be; the text bears a secret meaning within its surface appearances.

We have to manage a double reversal here. First, Dante says that the key figure in the canzone is not what people thought. The lady he saw gazing at him from a window, whose beauty eclipsed his devotion to Beatrice, is an allegorical construction, not a real woman. She is the focus of Dante's pursuit of Truth, the Lady Philosophy. In the *Convivio*'s reading she is represented as a wholly positive figure.

Her virtue defines the *Convivio*'s second reversal of meaning. In *La Vita Nuova* Dante's attraction to this lady of the window appears a kind of relapse from his love for Beatrice. However one interprets the point of this relapse, the narrative of *La Vita Nuova* moves on to show Dante recovering his former devotion to Beatrice. But in the *Convivio* he returns to that earlier writing scene to argue an interpretation he knows will startle his readers, so different does it seem from that given in *La Vita Nuova*. The *Convivio* argues that the lady of the window came into his life to escort Dante beyond his Beatricean devotions to a set of even more exalted pursuits. In terms of his work as a poet, philosophical poetry replaces what Dante called in a related canzone "the sweet songs of love."

This kind of moral or conceptual reclamation of imaginative work is fundamental to what we learn and teach in our schools. Less critical methods—Walter Pater called them "appreciations"—don't try to move against the work's original grain, as Dante does here. Nonetheless, both critical and appreciative interpretations promote some kind of intellectual or theoretical agenda. Emily Dickinson's thought is different. When she talks of reading poems backward she is thinking of recitation, whether silent or articulated. She proposes that an intellectual "overtaking" may come if one recites a poem from end to beginning, last line to first line (or is it last word to first word?).

Implicit in her proposal is a romantic apprehension: that the rhetorical power of a work of art will ultimately work against itself, dulling our sense of its own freshness. Dante's rereadings develop from a different ground altogether. For him a poem has a determinate conceptual intelligibility, and while one may mistake it, or grasp it partially or inadequately, it nonetheless subsists, just as a transcendentally intelligible Word subsists behind or within all creation. Dickinson, however, dwelt not in the intelligible but in the *possible,* as she famously observed. In such an existence, intelligibility is the consequence of a poetic action and ideas are forms or fields of experiment.

In this perspective, the critical and interpretive question is not "what does the poem mean?" but "how do we release or expose the poem's possibilities of meaning?" Dickinson's reading proposal has nothing to say about "meaning" at all, new or old. Her thought, her *idea,* is not a reimagined meaning but a project for reconstituting the work's aesthetic form, as if a disordering of one's senses of the work would make us dwellers in possibility. In offering this proposal Dickinson recognizes the uncommonness of her thought—this is the point of her rhetorical question—but she seems willing to believe that the thought may be entertained. Poems, after all, aren't transmitters of information, and if we usually read them in a linear mode, we know that they also (and simultaneously) move in complex recursive ways. Tennyson wrote of their strange diagonals. For Dickinson, a conception like "the poem itself" obscures not only how poetry functions but how language itself is constituted. For her, as all her letters and poetical writings show, language is an interactive medium. Moving backward through a poem, we expose its reciprocal inertias in performative and often startling ways.

We use Dickinson's proposal for reading poems backward, then, as an emblem for rethinking our resources of interpretation. It is a splendid model for what we would call deformative criticism. Her procedure, as we have suggested, follows from a romantic awareness, famously articulated by Shelley, among many others, that poems lose their vital force when they succumb to familiarization. Dickinson's is a protomodernist strategy of estrangement. But while we recognize her affinity with these traditional lines of aesthetic modernity, we shouldn't lose sight of the difference. Dickinson's critical model is performative, not intellectual. Indeed, in an important sense it is antitheoretical: not because it is opposed to theory (i.e., speculative thought) but because it places theory in a subordinated relation to practice.[1] In this respect her proposal recalls what Blake says about the difference between a Swedenborg and a Shakespeare, between Dante and his interpreters. For Blake the exegete is an "angel," a "philosopher." Either pitiful or presumptuous in Blake's eyes, such exegetes lift intellectual candles before the suns of vision.[2]

Interpretation as Performance: The Case of Dante, the Coda of Shelley

Blake's contempt for the "Cunning & Morality" of interpreters, however radically they present themselves, defines his artist's response to forms of conceptual or thematic interpretation. His life's work was an imaginative argument—an argument mounted in works of imagination—against all nonperformative styles of interpretation. Interpretation of works of imagination called for responsive works of imagination, not reflexive works of analysis. While Dickinson certainly thinks and works in the same spirit, her comment about reading backward introduces an interesting and important variation. Reading backward is a deformative as well as a performative program. It recollects the argument that Dickinson's contemporary, Humpty Dumpty, threw in Alice's face to unhinge her conventional imagination of language (see chapter 1).

Recalling that Dante himself was engaged in a thoroughgoing poetical deformation, we too might ask Humpty Dumpty's question: Who is to be master—the later Dante or the earlier? This is not a question to be settled with an answer; its point is gained when the question is put. The later Dante argued that he was to be master, and he argued further that mastery lay in an interpretation directed toward thematic and philosophical goals, rather than to affective and stylistic purposes. But according to both Dante's and Humpty Dumpty's views of the matter, mastery comes through rhetoric, in the acts of formation and deformation that Dante carried out, early as well as late. The significance of the *Convivio* lies less in the ideas it proposes than in the execution of the proposals, and in the imaginative overthrow that bears them violently along and away. The *Convivio* does not deconstruct but instead deforms *La Vita Nuova,* which is forced to take on meanings of which it was not originally possessed. In this respect the critical work treats the autobiography to the same kind of deformation that *La Vita Nuova* visited upon poems like "A ciascun alma presa," written by Dante years before the autobiography and the events it recounts but placed in the text as if it were involved in *La Vita Nuova*'s immediacies.

Here we observe instruments of expression functioning in performative, and often deformative, ways. Poetical works regularly operate in such ways. Prose, on the other hand, has come to appear a genre of transparency, as if it might be made a vehicle of noise-free information transmission or information representation. Working in that spirit, the *Convivio* means to set down the *ragionamento* of poems like "Voi ch' intendendo il terzo ciel movete." We do not have to deconstruct Dante's text in order to see that this *ragionamento*—its meaning and its information—is riven with discrepancies that will outface each other for ever.

Coming before the historical period when prose gained its scientistic function, the *Convivio* is especially important: for it is also the work that models and licenses many of our most basic hermeneutic procedures. The force of its interpretive desire is so great, and has been so successful, that it still imbues our own most common interpretive modes.[3] Dickinson's reading proposal discovers its special importance in this situation. For if we *believe* Dante's arguments in the *Convivio* (rather than give them our most serious attention), all forms of poiesis are threatened with prose possession. Reading backward short circuits the sign of prose transparency and reinstalls the text—any text, prose or verse—as a performative event, a made thing. In so far as Dickinson's verse does make a connection to prose discourse, it imbeds itself in highly personal and idiosyncratic prose textures—in personal letters and diaristic scriptures, like the notation on reading backward. Of course Dickinson is not a better or worse writer or thinker because she lacks Dante's passion for *ragionamento,* or for meaning that can be systematically articulated. She is just different. But her difference can help us recover a new (or perhaps renascent) appreciation of Dante's work, which is after all poetical, not philosophical (systematic or otherwise).

Recall again, for example, that in his later life Dante reserved the critical function of poiesis to work that sought moral and political goals: the *rime petrose* and the *Commedia* search and revise the "sweet songs of youth." This change of view in Dante is not, however, a change in basic critical (that is to say, poetical) method. He is looking at his work from a new angle. *La Vita Nuova* itself, as we noted, involves a critical translation of texts written earlier. This method, if it can be so called, suffuses the writing practice of Dante and his late-thirteenth-century circle. When these poets wrote exegeses of contemporary work, they commonly chose verse as their critical form. The opening sonnet of *La Vita Nuova* explicitly calls for the "true interpretation and kind thought" of other poets. The call is an interesting one to make: Why should Dante want his fellow poets to interpret his dream and its related sonnet? What could they have to say that would clarify the strange vision that opens the narrative of Dante's autobiography?

The readings they gave, the sonnets on Dante's initial sonnet that descend to us, do not settle such questions but instead complicate them. Cavalcante, Cino, and Dante da Maiano, who wrote the best-known interpretations of Dante's sonnet, all take a different view—as we might expect, as Dante himself might have expected. But perhaps those differentials signal the critical point: that meaning is more a dynamic exchange than a discoverable content, and that the exchange is best revealed as a play of differences. Indeed, the exchange gets exposed most fully in forms that are as self-alienated and nontransparent as Dante's beseeching sonnet. And we want to remember that the sonnet itself does not pretend to possess its own meaning. Meaning is what it goes in search of.

Dante never doubts that if a poem has been properly made its structure and conceptual content can be cast into a prose description and paraphrase. His thought is clearly stated in the *Convivio*, but it is implicit as well in the regular formal descriptions he gives in *La Vita Nuova* after each of the interpolated poems. The question then arises: Why write in poetry at all, and especially why write intellectual and philosophical poetry? Dante's answer is classical: Verse adds delight and pleasure to instruction. Even in the *rime petrose*, we ask? And the answer is yes, even there, although the pleasures of those later texts come in more severe and often more abstracted forms.

Dante's thought is Thomistic and Aristotelian: "nihil est in intellectu quod non prius est in sensu." This priority is not temporal but logical, and perhaps ontological. In poiesis, the physique of language forms a dialectic with the text's *ragionamento*, the dialectic of pleasure and instruction. Even were it to be executed to perfection, however, the dialectic involves only human perfections. Dante understands that his work is supervened. The poem's action takes place within an encompassing "love that moves the sun and the other stars" (*Paradiso* 33). Consequently, the intellectual "content" of a poem, if it must be paraphrasable to have any authority whatsoever, cannot be imagined a final thought. If it is also a mastering thought (and for Dante it is), it functions in a Humpty Dumpty mode. The poem's *ragionamento* is regularly exposed to its human limits through a formal devotion to the artifices of surprising pleasures. Paradoxically, then, this structure of pleasure works to draw the intellect beyond what it is able to imagine. In this sense, the elementary, linguistic pleasure of verse becomes the manifest form of divine presence. Dante sees that presence as Beatrice when he is young and as Lady Philosophy when he is older: *dolce stil novo* as against *rime petrose.*

Dante's approach to the performative knowledge of poiesis is far removed from Dickinson's or Lewis Carroll's, and the latter read backward and upside-down at a very different historical moment. The turn of poiesis from performance to deformance marks an epoch when Dantean *ragiona-mento,* the dream vision of enlightenment, had grown vexed to scientistic nightmare. No one exposes this turn of events better than Shelley, whose allegiance to Dante's visionary hopes is unmistakable. When his friend Thomas Love Peacock put the case for a new kind of instrumental knowledge, scientific rather than poetical, Shelley responded—twice, in fact: once in prose, a second time in verse. The prose response is well known:

> We have more moral, political, and historical wisdom, than we know how to reduce into practice. . . . The poetry in these systems of thought, is concealed by the accumulation of facts and calculating processes. There is no want of knowledge respecting what is wisest and best. . . . But we let *I dare not* wait upon *I would,* like the poor cat in the adage. We want the creative faculty to imagine that which we know; we want the generous impulse to act that which we imagine; we want the poetry of life: our calculations have outrun conception; we have eaten more than we can digest. The cultivation of those sciences which have enlarged the limits of the empire of man over the external world, has, for want of the poetical faculty, proportionately circumscribed those of the internal world; and man, having enslaved the elements, remains himself a slave. (502–503)

This is a Dantean and not a Kantian thought about poetry, but the "Defense" is replete with Dante's ideas and expressions. If its rhetoric proved merely beautiful and ineffectual at the flood-tide of rationalist ideology, it may strike late-twentieth-century readers very differently. In any case, it helps us to see that a continuity of thought about poiesis, knowing, and action stretches between Dante's enthusiasms and Dickinson's extremities.

Shelley's place in that tradition is perhaps even more clear in the verse text that goes with the "Defense": the coded narrative of *Epipsychidion,* written just after Shelley finished his prose treatise. The poem lays bare the ambiguous truth of the "Defense" by staging it as a performance rather than arranging it as an exposition of ideas. As in Dante's work, *Epipsychidion* clarifies what it knows by becoming what it beholds. The prefatory "Advertisement" for the poem explicitly locates it in relation to *La Vita Nuova.* More than that, Shelley lets us know that his "version" of *La Vita Nuova* is the work Dante reconstituted through the *Convivio's* interpretation of "Voi ch' intendendo il terzo ciel movete." Shelley puts his free translation of the last strophe of Dante's canzone at the head of his poem, making what he calls a "presumptuous application" of Dante's work to his own. Thence unfolds Shelley's quasi-autobiographical reprise on *La Vita Nuova*—partly fictive, partly factive, as the "Advertisement" makes so clear, but in all cases thoroughly allegoristic. The poem is only superficially a veiled series of biographical anecdotes. What Shelley has made is an argument, as the title explicitly says, "on the subject of the soul." That is to say, it is an argument about the soul's desire, or love. More to the point, it is an argument addressed from and to persons who perceive the frustration of desire as a function of social circumstances and institutions.

No poem of Shelley's has been judged more recondite. To his admirers it is perhaps his most beautiful work, to his detractors his most ineffectual. And both judgments are not only persuasive but also underscore the poem's performative character. *Epipsychidion* is a love poem that realizes a dysfunction between desire and action. It imagines what it knows, and what it knows it represents in and as itself: that is, both the rule of this dysfunction and the unachieved desire to overcome it. The initial setting of the poem's action—"the noble and unfortunate lady . . . now imprisoned in [a] convent"—occasions an intense symbolic elaboration. The unfolding poem doesn't alter those imaginary circumstances; it fulfills them.

From Performance to Deformance

The foregoing discussion underscores two matters of special importance for our purposes. First, imaginative work has an elective affinity with performance: It is organized as rhetoric and poiesis rather than as exposition and information-transmission. Because this is so, it always lies open to deformative moves. Harold Bloom's trenchant theory of poetic influence spelled out some of the imagination's performative "ratios," as he called them. Certain of these ratios are aggressively deformative, as when Blake famously overturns both Milton's *Paradise Lost* and its chief precursor, the Judaeo-Christian Bible, or when Ronald Johnson selects from and revises *Paradise Lost* in his marvelous book *RADI OS* (1977).

What we have written here, however, is neither performative nor deformative; it is expository. And this fact raises a second matter of importance: that criticism (scholarship as well as interpretation) tends to imagine itself as an informative rather than a deformative activity. In the last section of this essay we shall address the informatics of criticism with a view toward shifting what we take to be the customary understanding of such work. Here we want to point out that lines of performative and deformative critical activity have always existed. Editions and translations are by definition performative. Elaborate scholarly editions foreground their performative characteristics. Sometimes translators do the same.

Let us briefly consider two examples of these critical performatives, simply to clarify what we mean when we say that editions and translations are *prima facie* performative. The first example is one we have already remarked upon, the Kane-Donaldson edition of the B Text of *Piers Plowman*. The edition performs its own meaning. Any other meaning it might have, or be given, could only enter the field as another performative act, another edition.

There is perhaps small need to illustrate the performativity of translations. D. G. Rossetti's comments on his great and influential book *The Early Italian Poets* (1861) are so telling, however, that he can be usefully called to speak for many. Because "a translation [involves] the necessity of settling many points without discussion," Rossetti observes, it "remains perhaps the most direct form of commentary" (283) that can be brought to literary work. T. S. Eliot's displeasure with Rossetti's book is as programmatic as the book itself, and the Kane-Donaldson *Piers* outraged various scholars for similar reasons. The critical thoroughness and integrity of both works is exactly the problem. It does no good to say, as some have, that Rossetti "mistranslates" certain passages, any more than demurs at individual readings in the Kane-Donaldson *Piers* can gain serious critical force. Eliot's disapproval of Rossetti is far more to the point, for he understood that Rossetti was using his translations to install a commentary on the relation between pagan and Christian spirituality. If editing is the paradigm of performative scholarship, translation is perhaps the same for criticism-as-interpretation.

Whereas in imaginative work the passage from performance to deformance is easily negotiated, the same is not true for critical work. Deformative scholarship is all but forbidden, the thought of it either irresponsible or damaging to critical seriousness. It exists nonetheless, and in certain cases it has gained justifiable distinction and importance. Despite its bad eminence, forgery is the most important type of deformative scholarship, and its contribution to the advancement of learning cannot be underestimated, as Anthony Grafton has recently shown.[4] Interesting as this type of deformance must be, we shall set it aside in order to concentrate on procedures of interpretive deformation. The latter are best exemplified in heretical and other kinds of non-normative readings of established cultural artifacts. *Sortes Virgilianae* and subjective appropriations of poetical works are types of interpretive deformation. So are travesty retextualizations, both deliberate and unpremeditated: The first type is exemplified in the work of Kathy Acker, the second in mistaken and deviant readings produced, for example, by students unaware of an ignorance in their historical or linguistic understanding.[5]

All these cases of interpretive deformation fall outside Dickinson's radical proposal of backward reading. In literary work, for example, invasions or distortions of the documentary foundation of the artifact are rare. That interpreters avoid such moves demonstrates, we think, something more than a ground of critical orthodoxy that readers are disinclined to attack. The reluctance shows, more interestingly, that interpreters—even radical ones—do not commonly locate hermeneutic vitality in the documentary features of literary works. Because meaning is assumed to develop as a linguistic event, critical deformance plays itself out in the field of the signifieds. The great contemporary exception proving this rule is the remarkable work of Randall McLeod, whose "transformissive" explorations of (mostly Renaissance) works comprise, we believe, one of the most important, and clearly one of the most imaginative, bodies of critical writing of our time.[6]

Critical and interpretive limits are thus regularly established (and for the most part quite unselfconsciously) at the Masoretic wall of the physical artifact, whose stability and integrity is taken as inviolable. From an interpretive point of view, this assumption brackets off from attention crucial features of imaginative works, features wherein the elemental forms of meaning are built and elaborated. These forms are so basic and conventionally governed—they are alphabetical and diacritical; they are the rules for character formation, character arrangement, and textual space, as well as for the structural forms of words, phrases, and higher morphemic and phonemic units—that readers tend to treat them as preinterpretive and precritical. In truth, however, they comprise the operating system of language, the basis that drives and supports the front-end software.

That computing metaphor explains why most readers don't fool around with these levels of language. To do so entails plunging to deep recesses of textual and artifactual forms. Linguists, semioticians, bibliographers, and cognitive theorists regularly explore these territories, but their work is not normally concerned with interpretation in the customary sense—that is, with explaining aesthetic and stylistic features of works in formal and/or thematic terms. Reading backward is a critical move that invades these unvisited precincts of imaginative works. It is our paradigm model of any kind of deformative critical operation.

Such a model brings to attention areas of the poetic and artifactual media that usually escape our scrutiny. But this enlargement of the subject matter of criticism doesn't define the most significant function of deformative operations. Far more important is the stochastic process it entails. Reading backward is a highly regulated method for disordering the senses of a text. It turns off the controls that organize the poetic system at some of its most general levels. When we run the deformative program through a particular work we cannot predict the results. As Dickinson elegantly puts it, "A Something overtakes the Mind," and we are brought to a critical position in which we can imagine things about the text that we didn't and perhaps couldn't otherwise know.

There is one other important result. A deformative procedure puts the reader in a highly idiosyncratic relation to the work. This consequence could scarcely be avoided, since deformance sends both reader and work through the textual looking glass. On that other side customary rules are not completely short-circuited, but they *are* held in abeyance, to be chosen among (there are many systems of rules), to be followed or not as one decides. Deformative moves reinvestigate the terms in which critical commentary will be undertaken. Not the least significant consequence, as will be seen, is the dramatic exposure of subjectivity as a live and highly informative option of interpretive commentary, if not indeed one of its essential features, however neglected in neoclassical models of criticism that search imaginative works for their "objective" and general qualities.

Examples and Experiments

Pictorial deformation is a mode not explicitly addressed or exemplified here, for reasons of space and medium. Readers are referred to the critical deformations carried out on a painting by Dante Gabriel Rossetti, the Fogg Museum's copy of *The Blessed Damozel*.[7] Here we focus instead on poetic deformations, which we have so far organized into four types: reordering (for example, reading backward), isolating (for example, reading only verbs or other parts of speech), altering (exteriorizing variants—potential versions—of words in the work; or altering the spatial organization, typography, or punctuation of a work), and adding (perhaps the most subjective of our deformative poetics). Our focus will be on the first two types of deformance and on two works by Wallace Stevens, beginning with "reading backward" as our paradigm deformance. Stevens is peculiarly apt for deformance because his work has been alternately judged philosophically serious and poetically nonsensical—as is demonstrated by the divergent reactions of critics like B. J. Leggett and Hugh Kenner[8]—and so serves as a ground for the conflict between poetry-as-meaning and poetry-as-style. Without imagining a resolution to this conflict, we hope to go some ways toward clarifying how it operates. Approaching Stevens's poetry through its nonsemantic elements, we want to show how its pretensions to meaning are not so much a function of ideas as of style.

Our first case in point is "The Search for Sound Free from Motion" (1942), in which Stevens engages the issue of world sound versus human sound:

> All afternoon the gramophone
> Parl-parled the West-Indian weather.
> The zebra leaves, the sea
> And it all spoke together.
>
> The many-stanzaed sea, the leaves
> And it spoke all together.
> But you, you used the word,
> Your self its honor.
>
> All afternoon the gramophoon,
> All afternoon the gramophoon,
> The world as word,   ˙
> Parl-parled the West-Indian hurricane.
>
> The world lives as you live,
> Speaks as you speak, a creature that
> Repeats its vital words, yet balances
> The syllable of a syllable.

Before deforming this text, let's consider how we might analyze it in a normative conceptual way, "figuring out what it means." The final stanza grammatically conflates "the world" and "you"—where "you" is both reader and poem—into "a creature," which is then the reference of all three: world, reader, and poem. All three "repeat" life as language ("its vital words") in the seemingly nonexistent space indicated by "The syllable of a syllable."

Each stanza carries on a similar layering conflation: gramophone, weather, leaves, sea, you, word, hurricane, creature, syllable. In this case, as Charles Olson might have argued, our reality is "no longer THINGS but what happens BETWEEN things."[9] Pondering between-ness itself, we move to search out Stevens's nonhierarchical verbal space, where organizing properties like motion or syllables—and thus divisive temporality—can be undone, where sound can be free from motion. In this interstitial realm, the syllable of a syllable is perhaps the ultimate straddler. It can be the sound the syllable makes in the spoken version of its written production— the life of its print, the sign of the imperative that the marks of printed language are only one part of a language event also spoken. The syllable of a syllable can also be the letters, which are the smallest units of any syllable, the shifting territory between and alongside of phonemes and morphemes, as well as phonemes and morphemes themselves. It can also be the *idea* of the syllable, the Platonic syllable's "signified." Stevens's phrase, as we grope to explain it, to paraphrase it, emerges as an imagination of something we don't know.

The poem's culminant line summarizes a linguistic action that observes forms of discursive order that exceed conceptual formulation. But this incomprehensibility has been with the poem all along: "All afternoon the gramophoon" announces the pleasing nonsense that ordinary words cultivate, seeming to long for, arbitrarily. The decision to generate a gramophoon from an afternoon is finally a human one. But the decision will be riven with paradox, as the equally determinate title, so resolutely paradoxical, declares.

This lineated text, moving forward, becomes an instance of the "search" named in the title. It is (literally) a textual passage to impossibility. How then are we to understand it? A deformance of the text becomes useful at this point: What if we retrace the poem's path, moving in a reverse quest over the way it seems to have come? In fact, "sound free from motion" accompanies sense free from direction. The languaged "world as word" can be free from the world as regular rotating object, and we can read this poem backward, as Dickinson prompts us to do:

The syllable of a syllable
Repeats its vital words, yet balances
Speaks as you speak, a creature that
The world lives as you live,

Parl-parled the West-Indian hurricane.
The world as word,
All afternoon the gramophoon,
All afternoon the gramophoon,

Your self its honor.
But you, you used the word,
And it all spoke together.
The many-stanzaed sea, the leaves

And it all spoke together.
The zebra leaves, the sea
Parl-parled the West-Indian weather.
All afternoon the gramophone

The point of such an exercise is not only to see the poem afresh. It is more important to see that the poem yields to such a remapping. The arbitrary imposition of a reversed order on the original layout indicates that the poem possesses its own means for evading temporal determinateness.

Reconsider the new "first" stanza: "The syllable of a syllable" is now the opening subject instead of the concluding object. We may fairly argue that it thus acts as a hidden subject repercussively, retrospectively, in the original order of the poem. Here its act turns explicit: the morpheme of the morpheme, the word of the word (other ways of saying "the syllable of a syllable") is involved in repetition: It speaks over and over again "its vital words." We do not know what these words are, but we do see that the poem embeds the knowledge of them in itself, makes an absolute of the existence of "vital words." The poem, then, knows what is vital, knows that the vital gets repeated in and as verbal interstices. This knowledge appears not as a developed, least of all a completed, understanding but as an original idea. At the same time, that interstice ("the syllable of a syllable") "balances": The repetition of the vital is a unified reinscription, but nevertheless there is a duality, there is something to balance. In the discovered syntax of backwardness, that something is both the subject itself (the syllable of a syllable must balance itself) and the object (it must also balance "its vital words").

The next line can be read as a continuation: The subject "balances / Speaks," juggles multiple *paroles*. It can also be read as a new verb phrase for our subject ("The syllable of a syllable / . . . / Speaks as you speak"). In this second reading, the interstitial subject is now linked to the indefinite "you," which in the absence of more specific definition the reader may take as herself, or as another within the confines of the poem. The backward reading retains the ambiguity of "a creature" but now restricts it only to the subject (the interstitial "syllable of a syllable") and to the "you." This restriction makes it possible to argue that the "world" has a diminished importance in the constellation of the final stanza, in the same way that we recognize the new subject position of "the syllable of a syllable" as throwing back its meaning on the text in its original lineated order. What happens to this "creature" in the next line? It is "a creature that / The world lives as you live": It is a creature that the world enlivens (now reading "lives" as a transitive rather than as an intransitive verb) as it enlivens "you." Or the backward reading strips the pronoun "that," in the third line, of any object and throws us into the fourth line as into an absolute statement: "The world lives as you live."

This backward reading not only shows more than the poem's temporal instability. It demonstrates the repercussive effects of the alternate (backward) meanings on the original order. In the repetitions of the poem, "its vital words," are the variations of the poem, as we glimpse in the suggestive lines "But you, you used the word, / And it all spoke together." Because this is not a message, we read it more than once. Because we read it over and over again we "hear" the variations in order and meaning.

As we see in this commentary, deformance does not banish interpretation. The reversed text is still subject to, still giving of, interpretive readings. Deformance *does* want to show that *the poem's intelligibility is not a function of the interpretation, but that all interpretation is a function of the poem's systemic intelligibility.* Interpreting a poem after it has been deformed clarifies the secondary status of the interpretation.

Perhaps even more crucially, deformance reveals the special inner resources that texts have when they are constituted poetically. Nor do judgments about the putative quality of the poem matter. Good, bad, mediocre poems, by whatever measure or judgment: In so far as they are poetically made, they share this special kind of intelligibility.[10] Once a textual poiesis is undertaken, then, language is set beyond the order of conceptual and expository categories. Not outside those categories—poems deal with expository meaning because they deal in language—but beyond them.

Another example from Stevens is an experiment in isolating deformation: eliminating everything from a poem except certain words, to see what happens when they are alone on the page. One might try reading only the verbs of poems, which helps to isolate the energy or dormancy of the poem's action. One might also try reading only nouns, in order to throw into relief whether they are mostly abstract or concrete, whether the poem is or is not noun-heavy. For this example of isolating deformance we use Stevens's "The Snow Man":

> One must have a mind of winter
> To regard the frost and the boughs
> Of the pine-trees crusted with snow;
>
> And have been cold a long time
> To behold the junipers shagged with ice,
> The spruces rough in the distant glitter
>
> Of the January sun; and not to think
> Of any misery in the sound of the wind,
> In the sound of a few leaves,
>
> Which is the sound of the land
> Full of the same wind
> That is blowing in the same bare place
>
> For the listener, who listens in the snow,
> And, nothing himself, beholds
> Nothing that is not there and the nothing that is.

Again we start with some normative interpretive moves to suggest why deformance is a good way to engage the poem's stylistic orders. The poem enacts an otherness, what it calls the "nothing" of its experience, discouraging other standards (not thinking outside winter, of spring with its full trees and therefore of winter's bareness as miserable). One's senses are shifted inside the poetic space: the "listener" "beholds" rather than hearing, "one" has "a mind of winter" but doesn't in fact escape from the potential "misery" of realizing the difference between cold and other weather.

Once we have noted the self-sufficient "nothingness" of this poem, two related points immediately rise up: What do we say about the poem's unexportable meanings—its wintry resistance to the spring of comparison and prose translation—and how do we say it? Say that Stevens's poetic "nothing" is not (necessarily, at least) the negative force we tend to associate with that word. If this poetry makes "nothing" happen, what does "nothing" make happen? How do we talk about "nothing"? Which is another way of asking: What are the prosodic tools proper to the incommensurate?

We can try to answer these questions by deforming "The Snow Man," first making it more prose-like and then stripping it of clarifying context and syntax. First, to help analyze the extent of its syntax or sense, let's set it out typographically as prose[11]:

> One must have a mind of winter to regard the frost and the boughs of the pine trees crusted with snow; and have been cold a long time to behold the junipers shagged with ice, the spruces rough in the distant glitter of the January sun; and not to think of any misery in the sound of the wind, in the sound of a few leaves, which is the sound of the land full of the same wind that is blowing in the same bare place for the listener, who listens in the snow, and, nothing himself, beholds nothing that is not there and the nothing that is.

This prose setting demonstrates that the original poem is more like prosaic free verse structured into visual tercets than like a descendent of trimeter or tetrameter couplets—hence we might expect limited success with a critical analysis that relies on metrical prosodies. The poem moves from an independent clause (before the first semicolon) to a clause that depends on the subject of the first clause (between first and second semicolons) to a final long dependent clause that undoes the independence of the earlier clauses by modifying them without achieving grammatical closure. This modification is especially prominent after "a few leaves, which is the sound of the land," etc. What seems independent loses its subject and then loses its independence; in terms of grammar and syntax, the poem enacts an independence-dissolving progress. In terms of "meaning," however, the last half of the poem is more vibrant and mysterious: The first clauses are (merely) descriptive, while the final dependent clause is replete with some kind of philosophical or ontological import.

Read as prose, then, the poem disassembles itself grammatically but increases in "meaningful" assertion. The independence of the "sentences" comes undone, so if readers want to form some completion of the poem's sense they must do so nonsyntactically, willfully, joining the first and second parts of the poem, undoing its grammar, and flouting punctuation rules. Imagining the reading process this way, we might say the reader brings independence into existence; the poetic "nothing" makes readerly independence happen.

If this is so grammatically and syntactically, is it also so semantically? We can explore this question through a double deformation of the poem, examining it in isolated pieces. Start with a noun reading, keeping the words in their same positions relative to the complete poem:

> mind   winter
> frost   boughs
> pine-trees   snow;
>
> time
> junipers   ice,
> spruces   glitter
>
> sun;
> misery   sound   wind,
> sound   leaves,
>
> sound   land
> wind
> place
>
> listener,   snow,
> nothing himself,
> Nothing   nothing

What does such deformative diagramming help us to *see?* First, and tellingly for this poem, it enhances the significance of the page's white space, which now appears as a poetic equivalent for the physical "nothing" of snow. It also enhances one of the poem's salient semantic features (nouns, in this case), calling into question and perhaps exposing more of their inset importance. Stevens's poem is exposed as both noun-heavy and noun-balanced. In each stanza, a fairly equal distribution balances the moorings of nouns and the airy nothing of the (temporarily invisible) words that string nouns together and help determine their interrelations. When nouns are so crucial, do so much to "tell" a poem, might we read it as a poem of quiddity, perhaps?

Perhaps, and this holds especially when we see that the first four stanzas have only one abstract noun apiece—"mind," "time," "misery," and "place"—

and that these are outnumbered by concrete, physical nouns. But this imbalance changes in the final stanza, whose three abstract nouns, repetitions of "nothing," might be said to overmaster both abstract and concrete forerunners. Furthermore, the triad "sound wind," "sound leaves," and "sound land" matches the triad of "nothing," "nothing," "nothing." We might say that the (concrete) nouns implant their own (abstract) cancellations, especially when we also see that the opening noun, "mind," arcs to "nothing" in the end. In spatial terms, this isolating deformance highlights the gap of the final line: The final two nouns—"Nothing   nothing"—are further apart from each other than any others in the poem, and the first "nothing" is the only capitalized noun, anchoring the physique of the poem like a cornerstone.

And yet the poem has such palpable senses: Those concrete nouns never go away, planted as they are in "nothing." To help us consider the poem's senses, we can turn from deforming the poem through the intellectual geography of its nouns and instead isolate all of the verbs, those words that might be said to effect the action and feeling of the poem:

        must have
        regard
            crusted

        have been
        behold   shagged

            not to think

        is

        is blowing

            listens
            beholds
        is not   is.

Here too we have a balance: between four verbs of action and four of absolute being. "To regard," "to behold," "not to think," and "listens" begin to interweave, in the fourth stanza, with four repetitions of "is," which has (is) the last word. But this is clearly less a poem of verbs than of nouns. The final "is not is" declares the simultaneous presence and negation of verbal being; it also anchors the final state of being on the far right side of the poem's base, literally on the other side of the capitalized "Nothing." The strong but unspecific "not to think" is followed by a long verb-free space, and then "is" "is blowing" around. "Not to think" contains the action it cancels just as the final verbs here declare the presence ("is") that the final nouns ("Nothing nothing") negate.

Why are the verbs here so attenuated—or, in the case of "is," simultaneously weak and strong absolutes? As the noun arc is from "mind" to "nothing," the verb arc is from "have" to "is," from (imperative, self-) possession to (indeterminate, absolute) being. In informative terms, we might see this as the linguistic relinquishment of the poem to the reader, a giving up similar to the way the "prose" version of the poem leaves sense-making to the reader's independent mechanisms. If both nouns and verbs become increasingly inhabitable ("is" and "nothing" open space as "have regard crusted" and "mind winter frost boughs" do not), then their poem does as well. Which may be why Stevens's poem is so popular: Its syntax, nouns, and verbs slowly arc into inhabitability.

Finally, let's reshuffle our diagram to the following mixture of *selected* nouns and verbs, isolating the poem's linguistic moves towards inhabitable emptiness:

>   mind winter
>   regard   boughs
>   snow;
>
>   time
>   behold   ice,
>   glitter
>
>   not to think
>   misery sound   wind,
>   sound   leaves,
>
>   sound land
>   wind
>   is blowing   place

>   listener   listens
>   nothing   beholds
>   Nothing is not   nothing is.

Here, clearly demarcated, is this poetical nothing's paradoxical *somethingness.*
One wants to turn it slowly around before one's eyes, the way one turns
around a decorated vase or sculpture to see it from different perspectives.
Take this concatenated text of nouns and verbs and reconstruct it in
reverse. You will see it revealed again, in a further range of its visible intelligibility.

In this deformance we also enact a critical subjectivity: This version isolates only *some* of the poem's nouns and verbs. Such selectiveness instances
the critic's position as reactive reader, choosing certain recombinations that
exteriorize the variable attention we pay to parts of the poem. And what
we see in this deformance is that Stevens's poem harbors the redeemed
form of that "Positive Negation" Coleridge sought in fear and trembling
and could not find, perhaps because he sought it in the "Limbo" of conceptual forms rather than on the page that bears his act of writing. Not
that Coleridge's poem "Limbo"—which is a kind of obverse of Stevens's—
is therefore to be imagined a lesser poiesis than "The Snow Man." In certain ways Coleridge's poem is more impressive, the way Byron's dark poetry
is always so impressive. They are poets, to use Stevens's own thought, who
"go in fear of abstractions," and entering the realm of that fear is their hon-
orable feat.

As a final suggestion, we could take Coleridge's "Limbo" and read it
backwards. Couplet verse is especially apt for such treatment: Turn it over
to different kinds of transformation; eliminate everything but the capitalized nouns; isolate the adjectives, those stylistic signatures of a romantic
style. Open the poem to its variable self.[12]

Conclusion: Deformance and Critical Dialectics

These examples of interpretive deformance have been chosen partly as
incentives to critical speculation and partly for their programmatic clarity.
Although they do not represent the mainstream of twentieth-century
interpretive procedure, a confederacy of such work can be found, especially
among artists and poets, for whom interpretation regularly involves some
kind of performative element. Blake, Rossetti, and Dante, as we have seen,
have been notable exponents of these interpretive ways. Scholarly uses of

such methods are, however, rare. The work of Randall McLeod is the contemporary exception proving the rule: that interpretive deformance is an unlicensed critical activity, all very well for poets and artists, but inapt for the normative rigor of the scholar and critic.[13]

In our view, however, we may usefully regard all criticism and interpretation as deformance. Scholars murder to dissect, as Wordsworth famously observed, and as naive readers—typically, young students—often tell us when they recoil from our interpretive operations. "You've ruined the poem for me": That kind of comment, academically infamous, illustrates something far more important than a protest against scholarly sophisticates. Often coming as a kind of blanket judgment on reflexive interpretation, it implicitly asserts the deformative status of critical method in general.[14]

The truth-content of such views is further exposed when we reflect on the critical dialectics of the great Italian philologist Galvano della Volpe. At the heart of his *Critique of Taste* (1960) stands a view of interpretation—he calls it a "realist" view—that supplants, on one hand, the dominant idealist approaches broadcast through modernist and New Critical venues (both romantic and neoclassical), and, on the other, the various historicisms (Marxist and otherwise) that have gained increasing authority during the past 30 years. Like Dante, and in contrast to, say, Coleridge or Schlegel, della Volpe sees poetry as a type of "discourse" whose rationality—*ragionamento*—consists in its exploitation of the "polysemous" dimensions of language, whose structures are no more (and no less) difficult or even "mysterious" than processes of logical deduction and induction. For della Volpe, "intelligibility" is as much a feature of poiesis as of scientia.

Interpretation is the application of scientia to poiesis, or the effort to elucidate one discourse form in terms of another. Furthermore, the effort is not directed toward establishing general rules or laws but toward explaining a unitary, indeed a unique, phenomenon. A doubled gap thus emerges through the interpretive process itself, and it is the necessary presence of this gap that shapes della Volpe's critical thought. We may usefully recall here that when poets and artists use imaginative forms to interpret other such forms, they pay homage to this gap by throwing it into relief. Rossetti's famous sonnets for pictures, like all such works, from Cavalcanti to John Ashbery, do not so much translate the originary works as construct imaginative paraphrases. Rossetti's theory of translation, as we see in *The Early Italian Poets* (1861), follows a similar paraphrastic procedure.

Della Volpe's theory of interpretation runs along the same intellectual salient. When he argued that "critical paraphrase" should ground interpretive method, he was consciously installing a non-Hegelian form of dialectical criticism. In place of "a *circular* movement of negation and conservation of an original meta-historical unity of opposites," della Volpe offers what he calls "a dialectic of expressive facts"—the facts of the discrete poem and its discrete paraphrase—in which "neither of the elements of the relation can be reduced absolutely to the other . . . for . . . they . . . circulate only *relatively* within each other, in the *diversified unity of an historical movement*" (*Critique of Taste* 200). Interpretation for della Volpe, whatever its pretensions, always displays a gap between the work being examined and the student. But this gap does not represent a failure of criticism, or even a mysticism of poiesis. It locates the source and end and test of the art being examined. Della Volpe calls the gap a "quid," which comes into play as soon as the critic develops some "philosophical or sociological or historical equivalent of the poetic text," that is to say the "paraphrase . . . of the poetic thought or . . . content." Because this paraphrase will necessarily constitute "a reduction" of the original, "a comparison will necessarily be instituted between this paraphrase and the poetic thought or 'content' which it paraphrases" (193).

Critical interpretation develops out of an initial moment of the originary work's "degradation" via "uncritical paraphrase": "for in the case of the poetic, polysemic text, paraphrase—the *regression* to current linguistic use . . . constitutes the premise of an internal *progression* of thought . . . , an internal variation and development of meanings, which is disclosed . . . in a . . . philological comparison . . . of the paraphrase with that which is paraphrased" (133). Interpretation, then, is a constellation of paraphrases that evolve dialectically from an uncritical to a critical moment, from "regression" to "progression." The interpretive constellation develops as the "uncritical" features of each critical turn get exposed—as new turns are taken, as the paraphrase is successively rephrased. One moves so to speak from "degradation" to "degradation," or, as we would say, from deformance to deformance. Thus paraphrastics becomes "the *beginning* and *end* of a whole process" of comparative explorations that get executed across the "quid" or gap that a process of interpretation brings into being. Again, the process is open ended not because the "poem itself" possesses some mysterious, inexhaustible "meaning" but because its originary semiotic determinations must repeatedly be discovered within the historical space defined by the della Volpian "quid," where distantiation licenses "the method . . . of experimental analysis" (199).

Della Volpe carefully separates his theory of interpretation from the dialectics we associate with Hegel and especially Heidegger. The latter involves a process of thought refinement: Through conversation or internal dialogue, we clarify our ideas to ourselves. We come to realize what we didn't know we knew. This kind of reflection traces itself back to the idea of Platonic anamnesis. Della Volpe, by contrast, follows an Aristotelian line of thought, a "method . . . of experimental analysis." This method develops a process of non-Hegelian historical reflection. Interpretive moments stand in nonuniform relations with each other so that the interpretation unfolds in fractal patterns of continuities and discontinuities. Besides realizing, perhaps, what we didn't know we knew, we are also led into imaginations of what we hadn't known at all.

The deformative examples set forth in the previous section are conceived as types of a della Volpean "experimental analysis." Being a philologist, della Volpe pursues this kind of analysis through a series of searching historicist paraphrases of the texts he chooses to consider. To attempt a sociohistorical paraphrase is to experiment with the poetical work, to subject it to a hypothesis of its meanings. As in any scientific experiment with natural phenomena, the engagement with the originary phenomenon inevitably exposes the limits of the hypothesis, and ultimately returns us to an even more acute sense of the phenomena we desire to understand. So it is with della Volpe's paraphrases. By contrast, our "experimental analyses" place primary emphasis on the preconceptual elements of text. We do this because social and historical formations seem to us far less determinate, far more open to arbitrary and imaginative construction, than they appear in della Volpe's Marxist frame of reference.

If we follow della Volpe's method, then, we feel ourselves closer in spirit to the thought of, say, Blake when he remarks on the difference between the intelligence of art and the intelligence of philosophy: "Cunning & Morality are not Poetry but Philosophy the Poet is Independent & Wicked the Philosopher is Dependent & Good" (Blake 634). Our deformations do not flee from the question, or the generation, of "meaning." Rather, they try to demonstrate—the way one demonstrates how to make something, or do something—what Blake here assertively proposes: that "meaning" in imaginative work is a secondary phenomenon, a kind of metadata, what Blake called a form of worship "Dependent" upon some primary poetical tale. This point of view explains why, in our deformative maneuvers, interpretive lines of thought spin out of some initial nondiscursive "experiment" with the primary materials. "Meaning" is important not as explanation but as residue. It is what is left behind after the experiment has been run. We develop it not to explain the poem but to judge the effectiveness of the experiment we undertook.

One could do worse than to recall, even in this special aesthetic frame of reference, Marx's last thesis on Feuerbach. Only philosophers try to understand art. The point is to change it. (Editorial efforts to preserve our cultural inheritance are themselves types of "change"). Our actions on these works, as on anything else in our experience, allow us to begin to understand our thinking about them. To essay a more direct application of "interpretation" to poetical work runs the risk of suggesting that interpretation can be adequate to poiesis. It cannot; it can only run a thematic experiment with the work, enlightening it by inadequacy and indirection. In a hermeneutic age like our own, illusions about the sufficiency of interpretative meaning before the work of art are especially strong. At such a historical moment one might rather look for interpretations that flaunt their subjectivity and arbitrariness, interpretations that increase their value by offering themselves at a clear discount.

To deliberately accept the inevitable failure of interpretive "adequacy" is to work toward discovering new interpretive virtues, somewhat as Lyn Hejinian claims that the supposed "inadequacy" of language "is merely a disguise for other virtues."[15] Interpretations that parody or ironize themselves become especially apt and useful, as we see in Derrida's textual games, in the brilliant philological studies of Randall McLeod, in Barthes's *S/Z,* and in Laura Riding's attitude toward language and understanding: "our minds are still moving, and *backward* as well as *forward;* the nearest we get to truth at any given moment is, perhaps, only an idea—a dash of truth somewhat flavouring the indeterminate substance of our minds."[16] This attitude toward literate comprehension, and the kind of criticism it inspires, gains its power by baring its own devices. We take it seriously because it makes sure that we do not take it too seriously. Examples of such critical approaches are legion: we just need to remember to look for them, and perhaps how to look for them.

Appendix to Chapter 4

[We give here, without comment, a series of deformative moves on Stevens's "The Snow Man," as well as a deformance of Coleridge's "Limbo." These illustrate a few other operations that might be undertaken with poems.]

Wallace Stevens's "The Snow Man"

1. Reading Backward

> Nothing that is not there and the nothing that is.
> And, nothing himself, beholds,
> For the listener, who listens in the snow,
>
> That is blowing in the same bare place
> Full of the same wind
> Which is the sound of the land
>
> In the sound of a few leaves,
> Of any misery in the sound of the wind,
> Of the January sun; and not to think
>
> The spruces rough in the distant glitter
> To behold the junipers shagged with ice,
> And have been cold a long time
>
> Of the pine-trees crusted with snow;
> To regard the frost and the boughs
> One must have a mind of winter

2. Reordered Deformance

> One must have a mind of winter
> And have been cold a long time

> To regard the frost and the boughs
> Of the pine-trees crusted with snow;
> To behold the junipers shagged with ice,

                                        The spruces rough in the distant
                                        glitter
                                        Of the January sun;

    and not to think
    Of any misery   in the sound of the wind,
                                        In the sound of a few leaves,
                                        Which is the sound of the land
                                        Full of the same wind
                                        That is blowing in the same
                                        bare place
                                        For the listener,

    who listens in the snow,
    And, nothing himself, beholds
    Nothing that is not there and the nothing that is.

3. Isolating Deformance, All Nouns and Verbs

            must have   mind   winter
        regard   frost   boughs
            pine-trees crusted   snow;

        have been   time
        behold   junipers shagged   ice,
            spruces   glitter

                    sun;   not to think
            misery   sound   wind,
            sound   leaves,

            is   sound   land
                    wind
        is blowing   place

            listener,   listens   snow,
                nothing   beholds
        Nothing   is not   nothing   is.

4. *Isolating, All Words Other than Nouns and Verbs (Plus Punctuation)*

One   a   of
To   the   and the
Of the   with   ;

And   a long
To   the   with ,
The   rough in the distant

Of the January   ; and
Of any   in the   of the ,
In the   of a few   ,

Which   the   of the
Full of the same
That   in the same bare

For the   , who   in the   ,
And,   ,
     that   there and the   that .

5. *Altering Deformance*

one m ust halve a mine dove w inter
to re guard the f rost and the bows
of the pine trees c rusted with s no

and halve been c old along time
to be hold the junipers sh agged with ice,
the spruces ruff in the dis t ant g litter

of the January son   and not to th ink
of any miser y in the s ound of the win d
in the s ound of a few l eave s

witches the s ound of the l and
full of the s ame win d
that is b low ing in the s ame b are p lace

for the listen er who list ens in the s no
an d no thing him self be hold s
no thing that is no t t here an d the no thing that is

Samuel Taylor Coleridge, "Limbo"

6. Altering and Reordered

The sole
true Something—
This, in Limbo's Den
It frightens
Ghosts, as here
Ghosts frighten men.
Thence cross'd   by flit of Shades,—unmeaning
Unseiz'd—and shall   they as moonlight
some fated hour   on the dial
Be pulveris'd   of the day! But that
by Demogorgon's power,   is lovely—looks
And given as poison   like Human Time,—
to annihilate souls—   an Old Man
Even now it shrinks them—   with a steady look
they shrink in   sublime, that stops his earthly
as Moles (Nature's mute   task to watch
monks, live mandrakes   the skies; but he is blind—
of the ground) creep back   a Statue hath
from Light—then listen   such eyes;—yet having moonward
for its sound;   turn'd his face
See but to dread,   by chance, gazes the orb
and dread they know not   with moon-like
why—the natural alien   countenance, with scant white
of their negative eye.   hairs, with foretop
                                               bald and high, he gazes still,—
'Tis a strange place,   his eyeless face
this Limbo!—not   all eye;—as 'twere an organ
a Place, yet name it   full of silent sight
so;—where Time   his whole face seemeth to rejoice
and weary Space fettered   in light! Lip touching lip, all
from flight, with night-mare moveless, bust and limb—

sense of fleeing
Strive for their last
crepuscular half-being;—
Lank Space,
and scytheless
Time with branny
hands barren and soundless
as the measuring sands,

Not mark'd

he seems to gaze
at that which seems to gaze
on him! No such sweet
doth Limbo den immure, wall'd
round and made a spirit—
jail secure, by the mere
horror of blank
Naught-at-all, whose circumambi-
ence
doth these ghosts enthrall.
A lurid thought
is growthless, dull Privation, yet that
is but a Purgatory
curse; Hell knows a fear far
worse, a fear—a future
state;—'tis positive
Negation!

Chapter 5

Rethinking Textuality

There are some "features" of the real world that are better lost in translation.
Perhaps the idea of a document having a single location is one of them.
—Steven Johnson, Interface Culture

As we have seen over and over again, complex problems emerge when you try to think about digital media through our inherited codex paradigms or vice versa. The collision of these two marking systems—for that is ultimately what they are—came up repeatedly in our conversations about one of Johanna Drucker's central concerns—what she calls "The Metalogics of the Book."[1] That subject shifted into useful focus when Drucker and I undertook a simple experiment with an OCR scanner. The point of the experiment was to use computer hardware to demonstrate what our thought experiments kept suggesting to us: that the rationale of a textualized document is an ordered ambivalence and that this ambivalence can be seen functioning at the document's fundamental graphic levels. By "rationale" we mean the dynamic structure of a document as it is realized in determinate (artisanal) and determinable (reflective) ways. By "ordered ambivalence" we mean the signifying differentials set in play when a rhetoric of intention is applied to a document. Textual differentials at any level are a function of the effort to control or even eliminate them.[2]

The implications of this demonstration are, we believe, considerable. For our own special field of interest—the study of literary, cultural, and aesthetic works, and especially those deploying textual elements—the demonstration brings a strong argument for the following ideas:

(1)a. That what we call "a text" should be understood as a document composed of both semantical and graphical signifying parts.[3]

b. That the heuristic distinction between bibliographic and semantic elements obscures the field of textual meaning by identifying the signifying field (its "rationale") with the semantic field.

(2)a. That there is no such thing as an unmarked text, and the markup systems laid upon documents to facilitate computerized analyses are marking orders laid upon already marked up material. (Thus all texts implicitly record a cultural history of their artifactuality.)

b. That while we recognize how the semantic elements of any given document encode a record of those elements' historical passage, the same is true of the text's bibliographical elements.

(3)a. That marked text, a document, is interpreted text.

b. That text documents, while *coded* bibliographically and semantically, are all *marked* graphically.

c. That the distinction between graphic and bibliographic textual features stands as an index of the text's archaeological condition in both its semantic and its bibliographical orders.

d. That marking any textual distinction—for example, between bibliographic and semantic elements—is a high order interpretive operation.

e. That distinctions may be marked for attention or for inattention. (So the interpretive procedure, now prevalent, that does not "reveal the codes" of its bibliographical rationale has marked them for inattention.)

(4)a. That texted documents are not containers of meaning or data but sets of rules (algorithms) for generating themselves: for discovering, organizing, and utilizing meanings and data.

b. That since the demise of classical rhetorical theory and the emergence of advertising, bibliographical codes constitute a text's clearest display of its generative rules.

c. That these rules—the rationale of the texted document—are necessarily ambiguous because the rules are being repeatedly reread (i.e., executed), whether the reader is conscious of this or not.

d. That the marked text, as a record of its historical passage, is ipso facto a record of its previous readings, that is to say, its generative rules.

e. That the rules of marked text—the descriptive/performative protocols—can be made apparent (rendered visible) *as such* through another marking program. (But many of these rules, now so historically remote, will have become too obscure to recover.)

(5). That a certain class of texts—poetical texts, so called—are normative for all textual documents because their generic rationale is to maximize attention to the structure and interplay of the textual orders.

Understand that as we undertook our experiment this sequence of ideas had reached only the loosest state of articulation. Several were altogether unformulated at the beginning of our work, and at this point some are hypotheses for guiding our planned work. They emerged in a determinate form only after some months of preliminary theoretical conversations and initial experiments. A dialectical/experimental process came to clarify and unpack these inchoate ideas and direct the process of exploration. Nevertheless, I place them here so that you can follow and assess the adequacy of what we're doing and why we came to these first conclusions.

The Initial Experimental Context

The project began out of a general dissatisfaction with two approaches to textuality and text interpretation that have great authority in the community of literary and linguistic scholars. One, a recent power, gained its position with the emergence of humanities computing. The logical system of text markup developed for computers, SGML, fully represents this view. This hypergrammar treats its documentary materials as organized information, and it chooses to determine the system of organization as a hierarchy of nested elements; or, in the now well-known formulation: "text is an ordered hierarchy of content objects" (the so-called OHCO thesis).

This approach to textuality only became problematic when it was undertaken and then implemented by the Text Encoding Initiative (TEI), as several of its principal advocates pointed out in 1993: "the experience of the text encoding community, as represented and codified by the TEI *Guidelines,* has raised difficulties for the [OHCO] thesis."[4] As we know, TEI set about formulating a special subset of SGML that would be useful, in its view, for encoding cultural documents (as opposed to business and administrative documents) for computerized search and analysis. TEI is now a standard for humanities encoding practices. Because it treats the humanities corpus—typically, works of imagination—as informational structures, it ipso facto violates some of the most basic reading practices of the humanities community, scholarly as well as popular.

The revulsion that many humanists express for the emergence of digital technology reflects this sense that computerized models are alien things:

if not alien to imaginative practice as such, then certainly alien to the received inheritance of literature and art.

This traditional community of readers comprises the second group to which our project is critically addressed. For this group textual interpretation (as opposed to text management and organization) is the central concern. In this community of readers, the very idea of a "standard generalized markup," which is to say a standard generalized interpretation, is either problematic or preposterous. The issue hangs upon the centrality of the poetical or imaginative text for cultural scholars, though it applies equally well to students of art, history, anthropology, politics, law, and any discipline in which procedural rules of interpretation are perceived as more or less context-based, flexible, manipulable: "reader" or "community" organized—dialectical—rather than structurally fixed.

But while our specific project consciously addressed this duplex audience—each at once a set of adversaries and a set of comrades—it became a practical focus only after a set of (so to speak) prehistorical events had unfolded. Here I speak only for myself, not for Johanna Drucker, who at the time (1992–1993) was working elsewhere and whom I did not know, though I knew her work pretty well.

The determinate matter here is the project of *The Rossetti Archive*. As we have seen, this came about in late 1993, about seven years after I had first encountered computerized technology and hypermedia methodology during my tenure at Caltech. At that time I knew I would undertake a project like the archive should the chance arrive. This was a clear decision based on the idea that a hypermedia "edition" or "archive" would make it possible to study literary and aesthetic works in entirely new ways. The innovative possibilities were, in my view, not just a function of the computational resource of these new tools. Two other matters interested me more. First, digital imaging resources offered hopes that students would be able to carry out their studies in a more direct relation to primary documentary materials. This was important to me because my previous work as an editor of such materials had shown me that what traditional interpretation sought as "meaning" in a text was always deeply funded in a text's material features—its "bibliographical codes," now so called. Second, I was struck by the interpretive opportunities released in those relational organizations fostered by computerization: hypertext and hypermedia.

When we began building *The Rossetti Archive* in 1993, I was introduced to SGML and TEI as tools for enhancing the analytic power of the archive's resources. The usefulness of these tools became apparent fairly quickly and so with the help of some people who had a deep understanding of logical markup forms, we created a specialized version of SGML to organize the data in the archive.

Then followed seven years of practical implementations of our initial plans and ideas. These were years filled with those splendid, even ravishing enlightenments that only come when your plans and ideas are thwarted and overthrown. "In a dark time," as Theodore Roethke famously wrote, "the eye begins to see."

So, as we proceeded with the practical construction of the archive we began to see the hidden fault lines of its design structure. As I've already pointed out, what began as a project to put out a certain product—an image-based design for electronic editing that would have wide applicability—bifurcated. Our initial purpose acquired a new one: to use the archive's process of construction as a laboratory for reflecting on the project itself. That second purpose led inevitably to a regular set of critical inquiries into the basic organizing ideas of the archive and its procedures. This new set of interests inevitably delayed the appearance of the archive itself—a frustrating event in certain respects but immensely fruitful in others.

One result of these new interests is Drucker's "Metalogics of the Book" project. In my case the project emerged directly from a reflection on three types of problem that the building of the archive exposed. The first, which I've already noted, involved the weaknesses in "the OHCO thesis" of textuality that we found when implementing the archive. The second problem centered in the way we were handling digital images. That is to say, the archive's logical design had no means for integrating these objects into an analytic structure. Finally, interface—or rather, the failure to consider interface in a serious way—constituted yet a third problem. This last case was in certain respects the most interesting as well as the most surprising. For when we worked out the archive's original design, we deliberately chose to focus on the logical structure and to set aside any thought about the Interface for delivering the archive to its users. We made this decision in order to avoid committing ourselves prematurely to a delivery mechanism. The volatile character of interface software appeared so extreme that we determined to proceed in such a way that, when we were ready to deliver the work, we would have a product that could be accommodated to whatever software seemed best.

The Rewards of Failure

A great virtue of computerized tools is that they are simple. Consequently, to get them to perform their operations you have to make your instructions explicit and unambiguous. To do that means you have to be very clear in your own mind about what you're thinking, meaning, intending. The simplicity of the computer is merciless. It will expose every jot and tittle of your thought's imprecisions.

What I've just said is news to no one. It is a banality. But we want to remember that time when we thought differently about computers and about cognitive precision. The recollection is important here because it will help to clarify our project.

Here is my recollection circa 1983. Introduced to UNIX multitasking and to the possibilities of digital hypermedia, I was drawn to my initial imagining of something like *The Rossetti Archive*—a critical and scholarly environment for studying aesthetic works in novel and hitherto impossible ways. When the chance came some ten years later actually to build such a work, I thought I had come to the Promised Land.

It was Middlearth after all, I would soon realize. But in fact also a land of promise, although promising in a way I had not expected.

The simplifying rigors characteristic of digital systems have not been prized by humanities scholars for a long time. They are associated with disambiguated scientific—or at least scientistic—thinking. Humanities scholars pledge their allegiance to a different kind of rigor and precision. Or so we have always said. But what *is* that kind of precision, precisely?

Responding to that question is a primary, and in all likelihood longterm, goal of the "Metalogics of the Book" experiment. Our general goal is to study how digital tools fail to render or realize complex forms of imaginative works (the works of Rossetti, for instance). The purpose, however, is not to "correct" these "failures" but to try to understand their significance and meaning.

So we're trying to use computational operations not to realize our purposes and ideas but to derealize them, as it were. Why do we want this? Because our subjects of interest are works that realize themselves not *in* standardized and disambiguated forms but through their active relation to such forms. This relation shows why computerization can only realize imperfectly and imprecisely the projects most dear to scholars who study imaginative works. The problem does not lie "in" the computers but in the strategies of those who design them. This inevitable dysfunction, however, is no reason at all to dismiss computerization from the principal research interests of humanities scholars. On the contrary, these new tools offer an unprecedented opportunity for clarifying our thinking processes. Indeed, they license us to implement in more rigorous ways della Volpe's dialectical model of interpretation (see chapter 3).

This project means to use computerized resources to clarify—to define precisely—what we imagine we know about books and texts. Because our computer tools are models of what we imagine we know—they're built to our specifications—when they show us what they know they are reporting ourselves back to us.

The Experiment

Ask this question: "Can a computer be taught to read a poem?" The answer is "yes." TEI is a grammar that computers can understand and manipulate. When you mark up text you are ipso facto reading and interpreting it. A poetical text marked up in TEI has been subjected to a certain kind of interpretation.

But of course sophisticated readers of poetical works recoil when such a model of reading is recommended to them. Poems are rich with nuances that regularly and, it seems, inevitably transcend TEI protocols.

But suppose one were to step away from complex forms like poetry. Suppose one were to try to begin a computerized analysis of texted documents at a primitive level. The first move in this case would be to choose to "read" the document at a presemantic level. The focus would be on the document's graphical design, the latter being understood as a set of markup features comprising a reading of the document, that is, a set of protocols for negotiating the textual scene. The idea would be to construct an initial set of elementary text descriptors that would be fed to a computer. The computer would use these to parse the document and then deliver an output of what it read.

Our hypothesis was that it would deliver multiple readings.

This initial model for the experiment did not survive a series of critical interrogations. Conversations we had with Worthy Martin (one of our colleagues at IATH and a specialist in computer vision) exposed the difficulty of constraining the text descriptors so that we would get usable results. To do this was theoretically feasible but would take a great deal of mathematical analysis. These conversations brought another important realization: that the text primitives we were trying to articulate would comprise an elementary set of markup codes. And that understanding brought out a crucial further understanding about textuality in general: that all texts are marked texts.

At this point let me quote Johanna's notes on our investigation as it then stood:

> JJM said that his idea of automated mark-up was not simply to insert tags identifying semantic or syntactic or content features, but to show that texts

were already "marked" in their written form. This suggested to me the idea of the "reveal codes" command in a digital document, since it would make evident what is usually unacknowledged and unseen: the commands and protocols according to which the file is encoded.

Though "reveal codes" was the first term that galvanized discussion, it was quickly evident that Jerry and I came at it from two different directions and with two different, but curiously complementary agendas. Jerry saw "reveal codes" as an aspect of "deformance" and I saw it as a first step in a "meta-logics of the book." Thus we split from the outset between interpretation and analytic description, between a desire to create a demonstration of deformance as a mode of reading and an interrogation of book form and format as interface. In both instances, the point of commonality that links our project into one is the conviction that the graphic format of a text participates in the production of textual signification in ways that are generally unacknowledged. Our shared aim is to demonstrate this—JJM leading us through experiments in computer misreading of graphic features and me trying to push the analysis of graphic form by developing a critical vocabulary for it. (Notes 1)

As we tried to relate and define more precisely our two lines of inquiry, it occurred to us that we might take advantage of the elementary reading operations carried out by Optical Character Recognition (OCR) programs. Even the best of these programs, as we knew, produced deformed readings of the documents they scanned. We therefore decided to see what could be discovered from the deformations generated by a good scanning program. We used Omnipage 10.0. We also decided to work with prose texts rather than with poetry. But the prose texts would be of two different kinds: first, a document with some complex display features, and second a relatively straightforward piece of prose formatted margin-to-margin in standard block form. We report here only on the first document.

We chose an advert page from the 20 August 1870 issue of the Victorian periodical *The Athenaeum* (page 256). We set the scanner at True Page/Greyscale. The plan was to run the page through several successive scannings, in this order: (1). An initial scanning; (2). A reprocessing (NOT a rescanning) of the document at exactly the same settings and without moving the document; (3). A repetition of operation 1, that is, a rescanning of the document keeping all original settings and with the document unmoved; (4–6). A repetition of operations 1, 2, and 3 but at a black and white setting; (7–12). A repetition of operations 1–6 except we would lift the document and replace it in as nearly the same position as we could. We had other similar repetition/variation scans in mind as well, but before planning them we judged it best to assess the results of these first 12 operations.

As it turned out, the results we obtained in the first two operations led us to modify these initial plans. We performed instead a second repetition of the initial scan and then went on to perform only a selection of the other operations.

Operation 1. The first scanning pass produced the usual double output: a rough image highlighting the page sectors, and a standard output of the alphanumeric text. The scan produced a text divided into 21 zones plus an alphanumeric text with a series of misreadings and error messages.

Operation 2. The reprocessing of the first scan produced a startling double result: the output this time divided the document into 20 zones and displayed slightly different alphanumeric text.

Operation 3. The rescanning of the document produced yet further variances in both the sectoring and the alphanumeric output. This time 17 zones were distinguished and new variances appeared in the alphanumeric text.

The results of operations 2 and 3 convinced us to repeat operation 3, which produced this time 18 sectors and new variances in the alphanumeric text. At this point we had results that were significant for our purposes, so we curtailed the rest of the planned experiment. We did two more rescannings: a scan at black and white settings, which reproduced the sectoring of operation 1 but output a new set of alphanumeric variances; and a rescanning after the document had been lifted and then replaced on the scanner. This operation yielded 22 sectors plus new alphanumeric variances.

Several important consequences flowed from these experiments. First, we now possessed a powerful physical argument for a key principle of "textual deformance" and its founding premise: that no text is self-identical.[5] Whatever the physical "causes" of the variant readings, and however severely one sought to maintain the integrity of the physical operation, it appeared that variance would remain a possibility.

Second, the OCR experiments showed that textual ambivalence can be located and revealed at graphical, presemantic levels. This demonstration is important if one wishes to explore the signifying value of the bibliographical codes of a textual document. For it is a commonplace in both the SGML/TEI and the hermeneutic communities that these codes do not signify in the way that semantic codes do.

Third, the experiments strongly suggested that while every text possesses, as it were, a self-parsing markup, the reading of that markup can only be executed by another parsing agent. That is to say, there can be no such thing as an "unread" text. (And while the experiments did nothing to argue for the following conviction, it remains strong with both of us: that every text "contains within itself," so to speak, a more or less obscured history of the readings/parsings, both semantic and bibliographical, that transmit the document to any immediate moment of reading/parsing.)

The Present Situation

Out of these experiments emerged the theses I set out at the beginning of this chapter, and the issues raised through the theses have set Drucker and myself on a pair of new courses. First, here are Drucker's notes for developing 4D interface design models.

> Rather than visualizing the thematic/semantic contents of a text in abstract form I now want to be sure to map it into a visualized spatialization of the book. Thinking of the book as a space, one that also unfolds along the temporal axis (or axes) of reading, I can envision a 4–d model of the book.
>
> In this model every graphic element is actually a structuring element. Thus, for instance, a table of contents is not a simple notation lying on a thin sheet in the front matter, but is means of dividing the sculptural form of the book into a set of discrete spaces, each demarcated in relation to that original point of spatial reference, and located relationally within the whole. This sounds terribly empirical, I know, and insofar as I am interested in describing an object in material, schematic, and logical terms, I intend for it to suggest a faith in what Worthy calls "the properties of things themselves." I would stop short of any suggestion that these are "self-identical" properties, or that a specific signification inheres in these properties, or that there might be a lexicon of values attached to such properties. Instead, I suggest that as organizing schemata, these format features function as an integral portion of the text because they function as an interface.
>
> In a several stage process, I want to make a visualized model of a book, a wire-frame image of its format features down to their specifics and particularities, and then flow the text through that so that semantically/syntactically tagged features can be displayed (why? first to see what patterns figure forth from such a demonstration, and second, to be able to morph this display as another act of deformance).
>
> JJM suggests a second form in this model, a second "book" that would emerge as an image of the discourse of reading, the trace of intercourse of reader and text. This begins to suggest the holographic projection of my original graph of deformance as a space between discourse and reference.

Now I see that that space is in fact the space of reading—with reading defined as deformance. (Notes 7)

This new project intends to deepen the exploration of the "nature" of paper-based documents. And while my work with *The Rossetti Archive* "as a theoretical pursuit" has been directed almost exclusively in that direction for the past five years,[6] I am beginning to see a need to clarify the critical possibilities of digital environments and tools at the user end. So the following questions begin to pose themselves. First: what practical difference does it make to understand documents as "difference engines"? At one time we thought (I think) that a person might usefully engage in "endless play" with "the text," but the tediousness of such a thought is now apparent to (nearly) everyone. It is the dead-end of our 1500–year experiment with the game of silent reading. The game will probably never cease to have its charms, but it is a game now often spinning the wheels of its own conventions. (That is the "meaning" of a work like *If on a Winter's Night a Traveller* [Calvino], though I should add that since Poe the meaning has been as available as the purloined letter.) Second: what good are cybertools for elucidating these difference engines?

Those two questions will be addressed in a practical way by asking two other questions: What use-functions distinguish cybertext from docutext? And (how) might any of those functions promote our appreciation of texts as difference engines?

A Brief Digression

Some of the most reliable promoters of cybertext—whether critical (like Espen Aarseth) or inspirational (like Janet Murray)—have themselves, I think, obscured the issues. Murray, for example, distinguishes four central properties of digital environments: two interactive properties (procedural, participatory); and two immersive properties (spatial, encyclopedic) (Murray 71–90). It can be shown, however, that none of these properties are peculiar to digital environments. They are even essential properties of the docutexts that control the way Murray thinks about digital tools. Her interest is in fictional narrative, and if one thinks seriously about such narratives one easily sees that these four properties characterize their operational status. This fact is most apparent from Murray's own book, for when she introduces her view of the digital environment, she uses a number of paper-based works she calls "Harbingers of the Holodeck." All of her harbingers are recent, but the truth is that these harbingers go far back—the

Bible being one of the most apparent. Murray chooses recent ones in order to seduce us into thinking these environments are recent phenomena. But they aren't, as book scholars have often pointed out to cyberiots.

Aarseth has proposed an elaborate taxonomy for texts in general in order to construct a distinctive set of criteria for understanding what he wants to call "cybertexts." Unlike Murray, Aarseth recognizes that books have "dynamic" functions and hence that "new [cybernetic] media do not appear in opposition to the old [paper media] but as emulators of features and functions that are already invented" (Aarseth 74). Despite this remark, however, Aarseth makes a sharp distinction between what he calls "linear" and "ergodic" texts and he locates "ordinary text"—including "hyper"ordinary texts—on the linear side of the distinction. Cybertexts, by contrast, are "ergodic" in that they have dynamic user-function(s) beyond the purely interpretive function common to all texts (Aarseth 62–67). (He distinguishes three other user functions: explorative, configurative, and textonic, the last signifying the user's ability to add permanent traversal functions to the text.)

Useful as Aarseth's study is, however, he too, like Murray, misconstrues "ordinary text" as "linear." One does not have to recall Mesoamerican *quipu* or any number of ideographical texts to recognize the nonlinear character of various kinds of precybertexts.[7] Every poem comprised in our inherited Western corpus could fairly be described as a nonlinear game played (largely) with linear forms and design conventions, but often with nonlinear forms as well. Nonverbal texts are useful to consider in this context because they highlight the sociohistorical nature of "linear textuality." Epitomized by documents constructed from alphanumeric characters and by a "clockwork" temporality, even the most abstract linear texts contain residues of nonlinear semiotic functions and relations. The residues appear when textual spaces are treated as maps, when algorithms of traversal are deployed (as with glosses, footnotes, and such), or when the form taken by scripts and typefaces functions rhetorically (operates beyond an abstract and transparent informational function). C. S. Peirce's turn-of-the-century effort to replace the alphanumeric text with what he called existential graphs in order to achieve a greater range and clarity of logical exposition is an extremely important event in the history of Western textuality. The graphs were an effort to develop a language for nonlinear relations.[8]

Material Messages

Aarseth's and Murray's views about the differences between traditional and cyber textualities are common and widely accepted. That fact underscores the need for a thoroughgoing retheorization of our ideas about books and traditional textuality in general. Since our immediate purpose is to "rethink textuality" in relation to digital resources, we will settle for something much more modest at this point. Three points are especially important. First, we want to recover a clear sense of the rhetorical character of traditional text. Rhetoric exposes what texts are *doing* in saying what they say. It is fundamentally "algorithmic." Secondly, we want to remember that textual rhetoric operates at the material level of the text—that is to say, through its bibliographical codes. Both matters are crucial if we are to build digital tools that can exploit the resources of traditional texts. Finally, we have to preserve a clear sense of the relation of those two features of traditional text and the inherently differential, underdetermined character of textual works. Texts are not self-identical, but their ambiguous character—this is especially clear in poetical texts—functions in very precise and determinate ways.

Of first importance is the analysis of the elemental formality that makes text possible: textspace, or the confines that invite the appearance of text in any form at all. We think of this as some kind of pagespace or its equivalent, but in fact text can be entertained in spaces whose elements are distributed in linear or nonlinear arrangements, or both. In the case of nonlinear, the topology may be open or closed (a cave wall, say, versus a bowl, a vase, a knife, etc.). Those spaces represent different executable programs for the deployment of text. If we think in terms of pagespace exclusively, the formal options for deploying text (or text plus shapes, or text plus shapes and/or images) are both complex and determinate. Any given pagespace could be analyzed for its textual deployment rules, and one could also go on to lay out a higher order set of rules for pagespace in general—a set that would be generalized from an inductive study of a comprehensive body of documentary instances. The atomic documentary unit of any pagespace would be a textual mark, that is to say, an alphanumeric or a syllabic (or perhaps an ideographic) mark along with the space that has interpellated the mark. That unit of marked space can then generate, through rule-governed procedures, the higher-order textual constructions that are available within pagespace.

Textspace is only partly distinguished in such documentary terms, however. For one thing, those terms are purely formal ones and say nothing about the generative capabilities of a textual document considered with respect to its materialities (whether semantic or linguistic). For another, although the formal structure of pagespace is planar and two-dimensional, the forms of pagespace can be made to generate themselves through n-dimensional orders (see chapter 7). Furthermore, beyond the documentary state of the text stand many other rule-governed orders of textuality—rules of grammar, rhetoric, genre, and their subsets of rules. And informational as opposed to poetic texts illustrate a crucial *generic* distinction, as everyone knows. Those two great genres proliferate through numerous subgenres that are framed by coded instructions. Any given textual form represents a complex set of transactional codes written for simultaneous and/or sequential execution.

In all these cases we are considering what texts are *doing* in saying what they say. I have deliberately kept the analysis from considering any more complex, higher-order types of textual performatives—for instance, from considering the ideological dimension of textuality, which is perhaps the one area of textuality where injunctive processes have drawn regular—if not especially rigorous—critical attention. The point is to keep the form of the analysis as sharply defined as possible so that we can get a clear view of the rhetorical scene at a general level, because the complexity of text-space and its coding options are very great.

Let's shift, then, from these spatial grammatologies to consider textuality in terms of the lexicon. Any textspace can, in the abstract, deploy any lexicon. But in fact any text coded into any textspace brings with it certain discursive instructions, that is, certain rules that delimit the discourse(s) being deployed in the textspace. Bakhtin's celebrated discussions of textual heteroglossia reference in a general way this discursive structure for fictional texts. Or consider the brief opening chapter of G. Spencer Brown's *Laws of Form* (1969), where a discourse drawn from the (closely related) lexicons of logic and mathematics is being deployed.[9] What is important to remember—Wittgenstein forced us to this recollection, remember?—is that semantic materials are not units of atomized meaning. They are parts of a language game—more than that, they are instantiated instructions for playing a certain language game in a certain time and place for certain particular purposes.

That truth about text was first brought home to me years ago in Chicago. I and some of my students interested in poetry used to play a game with brief texts of verse. One person would choose a short and more or less obscure poem (unknown to the others), break it down into an alphabetized list of its constituent words (including the number of times any word appeared in the poem), and then give the list to other persons in the group. The game was to construct a poem from the list of words. Playing the game we soon discovered that our reconstructed poems were often uncannily similar to each other; more, they seemed borne along by a kind of fate back towards the original poem. We then changed the game and made our object the reconstruction of the original (unknown) poem from the given word lists. We gave up the game when it became obvious that we could do these reconstructions—not because we were especially clever, but because (a) we could access the discourse of poetry in various dialects, and (b) the word lists represented brief excerpts of a complete language game. The apparent randomness of the lists comprised a second order illusion that threw into relief the coded character of the original texts. We weren't dealing with code and output. Everything was code and output simultaneously.

Implicit in this discussion is the (theoretical) possibility, long cherished by structural linguists, of deducing the rules for writing the codes that generate traditional text output. In my view such an effort would be most usefully pursued toward broadly semiotic, rather than more restricted linguistic, codes because the latter depend for their operation on a (logically prior) semiotic space. Besides, that space, being more primitive, displays textual laws of form in structural terms that are simpler to see and read.

The complexity of such a project of deduction, known to all and lamented by many, is a function of our different ways of parsing semiotic and linguistic space. To structure or analyze semiotic or linguistic space we need, we believe, some standard code for description and measurement. But such a standard code flees us for exactly the reason set out by Spencer Brown: you cannot obtain a standardized system of measurement when your acts of analysis are drawn from and make up a part of your subject of attention and inquiry. We get fixed standards—rules of naming and rules of relation—only when we make an impermeable distinction between subject and object. In a textual condition, while such a distinction can be drawn, it can only be maintained arbitrarily. Even structural linguistics is riven by difference, and its best practitioners, conscious of those differentials, have always tried to make them as explicit as possible.

What has this to do with the possibility of using digital technology to improve the study of traditional text? The discussion may perhaps appear simply to have spun to a dismal conclusion about that possibility. But my argument is that we (necessarily) reach dismaying conclusions in these matters when we discount or miss the algorithmic character of traditional text. Text generates text, it is a code of signals elaborating itself within decisive frames of reference. A text is a display and a record of itself, a fulfillment of its own instructions. Every subsequent re-presentation in whatever form—editorial or interpretive—ramifies the output of the instructional inheritance. Texts are like fractal derivations.

From an analytic perspective, what is especially interesting about those re-presentations is their unmistakable errancy with respect to the "original text." Whereas the latter appears self-identical, the former seem alien interventions brought—paradoxically if not ludicrously—to reveal the truth about an original object that—paradoxically if not mystically—seems difficult to access despite its clear *integritas*. But because text is a field of dynamically unfolding elements and relations, every "state" of a text represents an arbitrary form "taken out of The Form," as Spencer Brown might put the matter (see chapter 7). These forms are de-forms and their usefulness for text analysis lies exactly in the set of differential possibilities they call to attention.

Every text is a network of roads taken and not taken. Some of the roads have never been taken, so far as we know, and of the roads known to have been taken, some are well traveled and some hardly traveled at all. Who traveled which roads, and when, and where, are matters of consequence to anyone studying the texts. Roads identical in one respect or another may be seen as very different roads if viewed from a different vantage—and of those different points of view, many will be possible.

—"But those are mere figures of speech," you will say, "how do you translate them into digital instructions?"

—"Look for the protocols of figuration. Here the graphic text may serve as an instructive figure—a clear instance—of an elementary set of instructional options (not 'figures of speech' but typographical figures—so to speak). The instructions are always instructions to mark and hence to deform/transform. So take any given poem and make a schedule of its transformations. Readers do this as a matter of course as they move through a text and make *themselves* the measure of a process of transformation. Scholars searching the text develop those transformations to exponential degrees. Let the transformations be marked and let their forms be stored in a network of related forms. Let that network of forms search itself and generate further forms out of itself, and let the process replicate. Ask the network to display the forms realized or not realized in any given text or set of texts."

We don't want to discover what the texts mean but what they might be imagined to mean or to have meant. Those meanings are a function of what texts might or might not do, given their rules of engagement; and those rules are determined from what they have and have not done, as well as what they might have done or might be made to do given their historical descent.

The initial search should, I believe, be undertaken at the elemental level of figuration—that is to say, in the metaphoric field where (so to speak) graphemes are carried across to phonemes and vice versa. The phoneme is a metaphor for language expending itself without record or trace other than the evidence implicit in what Shakespeare called lust in action. Blake saw this as the language of eternity when he wrote, in *The [First] Book of Urizen,* that before there was any "Earth . . . or Globes of Attraction," "Eternal Life sprung" (plate 3). By contrast or differential, the grapheme is, as Derrida showed, the trace, or a metaphor for language not as an "expense of spirit" but as a reflexive record of itself. Both grapheme and phoneme are forms of thought and not facts—not character data but parsed character data, or "data" that already functions within an instructional field.

The elemental scene where those metaphoric transformations expose themselves is the marked field, the graphical or auditional record. Because this will be a record of rule-governed differences, one can extract from that field a dataset of (hypothetical and arbitrary) rules that could replicate analogous differences in comparable fields (including the original record as it might be augmented and transformed by replicant operations). The output of such operations would be collated as a calculus of variants and delivered to us for study. Throughout, the operation assumes that the representation of knowledge involves the construction and display of difference. That assumption appears in every final "output" as a confrontation between a digital display of knowledge and a human reflection of/on the display.

Instructional Examples from The Garden of Forking Paths

A. Byron's "To the Po" / "Stanzas to the Po"

There are two holograph manuscripts, a draft (MS. M, 1819, Morgan Library) and a fair copy (MS. B, 1820, New York Public Library). Both are titled "To the Po. June 1819,"[10] both are in continuous units rhyming like abab quatrains. Because no space breaks come between those rhyming units, the rhyme scheme could as well be described ababcdcdefef . . .[11] Several copies were made from manuscript M during Byron's lifetime by other persons, all arranging the poem in distinctly spaced quatrain units; all are titled, however, as the holograph manuscripts. The poem was first printed after Byron's death (1824) without a title from one of those dependent nonholograph copies, and it was first printed in an authoritative collected edition in 1831 from a modified version of the 1824 text. The 1831 text is in quatrains and is titled "Stanzas to the Po." All subsequent editions follow the 1831 version until 1986, when the text was printed as it was left by Byron[12]—that is to say, *not* in space-marked stanza units but as a continuously unfolding text built from quatrainlike units that are sometimes end-stopped and sometimes enjambed.

These two basic textual forms represent different sets of reading instructions for the work. Choosing one or the other radically affects both how
one physically negotiates the work and how one interprets it for meaning.
Furthermore, the existence of both of these forms points toward a general
set of rule-governed options available for textspace scripts.[13]

Let us look at the opening 20 lines of the poem in diplomatic tran-
scriptions of Byron's manuscript text, on one hand, and the influential
1831 printing, on the other. First, then, the manuscript text of 1819:

> To the Po. June 2nd 1819.
> River! That rollest by the ancient walls
>   Where dwells the lady of love, when she
> Walks by thy brink, and there perchance recalls
>   A faint and fleeting memory of me,
> What if thy deep and ample stream should be   5
>   A mirror of my heart, where she may read
> The thousand thoughts I now betray to thee
>   Wild as thy wave and headlong as thy speed?
> What do I say? "a mirror of my heart"?
>   Are not thy waters sweeping, dark, and strong,   10
> Such as my feelings were and are, thou art,
>   And such as thou art were my passions long.
> Time may have somewhat tamed them, not forever
>   Thou overflow'st thy banks, and not for aye
> The bosom overboils, congenial River!   15
>   Thy floods subside, and mine have sunk away,
> But left long wrecks behind us, yet again
>   Borne our old career unchanged we move,
> Thou tendest wildly to the wilder main
>   And I to loving one I should not love   20

Now here is the text first printed in 1831 and subsequently followed by all
of Byron's editors until 1986:

> Stanzas to the Po.
> River, that rollest by the ancient walls,
>   Where dwells the lady of love, when she
> Walks by thy brink, and there perchance recalls
>   A faint and fleeting memory of me;

What if thy deep and ample stream should be   5
    A mirror of my heart, where she may read
The thousand thoughts I now betray to thee,
    Wild as thy wave, and headlong as thy speed!

What do I say—a mirror of my heart?
    Are not thy waters sweeping, dark, and strong?   10
Such as my feelings were and are, thou art;
    And such as thou art were my passions long.

Time may have somewhat tamed them,—not for ever;
    Thou overflow'st thy banks, and not for aye
Thy bosom overboils, congenial river   15
    Thy floods subside, and mine have sunk away—

But left long wrecks behind: and now again,
    Borne our old unchanged career we move,
Thou tendest wildly onwards to the main,
    And I—to loving *one* I should not love.   20

The linguistic changes that come into the 1831 text shall not detain us, interesting as they are. We shall concentrate on bibliographical details only, and especially on the general graphical transformation of the shape of the poem as Byron originally wrote it.

Crucial to note is that Byron wrote the poem in metrical quatrains rhyming abab. By long-standing typographical convention such a verse form is normally arranged as in the 1831 printing, that is, in separate four-line stanzas. But when he wrote the poem Byron departed from that convention, nor is it difficult to see why: Running the quatrains without stanza breaks forces an approach to the affective pace of the poem that turns the graphic form into a *figure* of the dominant linguistic *figure* (headlong passion and headlong river). The eye registers the presence of the quatrains and the refusal of the stanza convention and then "reads" the relation between the two.

Much can and should be said about the implications of what we see here. At the most general level we remark the signifying character of even the most elementary typographical conventions of verse presentation. What we observe here of this four line stanzaic form should be extrapolated to the presentational character of all stanzaic forms, as well as to the visual segmentations executed at the text's lower—if no less significant—levels. Punctuation is the most crucial visible form in this case. We want to recall that this highly evolved set of marks represent signs that were originally introduced as notations both for oral articulation and syntactic differentiation, and that they function in both registers to this day. As a set of oral cues—whether in silent or in articulated reading—punctuation is a foundational element in the affective (as opposed to the conceptual) ordering of the poem. As a set of syntactic cues it is also a signifying system foregrounding dominant sets of conceptual relations in the text.

We see some striking illustrations of these matters in this Byron poem. Compare, for example, the terminal punctuation of lines 4, 8, and 13 in the two versions. In line 8, what a difference between the exclamation point and the question mark. Or consider lines 4 and 13. In the 1831 text the editors introduce an end-stopped punctuation that isn't present in Byron's manuscript, and they further alter the movement of the text by breaking Byron's word "forever" into two words. The two texts signal very different pacings—what Keats famously called "unheard melodies"—for the reader.

Furthermore, the 1831 punctuation of line 13 also directs the reader to a different conceptual understanding of the poem. In Byron's manuscript the enjambment at the end of line 13 places the phrase "not forever" in a zeugmatic structure such that we are asked to read it simultaneously in two different syntaxes (as modifying "tamed" and as modifying "overflow'st"). The 1831 punctuation is a visible signal to read the phrase in only one syntax. In this respect it replicates the meaning signaled in the 1831 decision to print the poem in four-line stanzas: to do that is not only to tell the reader that the poem's basic metrical unit is a quatrain, it is also to say that the quatrain and its textual presentation stand to each other in a relation of symmetry rather than a relation of tension. And *that* "statement" imbedded in the text's visible form plainly goes to the very core of this poem's intellectual and affective meaning.

We want to point out that in this example we have consciously chosen a poet who is not known for any special interest in exploiting graphical forms for poetical effect. We leave aside Blake, Rossetti, Dickinson, and pattern and concrete poetry precisely because we wish to show that the standard presentational and graphic features of text are signifying features *as such*. In the effort to articulate meaning, affective as well as conceptual, *one necessarily installs the visible resources of language.* For every text is comprised simultaneously of a beauty of inflections as well as a beauty of innuendoes.

Here are two further examples. I shall not elaborate explanations in these two cases but leave those exercises in particularities to the reader.

B. Byron's *"When We Two Parted"*

In this case we are dealing with equivalent texts that are migrating authoritatively through different textspaces. A simple example of this kind of situation in Byron's works involves the document he published separately in 1816 under the title "The Incantation" and the equivalent text that appeared in 1817 as part of Byron's play *Manfred*. Text is a spacetime manifold where these kinds of translations and reinvestments take place on a regular basis.

"When We Two Parted" is remarkable only because it illustrates how complex these relationships can become. Between 1812 and 1823 some or all of the text published by Byron in 1816 as "When We Two Parted" was incorporated by him in at least eight completely different kinds of textual document—as printed and manuscript documents; as singly authorized and collaborative documents; as integral poetic manuscripts and as parts of manuscript letters where the formal poetic status of equivalent texts are completely transformed by incorporation in new prose expositions; and finally, as integral poetic forms that exhibit completely different metrical organizations.

C. Byron's *"Fare Thee Well!"*

This is another case of migrating texts. In this case the textspaces differ because only some of the translations and reinvestments are deliberately authorized by Byron. The most common instance of this situation unfolds as the general transmission history of any particular work or author during and then after his or her lifetime. Because that history commonly appears to us as more or less integrated and continuous, eventuating at any point in a largely transparent and apparently self-identical text, "Fare Thee Well!" is a useful case. Although the lexical form of the poem differs hardly at all moment by moment across its process of transmission, this work is marked by many contradictions, tensions, and discontinuities generated through the bibliographical coding. Those contradictions are most apparent in the sequence of the poem's transmissions in 1816. Byron distributed copies in manuscript to various persons, and he had the poem printed twice. In the interstices of those acts of authorial transmission appear other acts of textual transmission—in manuscript as well as print—executed by other parties, many of these persons Byron's enemies who clearly "read" his poem in antithetical ways. This network of relations is highly dynamic and interdependent, with different texts emerging as responses or consequences of other texts. In all cases, while the linguistic level of the texts remains fairly stable, the material/transmissional forms stand as eloquent witnesses of radical changes in the poem's "meanings."

Knowing Games

What then *does* distinguish cybertext from traditional docutext? Without pretending to answer that question, I would call attention to the special kinds of simulation that can be realized in cybernetic environments. While both Aarseth and Murray discuss computerized simulations, their critical taxonomies permit the subject to come forward only at the interspaces of their studies.

Of course all traditional texts construct simulations, but with docutexts we engage these simulations as "readers." A project like Michael Joyce's celebrated hyperfiction *Afternoon* or my own *Rossetti Archive* are paradigms of the "humanities" cybertexts we see all around us now. Both were conceived and designed as high-order reading environments. *The Rossetti Archive* was imagined as a simulated syndesis of a critical edition of Rossetti's textual works with a complete collection of facsimile editions of those works and a complete set of illustrated catalogues of all his pictorial works, including the reproductions of those works. The whole, however, remains a study environment embedded in a reading environment.

In this context it helps to remember that Plato disapproved of these kinds of textual simulations as instruments of study, thought, and reflection. For Plato, the optimal scene for thinking had to be living and dialectical. Texts are inadequate because they do not converse: When we interrogate them, Plato observed, they maintain a majestic silence. But in MUDS (Multi User Domains) and with various kinds of cybergames like ELIZA, one enters simulated environments where the user's interaction is no longer a readerly one. This result comes from the construction of a textual scene that simulates in real time an n-dimensional spatial field. One thinks of the Chorus's speech to the audience at the opening of *Henry V,* except in cyberspace the "wooden O" of the Shakespearean stage has been extended to include the audience as characters in the action.[14]

Computer games exploit this new dynamic space of textuality by inviting the user to play a role in the gamespace. These are well-known role types like warrior, hero, explorer-adventurer, creator-nurturer, problem-solver, and so forth. And while players may well have to read at various points, their participation in the game is not readerly. When cybertext enthusiasts speak of the "passive" docutext and the "active-participatory" cybertext, they are calling attention to this differential. Traditional readers rightly point out that reading is a highly participatory activity and one that is commonly quite as "nonlinear" as any cybertext. When the examples from Byron show us that multiple coding operates at the elementary material level of textspace, they are simultaneously demonstrating the interactive nature of that traditional textual condition.

As a traditional literary text enters (or is translated into) a cyberspace, then, it will be laid open to "participations" that may or may not be readerly participations. Indeed, paperspace is a far more effective medium for reading than cyberspace. From the point of view of someone wanting to create imaginative works, however—narrative or otherwise—cyberspace is replete with inviting opportunities. But from the point of view of the scholar, or someone wanting to reflect upon and study our imaginative inheritance, the resources of cybernetic simulation remain underutilized. The difficulty is conceptual not technical. Even when we work with cybernetic tools, our criticism and scholarship have not escaped the critical models brought to fruition in the nineteenth century: empirical and statistical analysis, on one hand, and hermeneutical reading on the other.

What critical equivalents might we develop for MUDS, LARPS, and other computer-driven simulation programs? How would one play a game of critical analysis and reflection?

That question brought into view the idea for what we would eventually call "The Ivanhoe Game." It would be a multi-user game designed to expose the structures of imaginative works like Scott's famous romance—which is also to say the structures that any literary work like *Ivanhoe* makes possible through the double helix of its genetic (social) codes: its production history and its reception history. These are the content fields of the game of *Ivanhoe*—discourse fields, as their scholars call them. The game would be played in either of two available multi-user domains: a real-time environment and a list-serve environment. Players would enter one or both as they like, and they would engage with others either as themselves or under consciously adopted roles.

The game is to rethink *Ivanhoe* by rewriting any part(s) of its codes. Two procedural rules pertain: First, all recastings of the codes must be done in an open-text environment such that those recastings can be themselves immediately rewritten or modified (or unwritten) by others; second, codes can only be recast by identifiable game-players, digital or human, who have specifically assumed a role in the game.

Any number of roles might be played. There are the roles of the fictional characters first imagined by Scott for his romance and for its surrounding materials. But to these we add other possible roles: persons involved in the book's material production; Scott's precursors, contemporaries, and inheritors (literary and otherwise); early reviewers and any of its later readers, reviewers, critics, illustrators, redactors, translators, or scholarly commentators; in general, persons in the book or persons who might have been in it, real or imaginary, as well as persons who read the book or who might be imagined reading it, for whatever reason. The roles may be played in various forms: in conversation or dialogue, through critical commentary and appreciation, by rewriting any received text, primary or secondary, seen to pertain to Scott's work.

The goal is to rethink the work's textuality by consciously simulating its social reconstruction.

> VOICE OF AN ANGEL. But this is implicitly to propose that the works of our cultural inheritance have no meaning or identity *an sich*—that their meanings are whatever we choose to make of them. It is to make a mere *game* of the acts of imagination.
>
> VOICE OF THE DEVIL. Are we then to make a business or religion of those acts? If we see it as a business then we propose to *make something* of our inheritance and not simply bury it in the ground, lest it be lost. If it is a religion we propose to recreate the world anew exactly as did the demiurge of the Book of Genesis when he refashioned his pagan inheritance by pretending there were no strange gods before him and then making a rule forbidding any later ones as well.

Part III

Quantum Poetics: 1999–2000

The night sky's text is brilliant and clear, the constellations as orderly and mysterious—as readable—as they have always been. Here is our oldest book, a palimpsest of fate and ancient memory. Once again you let your vision sweep across the stellar spectacle to recollect what you know but cannot see: that your eyes are taking but a snapshot of an eons-old cosmic event in which you and your camera are engulfed and borne along. You are reading a text from what D. G. Rossetti called "an inner standing point."

Now you turn from this vast theatre of space-time, from your awareness of its quasi-eternal and infinite extent. You go inside and pick up what you were reading—let's say, Lord Byron's *Don Juan,* a *mappa mundi* tucked away somewhere within that larger *mappa coeli.* The quantum effect comes suddenly as you try to take the measure of the book you are holding, yourself, and the encompassing manifold. Byron's metatheater, the merest atom in a Newtonian view, begins to open up as a new order of breathtaking magnitudes. The identities and relations of things shift, mutate, reconform, and dissolve in what appears an endless process of formation, disappearance, and reformation. Holding this book you hold "Infinity in the palm of your hand," as Blake precisely remarked, and in that infinite world you now begin to see, tucked away somewhere within, yourself holding the book you are reading.

Why, how does this happen?

Why: because that work by Byron, like every work aesthetically constructed, is a mimesis of a world governed by laws of change and transformation. As we try to acquire greater and more precise understandings of such worlds, we move simultaneously through Euclidean and Newtonian and quantum mechanics. In this progress our understanding grows by growing more certain of its limits and more precise in the way we measure those limits. So we now find, in the imitations of the world we fashion for ourselves, reflexes and repetitions of that kind of understanding. How: by the operation, and the experience, of what we now know best as Gödel's theorem. In the poem (in the music, in the work of art) our views and understandings are encompassed/transacted by the manifold that we are trying to perceive, study, analyze.

What we need is a poetics grounded in an epistemology congruent with a quantum conception of phenomena and the critical reflections we construct for studying those phenomena. This would entail a framework for grasping the objective instability of the subjects of our study (the works and their relational fields), of our tools, and of the results (interpretations and meanings) generated through the study processes. Gaining that frame of reference will come along two reciprocal lines: first, by exposing the fault-lines of interpretational methods that implicitly or explicitly treat any part of the study process as fixed or self-identical; second, by proposing interpretational methods that operate through different critical protocols.

The second of these goals, which is naturally the more important, emerges at (and perhaps as) the interface of human beings and their simulacral creations. The critical tools we want to develop will emphasize and clarify the subjective limitations of their agents, a process we see as a powerful stimulus to the further development of critical and imaginative thought. Models for these kinds of tool descend to us through our culture in games and in role-playing environments. At our particular historical moment, digitization has brought fresh opportunities for exploiting the interactive potential of both of those simulational processes. The remarkable ability of computerized tools for storing, accessing, and transforming unimaginably large bodies of data opens the field of what we know to what we could not otherwise bring to or hold in the field of our disciplined attention—literally, not simply to imagine what we don't know, but to be able to choose to undertake such imaginings in precise and determinate ways. The magnitude of the datafield and its logical clarity necessarily expose those undertakings to new kinds and levels of critical reflection.

These chapters trace the last stages of an exploration by which we arrived at that conclusion. They call to the final section of this book, "Beginning Again and Again: The Ivanhoe Game," which reports on our initial critical experiments with an interpretation engine that would, we think, prove adequate as an initial foray into the kind of poetics we have in mind.

These chapters therefore culminate the theoretical re-investigation of traditional textual and semiotic forms that grew out of the initial scholarly project begun in 1993, *The Rossetti Archive:* to design and build an online model for critically editing multi-media aesthetic materials. The fault lines that appeared in the pursuit of that endeavor force us to examine more thoroughly certain aspects of bookish textuality that regularly go unnoticed but that have significant implications for building interpretational models and tools.

Why this regression? Because we are interested in exploring the functional relation that connects our new technical media to our traditional humanistic tools. Our inherited artifices resist abandonment, as they should, for we need them both as fact (so called) and as figure. We all understand that computerized tools generate digital transformations of books, music, and pictures. So we have no difficulty saying that these transformations generate *virtual* books/music/pictures. But we also want to see that those well-known objects are no more real or less virtual than their recent electronic apparitions. All are creatures of what Herbert Simon years ago called "the sciences of the artificial."

The dialogue we enter at the interface of man and machine sends us out in quest of digitized instruments that promote the kinds of critical reflection we have known for centuries in our ancient dialogue at the interface of man and book. So we come upon ideas like "The Ivanhoe Game." But to go forward (so to speak) we must also retreat, for even now we hardly understand the complexity of that great social artifice we call "the book." Our first retreats are made along lines that invite our return: so we go back to look for the continuities that pertain between Blake or Dickinson, Mallarmé and D. G. Rossetti. Such persons facilitate these second critical comings. But once an initial return is made, our doors of perception begin to open along previously dark and relatively uninviting avenues. The visible language of Lord Byron's texts? Although more than 20 years of my life as a scholar focused on those works, their complex materialities remained largely *invisible* to me. Not unknown, but invisible. Those kinds of visibility, exposed in chapter 7, come in here for more broadly ranging examination.

This blindness resulted from having been trained to study literary works within a New Critical horizon, along with the corresponding structures of intentionality that shape such a critical method. The New Critical object comes to attention as a relatively transparent and unmediated form. Certain works, like those of Blake or Apollinaire, flaunt their visibilities, but even in those cases the temptation is to imagine you have a WYSIWYG interface: "what you see is what you get." Studying the work of writers like

Scott or Dickens helps to break the spell of the illusion of a work's immediate transparency. But the social and material structure of Scott's and Dickens's works is so dramatic and manifest—like the immediate visibilities of Blake's work—that they tend to be taken as special cases. The truth is that all such works are "special" because they call attention to a crucial general feature of textuality as such: its social and historical determinations.

This matter would have less importance here were it not for the fact that, in my case, digital tools first drew my interest in terms of visual tropes (hypertext) and forms (digital images). *The Rossetti Archive* was thus a natural and easy imagining—in contrast, say, to a Swinburne Archive, an imagining I scarcely ever considered despite my passion and admiration for his work. As *The Rossetti Archive* emerged, however, its virtual forms began to expose the visible languages that play in all textual forms, even those that seem without them.

One wants to see this result coming about. It stands as an emblem of the kind of self-consciousness one looks to discover in the dialogue of interpretation that takes place at the interface of Man and all of her machines, books as well as computers.

Chapter 6

Visible and Invisible Books in N-Dimensional Space

*Let us not generalize about exceptional cases, that is all I ask: yet my charac-
ter is in the order of possible things. No doubt between the two furthest limits
of your literature, as you understand it, and mine, there is an infinity of inter-
mediate points, and it would be easy to multiply divisions; but there would be
no point at all in that, and there would be the danger of narrowing and falsi-
fying an eminently philosophical conception, which ceases to be rational,
unless it is taken as it was conceived, that is, expansively.*
—*Lautréamont*, Maldoror, Book 5

All the news organs have picked up the story:

> After five centuries of virtually uncontested sway, the Book seems to be fac-
> ing a serious threat to its power. Informed sources report a large computer-
> ized force continues its sweep through traditional centers of bookish
> institutional control. Resistance has been fierce in certain quarters, and vast
> areas remain wholly under Book authority. Spokesmen from both sides
> describe the situation as volatile. It has been reliably reported that major cen-
> ters of Book power throughout the country have been voluntarily joining
> forces with the Electronic invaders. According to leader of the patriotic
> militias, Sven Birkerts. . . .

That kind of report shapes much of the public discussion about the relation of books and an array of new computer-based tools generically

named hypertext and hypermedia. Nor is there any doubt that we are, at this millennial moment, passing through the first stages of a major shift in how we think about and manage texts, images, and their vehicular forms. From a literary person's point of view, the relevance of these changes can appear purely marginal: for whatever happens in the future, whatever new electronic poetry or fiction gets produced, the literature we inherit (to this date) is and will always be bookish.

Which is true—although that truth underscores what is crucial in all these events from the *scholar's* point of view: We no longer have to use books to analyze and study other books or texts. That simple fact carries immense, even catastrophic, significance.

Trying to think clearly in this kind of volatile situation is not easy. In fact, after working for most of a decade implementing *The Rossetti Archive,* I began to see some simple but fundamental truths about books, digital tools, and what we might think about or expect of them. These simplicities are what we should be caring about now. Simplicities and solidarities. For digital and bibliographical forms of thought and expression stand in a mutually critical relation to each other. Or at least they seem so—have been so—in my experience.

Let me start, then, with a fundamental misconception: that a digital field is prima facie more complex and more powerful than a bibliographical one. A moment's reflection spoils that thought, as it should. The fields simply manage knowledge and intellectual inquiry at different scalar levels. Our worlds are differently constituted by spoons on one hand and by steamshovels on the other. Nor is one instrument "better" or more powerful. They do different things. Right now and in the foreseeable future, books do a number of things much better than computers. There is no comparison, for example, between the complexity and richness of paper-based fictional works, on one hand, and their digital counterparts—hypermedia fiction—on the other. Nor does the difference simply measure a difference of writing skill—Italo Calvino, say, versus Stuart Moulthrop. The history of the book medium and the development of fictional conventions within that medium have evolved an extraordinarily nuanced and flexible set of tools for the imagination. The truth is that the hypermedia powers of the book, in this area of expression if not prima facie, far outstrip the available resources of digital instruments.

But the latter, even in this moment of their earliest history, confidently declare and establish their authority in other areas of knowledge processing and communication. A like situation emerged in the fifteenth century with the invention of movable type. The printed book quickly supplanted the manuscript as a primary vehicle for storing, retrieving, and transmitting information. On the other hand, even the finest early printed books—and there are many such—lack the expressive and intellectual resources available to works produced in the manuscript tradition. That clear deficiency, needless to say, did not hinder the development of printed works—on the contrary, it inspired and promoted that development.

Today we stand in a similar set of circumstances. The significance of the changes being wrought through digitization became widely apparent in 1993 when W3 broke across the scene. That event brought the clear realization that a new textual condition was at hand and that traditional literary and textual studies had an enormous stake in it. One could now see quite clearly that digitization was both the medium and the message concealed in the crisis that had been developing in literary and cultural studies since the mid-1960s.

Why? Because the web exposes how the technology of archival and bibliographical exchanges can be radically expanded in both spatial and temporal terms. Scholars can interact with each other anywhere in the world, can exchange their work in various new ways, and can access materials located in remote locations. They can also execute remarkable new critical transformations of their subject matter, thus opening unexpected opportunities for investigations of many kinds, bibliocritical as well as interpretational.

We are thus entering a period when the entirety of our received cultural archive of materials, not least of all our books and manuscripts, will have to be reconceived. The initial stages of this reconception, which is well underway, have been largely confined to work with archives and libraries, whose holdings are being digitally repossessed in many new ways. And since these depositories are the ground of all traditional scholarly work, these institutional changes will have—are already having—radical effects. This is very much a *material* revolution, and in negotiating it we all—not least of all traditional scholars—would do well to recall Marx's eleventh thesis on Feuerbach, which has acquired interesting new meanings beyond those originally conceived by Marx: "The philosophers have only *interpreted* the world in various ways; the point, however, is to *change* it."

Information scientists and systems engineers will be (already are) much involved with these changes. But it is the literary scholar, the musicologist, the art historian, etc. who have the most intimate understanding of our inherited cultural materials. Hence the importance that traditional scholars gain a theoretical grasp and, perhaps even more important, practical experience in using these new tools and languages. For "theory" in this volatile historical (and historic) situation will have little force or purchase if it isn't grounded in practice.

My special interests as an educator, a writer, and a scholar have brought me to engage the authority of our new digital tools. As already noted, we undertook the development of *The Rossetti Archive* in 1993 as an experimental effort to exploit the special powers of digital technology—specifically, to try to design a model for a critical edition that would overcome certain of the key limitations of critical editions organized in book form. Scholars need tools that can efficiently manage large bodies of related literary and artistic objects. This is exactly what the traditional critical edition does. But it's clear, prima facie, that digital tools can execute many of the tasks of scholarly editing much better, much more thoroughly, and much more precisely, than books can.

For instance, in certain important respects even works of imagination will and should be treated as we might treat ordinary "material objects" like (say) screwdrivers or business records. The corpus of Rossetti's visual and textual works is very large and its interrelations are very complex. Simply building a scholarly space that facilitates accessing these material objects for study and analysis, including complex kinds of comparative study and analysis, is a very useful thing to do. We see this in such splendid constructions as *The Perseus Project* or any of the electronic archives being developed, for instance, at IATH—electronic tools centered in the works of Blake, Dante, Dickinson, Rossetti, Whitman.[1] In certain ways digital space is much richer and more flexible than bibliographical space. So in 1993 we set out to explore and exploit that space by building *The Rossetti Archive,* and after seven years' work we aren't unhappy with the results. No paper-based book or set of books could have done what *The Rossetti Archive* offers to scholars. The book medium is physically incapable of the kinds of storing, integrating, and accessing operations we had held out as a basic scholarly demand for the archive.

This situation does not portend the death of the book and its typographical world. It does mean, however, that one heretofore central function of book technology will be taken over by these electronic media. Think about what books do. Like computerized information tools, the book performs two basic functions: It is a medium of data storage and transmission; and it is an engine for constructing simulations. That first is an informational, the second an aesthetic function. Computers will displace—are already displacing—most of the information functions of our bibliographical tools. The aesthetic function of books will remain, however, and it's clear to me that they will prove indispensable in this respect. This result is inevitable for an apparently paradoxical reason. As digital tools and environments develop, we grow increasingly aware of their aesthetic functions and of the importance of those functions. We appear to be passing from a bibliographical to an "Interface Culture." Indeed, the aesthetic resources of digital tools appear so vast and synaesthetic that our bibliographical anxieties might easily grow more acute in face of them. The truth is, however, that we have much to learn from those older, more highly evolved forms of textuality that are now being joined and modified by our new media. Not since the first period of its emergence has the study of the book been a more imperative need.

How do we exploit the aesthetic resources of digital media? The question brings to mind Edward Tufte's work.[2] Tufte is interested in the ways inventive people have used paper instruments to organize and elucidate various kinds of information. Of course his interest in aesthetic form is explicitly in its vehicular function with respect to information: How do we design pagespace in order to facilitate a clear transmission of data? His work makes no investigation into the semiosis of aesthetic form *as* such. Nonetheless, his studies underscore an important set of metaquestions that are too rarely asked: What is a page, what is a book, what are their parts, how do they function?

From the outset of my work with digital media I've been most interested in aesthetic works and the critical understanding of their cultural meanings. I began work on *The Rossetti Archive* because it was clear to me how digital tools brought great practical advantages over paper-based critical editions. The new engines could handle, in full and unabbreviated forms, vast amounts of data—far more than any book or reasonable set of books. They could also handle different kinds and forms of material data—not just textual, but visual and audial as well. These capacities made it possible to edit critically certain works that could not be adequately handled in a paper medium: the works of Rossetti, of course, but also those of Burns, of Blake, of Dickinson. Digital tools also exposed the critical deficiencies of the paper-based medium as such. Any kind of performative work—dramatic works, for example, and pre-eminently Shakespeare's dramas—gets more or less radically occluded when forced into a bookish representation. These differentials led to what I regarded at the time as an important general insight into books, computers, and their scholarly relation. I got a lot of satisfaction out of writing, in 1993, the following dicta:

When we use books to study books, or hard copy texts to analyze other hard copy texts, the scale of the tools seriously limits the possible results. In studying the physical world, for example, it makes a great difference if the level of the analysis is experiential (direct) or mathematical (abstract). In a similar way, electronic tools in literary studies don't simply provide a new point of view on the materials, they lift one's general level of attention to a higher order.[3]

While I wouldn't dissent from those sentences today, when I wrote them I was certainly unaware of much that they implied. My own levels of attention would be considerably raised as we undertook to implement the logical design of *The Rossetti Archive* between 1993 and 1997.

Some of these matters I have already discussed—for example, the dysfunction that arises when one tries to use standard markup forms, SGML and all its derivatives, to elucidate the functional structures of imaginative works.[4] The recursive patterns that constitute an essential—probably *the* essential—feature of poetry and imaginative works in general cannot be marked, least of all captured, by SGML and its offspring. At first we engaged this dysfunction as a set of practical problems for building, or modifying our original plans for, *The Rossetti Archive*. But this deep asymmetry between our primary bibliographical data and our digital tools forced us to realize that we would not get very far with our practical problems if we didn't begin to think more rigorously about a pair of difficult elementary questions—questions that we had hitherto treated far too casually, as if they did not involve problems, for us at any rate, at all.

Here are the questions. First, what is a literary work, what are its parts, how do they function? We assumed we knew how to answer such questions, but our attempts to translate our bibliographical materials into coded instructions showed us that we didn't. (The principle here is simple and known to every teacher: If you can't explain what you know to someone else so that they also understand, you don't really know what you think you know.) Second, what constitutes a critical representation of a literary work, and how does such a representation function? With one notable exception, every critical method and theory known to me assumes that the measure of critical adequacy is the degree of equivalence that can be produced between the object of critical attention and the critical representation of that object.[5] As we kept building *The Rossetti Archive* the flaw in that traditional understanding became more and more clear. A *hypermedia* work by choice and definition, the archive therefore obligated us to integrate in a critical way both textual and visual materials. Our efforts were continually frustrated, however, because while digital texts lie open to automated search and analysis, digital images do not. Consequently, our critical commentaries never adequately reflected the reality we knew was there. Indeed, so far as the mirror of representation was concerned, much of that reality might as well have been a large population of vampires.

Consequently, a major part of our work with *The Rossetti Archive* became focused on basic theoretical problems about literary and aesthetic works and the material nexus of their social and historical forms and determinations. As I have argued in Part II of this book, however, "adequacy" in a critical representation cannot be measured by a scale of equivalence. A true critical representation does not accurately (so to speak) mirror its object; it consciously (so to speak) deforms its object. The critical act therefore involves no more (and no less) than a certain perspective on the object, its acuity of perception being a function of its self-conscious understanding of its own powers and limitations. As della Volpe shows, it stands in a dialectical relation to its object, which must always be a transcendental object so far as any act of critical perception is concerned. This transcendental condition is a necessity because the object perpetually shifts and mutates under the influence of its perceivers. The critical act is a kind of conversation being carried on in the midst of many like and impinging conversations, all of which might at any point be joined by or merge into any of the others.

Aesthetic forms recreate—they "stage" or simulate—a world of primary human intercourse and conversation. As with their reciprocating critical reflections, they manipulate their perceptual fields to generate certain dominant rhetorics or surface patterns that will organize and complicate our understandings. An important critical maneuver, then, involves dislocating or "deforming" those dominant patterns so as to open doors of perception toward new opportunities and points of view. A dominant self-representation of *Paradise Lost* is to "justify the ways of God to men." That famous dislocater of texts, William Blake, accepted the literality of Milton's text but utterly deformed its meanings, as it were: to Blake, the words "justify," "God," and "men" signify in ways that Milton could hardly have imagined. The all but complete inversion that Blake's interpretive moves bring to Milton highlights one of the most important features of imaginative works: that they are incommensurate with themselves at all points.

The Blake/Milton relation highlights the general relation that critical deformations bear to aesthetic incommensurability. Blake knew very well that he had deformed the great Puritan, who was also his master spirit. Blake's works are what he called "Buildings of Los(s)," consciously written under the rubric "I must create a system or be enslaved by another man's." That famous declaration draws on a peculiar Blake lexicon, however, in which the word "create" and its cognates are synonymous with the word "error." This is why Blake will speak of "Error or Creation" and go on to assert that "Error is Created Truth is Eternal." His brief epic *Milton* is a deformed reading of *Paradise Lost* and *Paradise Regained*. Its acuity—that is to say, its power to elucidate Milton's work—is a direct function of the "errors" that it deliberately creates in relation to that work.

Critical deformations can be usefully undertaken either randomly or according to a set of pre-arranged protocols. I have found, for example, that when certain of the standard filter protocols in Adobe Photoshop are applied to paintings—D. G. Rossetti's paintings, for instance—interesting structural features get exposed to view. Using the edging protocol to make arbitrary transformations of a number of Rossetti's pictures revealed, for example, that many of the pictures, and almost all of his famous portraits of women, are dominated by patterns of interlocking vortices and spirals. He plays numerous variations on these patterns, which are evidently the result of conscious purpose. This key structural feature of Rossetti's pictorial work has not been previously noticed or commented upon. It is a feature that leaps into prominence when these random deformations are passed through the pictures.

We now see that a useful set of image-editing operations could be established that would have two important critical functions: first, to expose characteristic formal features of pictorial works; and second, to release perception from the spell of precisely those kinds of characteristic formal patterns and open a perception of different arrangements and patterns. For the truth about works of art—textual, pictorial, auditory—is that they are, in Tufte's word, "multivariate."

There is an interesting moral to the story I've just told about critical reading as a deformance procedure. Although I've been familiar with the idea since at least the mid-1960s, when I first read Galvano della Volpe and when my lifelong interest in Blake's work began, I did not come to realize its claim to generality until I encountered the recalcitrance of digital images. Unlike language objects, once a visual object—a painting or drawing or photograph—is digitally reconstituted, it resists further moves to mirror or translate it. Playing and doodling with digital images in Adobe Photoshop one day—it happened casually and with no deliberate goal in mind—I suddenly saw that the resistance of the image was in fact a critical opportunity and not an impasse at all.

That realization brought additional unexpected consequences for the way we were conceiving *The Rossetti Archive*'s digital texts and the problems we were having in marking them for automated computational analysis. We knew from the outset of the project that digital images stood apart from the computational resources of the new technology and we came quickly to realize how difficult it would be, except in the most elementary ways, to integrate automated text analysis into the information contained in digitized images. But it was dismaying to discover how much of Rossetti's poetry—how much of his strictly textual work—escaped our powers to represent it critically.

Our failures with implementing some of the goals of *The Rossetti Archive* were bringing a series of paradoxical clarities not only about our digital tools but even more about the works those tools were trying to reconstitute. We realized that we were making inadequate assumptions about such works, and that we were using tools designed through those assumptions. That realization turned us back to reconsider the logical and ontological status of the original works. I am convinced none of us will get very far with our new digital tools unless we first undertake a thorough reconsideration of this kind.

First of all, a little history. The discipline of humanities computing developed in the field of linguistics, where scholars realized that computers would be extremely useful for carrying out automated pattern searches across large bodies of linguistic data. As a consequence, the textual corpus, even if it was in *fact* a poetical corpus, was framed for computational purposes as if it were informational or expository. Consequently, the tools that emerged to mark electronic texts for search and analysis also assumed that their object would be the exposure of the informational content and expository structure of the text.

The problem is that poetical works, insofar as they *are* poetical, are not expository or informational. Because works of imagination are built as complex nets of repetition and variation, they are rich in what informational models of textuality label "noise." No poem can exist without systems of "overlapping structure," and the more developed the poetical text, the more complex are those systems of recursion. So it is that in a poetic field no unit can be assumed to be self-identical. The logic of the poem is only frameable in some kind of paradoxical articulation such as: "a equals a if and only if a does not equal a."

Let me illustrate the truth of that formulation with a couple of very traditional interpretive examples. I'll begin with a famous sonnet by Gerard Manley Hopkins that illustrates in a dramatic way how textual objects of this kind are not self-identical.

As Kingfishers Catch Fire

As kingfishers catch fire, dragonflies dráw fláme;
As tumbled over rim in roundy wells
Stones ring; like each tucked string tells, each hung bell's
Bow swung finds tongue to fling out broad its name;
Each mortal thing does one thing and the same: 5
Deals out that being indoors each one dwells;
Selves—goes itself; myself it speaks and spells,
Crying Whát I do is me: for that I came.
Í say móre: the just man justices;
Kéeps gráce: thát keeps all his goings graces;   10
Acts in God's eye what in God's eye he is—
Christ—for Christ plays in ten thousand places,
Lovely in limbs, and lovely in eyes not his
To the Father through the features of men's faces.

The first statement in this text offers a paradigm of its duplicities. The word "As" here operates simultaneously in a formal and in a temporal sense (so here it means both "Just as" or "In just the way that" and also "While" or "At the same time as"). The repetition of the word in line 2 underscores its variational possibilities because the poem's second statement introduces an altogether new grammar. Then comes what at first might be taken for a synonym of "As," the word "like," which introduces the sonnet's third syntactic unit (running from the third word of line 3 through line 4). This unit of syntax appears to have the same general form as the sonnet's opening unit, but when we press it more closely we watch it shapeshift into a new and unexpected grammar. Once again the move comes through duplicitous word usage. The word "like" here functions simultaneously as a conjunction (a synonym for "as"), as an adverb (meaning "alike"), and as a noun (in the sense of "kind," as in the word "mankind").

There's nothing unusual about this passage from Hopkins. Poets do this kind of thing all the time, it is the very essence of poetical textuality. I choose the passage not exactly randomly, however, but because its complexities are so apparent and so dramatic. In four lines an amazing kind of textual metastasis has unfolded and I have not even come close to an adequate exegesis of what is happening here. The phrase "catch fire," for example, normally suggests—as our dictionaries tell us—a passive eventuality, but in this case a feedback loop causes another textual metamorphosis, so that the word "catch" turns active, as if this kingfisher were catching fire as it hunts and catches fish. This transformation occurs because the phrase is affected retroactively, as it were, by the syntactic rhymes that immediately follow the phrase in the next two lines ("kingfishers catch fire," "dragonflies draw flame," "stones ring").

Imaginative textual objects regularly work through these kinds of transformations, feedback loops, and complex repetitions. All are forms or types of what we call "rhymes," that staple poetic device illustrating the algorithm I set out above: "a equals a if and only if a does not equal a."

The nonhierarchical character of these transformations and rhymings emerges very clearly in the sestet of this sonnet. Look carefully at lines 12–14. The word "plays," probably the pivotal word in the poem, involves a most cunning kind of textual wit. It conceals a pun whose "other meaning," so to speak, is "prays." Why is this so? Because the word is syntactically linked to a predicate complement that only comes to us in the final line, in the phrase "To the Father." The text of the poem generates the literal phrase "plays . . . To the Father." The oddness of that phrase doesn't reach us until we have transacted the hiatus of line 13, however, when we suddenly realize that the text has been (mis)leading us to reconstitute the phrase into something more linguistically apt. No one reading such a phrase in the poem's plain context of religious usages can fail to *hear* the absent but secretly prepared alternative phrase: "prays . . . To the Father." This is simultaneously a playful and a prayerful text.

But the text has not finished with its games of self-generation and self-transformation. For the play/pray wordgame regenerates itself yet again in a kind of conceptual metatext: The word "prays" means as well "praise." The poem as a whole is a kind of playful prayer of praise "for" Christ and "To" the Father, the word "Christ" being here the text's key figure of individuation, or what Hopkins called "selving."

In all this commentary I've tried to keep my remarks free from any kind of thematic or ideational/ideological references. Everything I've talked about has to do with Hopkins's text as a functioning sign system, a structure of signifiers and signifieds. I've done this not because I think "meaning" in a referential sense isn't a crucial part of every textual field, but because I want to demonstrate how full of meaningful activities these fields are even when their referentialities are held in abeyance. (And if we inquired into the acoustic features of the sonnet—a central concern for Hopkins in all his work—we would open up a new world of complex and interlaced relations.)

Look again at line 12 of the sonnet and think about how it prepares us to register the word game that only gets fully exposed in line 14. In line 12 Hopkins has made a text that our mouths will find difficult to transact:

"Christ—for Christ plays." The problem comes as we try to negotiate a passage from those three *r*'s to the *l* in "plays." Our mouths would find it easier to read "prays" here rather than "plays," we have to make some physical and mental effort to ensure that we get the given phonetic sequence right. The effort is a perceptual signal that our bodies will not let our minds forget when we come to line 14. And we are prepared for this exercise with *r*'s and *l*'s because the sonnet in fact opens its textual field in line 1 with a major deployment of just those phonetic signs.

What is this kind of text, really? First of all, it is both—and simultaneously—a perceptual and a conceptual event. Informational texts seek to minimize their perceptual features in the belief that texts calling attention to their vehicular forms interfere with the transmission of their ideas. The textuality of poetry reminds us of the intimate part that phonetics play in the signifying operations of language. It also reminds us of a second important feature of text: that while it may deploy ordered, even hierarchical, structures of ideas, its object (as it were) is to play with and within such structures and not be consumed by them. Are there such things as pure, nonlanguaged "ideas"? Perhaps. However that may be, when ideas function textually, they commit themselves to fields of perception as well as to systems of conception. So in the case of this sonnet we will want to see that while Hopkins's Scotist ideas play throughout the text and even comprise its argument, the sonnet is not comprehended in those ideas or reducible to a Scotist description or exposition. No textual event—not the Scotist word "Selves," not even the word "Christ"—is ever self-identical or self-transparent. Most especially is this true for imaginative texts—where alone we will see an effort to exploit the full resources of textuality.

Let me point out one other feature of this text, a moment of its physical visibility that we may hardly recognize as a visible thing. The wordplay realized in line 14 (Plays/Prays . . . to the Father") would fail in its remarkable effect were it not for the hiatus in lines 12–13, a hiatus that is constructed as a visible space and a temporal rhythm. I leave for another occasion any discussion of that temporal rhythm and its perceptual character because I want to concentrate here on the visible forms being deployed.

We tend not to notice an elementary fact about printed or scripted texts: that they are constituted from a complex series of marked and unmarked spaces. The most noticeable are the larger regular units—the lines, the paragraphs, or (in verse) the stanzas, as well as the spaces between them. Every one of these spatial units, as well as all the others on a page or in a book, offer themselves as opportunities for nonlexical expression. For a helpful comparison think of the cartoon strip with its sequence of frames separated by gutters. The force of cartoon narrative is always a function of the energy generated in those gutters, where the work's inexplicit but crucial relations are solicited in the reader's imagination. Ballad poems regularly treat their stanzas in exactly the same way, and all good writers learn to exploit the spatial fields of their texts. A procedural gap organizes the continuous play of differences between the physical lines of a poetic form and the grammatical order playing in the form. The divisions in long poems and prose fictions create opportunities for building relational nets across the framed areas of the text.

It is highly significant that readers of books move from recto to verso, that their field of awareness continually shifts from page to "opening" (i.e., the space made by a facing verso/recto), and that the size of the book—length, breadth, and thickness—helps to determine our reader's perceptions at every point. Texts are not laid out flat on plane pages, and if I were to open the subjects of typefaces or calligraphic forms, of ink, of paper, and of the various ways marks can be scripted or printed, the multivariate manifold of the book would be easily recognized. Entering those subjects shows why a fine press book is not just another pretty face—at least not the ones that have given thought to themselves. When William Morris reissued *The House of Life,* his friend Rossetti's masterwork, as a Kelmscott Press book, the point was to help readers perceive the sonnets more thoroughly than they might in the previous trade editions. The Kelmscott edition radically alters the spatiotemporal field of the sonnet sequence. It is nothing less than what we would now call a new "reading" of the sequence.[6]

But even these examples can be misleading if they suggest that bibliographical space is a matter of solid geometry. To help dispel that possible illusion I offer the example of a seventeenth-century poem titled "To the Post Boy." This example comes to shift our angle of focus, so to speak, and to expose networks of dispersed visibilities.

To the Post Boy

Son of A whore God dam you can you tell
A Peerless Peer the Readyest way to Hell?
Ive out swilld Baccus sworn of my own make
Oaths wod fright furies and make Pluto quake.
Ive swived more whores more ways than Sodoms walls   5
Ere knew or the College of Romes Cardinalls.
Witness Heroick scars, look here nere go
Sear cloaths and ulcers from the top to toe.

> Frighted at my own mischeifes I have fled
> And bravely left my lifes defender dead.   10
> Broke houses to break chastity and died
> That floor with murder which my lust denyed.
> Pox on it why do I speak of these poor things?
> I have blasphemed my god and libelld Kings;
> The readyest way to Hell come quick—   15
> Boy   nere stirr
> The readyest way my Lords by Rochester.

This work illustrates another mode of textual instability operating at a translinguistic level. The issue gets focused as a problem of attribution: We aren't sure who authored this work, and the uncertainty affects every aspect of the poem's textuality.[7] Most of the primary textual witnesses— late-seventeenth- and early-eighteenth-century manuscripts and printed texts—assign the poem to Rochester, hence seeing it as an astonishing piece of self-directed satire perhaps designed to frustrate and undermine his enemies and their literary devices. The dialogue-poem would show that Rochester could write satire, even against himself, that none of his antagonists could match.

But certain early witnesses, as well as some later scholars, don't read the poem as Rochester's but as the work of one of his enemies.

The issue, on current evidence, is in fact undecidable, although scholarly opinion today inclines toward favoring Rochester's authorship. (Not very long ago opinion went the other way.)

The poem therefore gets framed in three optional ways: as Rochester's work, as the work of someone else satirizing Rochester, and as a kind of duck-rabbit lying open to either *and* both readings simultaneously. Those frames, we want to remember, are part of the textuality of the work and they are deeply imbedded. But they run through the text in visibilities that extend far beyond what we might register as the work's plane or solid geometries. Indeed, they only appear as bibliographical and manuscript data scattered in disparate and disjunct materials—documents now housed separately in many libraries (the British Library; the Victoria and Albert Museum; Ohio State University library; the Osterreichische Nationalbibliotek, Vienna; and the Bodleian). In those documents and their complex interfaces we trace out that crucial and fundamental feature of every text: its transmission history—which is to say, we trace out the remains of those earliest readers who half perceived and half created this text.

Every document, every moment in every document, conceals (or reveals) an indeterminate set of interfaces that open into alternate spaces and temporal relations.

Traditional criticism will engage this kind of radiant textuality more as a problem of context than a problem of text, and we have no reason to fault that way of seeing the matter. But as the word itself suggests, "context" is a cognate of text, and not in any abstract Barthesian sense. We construct the poem's context, for example, by searching out the meanings marked in the physical witnesses that bring the poem to us. We read those witnesses with scrupulous attention, that is to say, we make our detailed way through the looking glass of the book and thence to the endless reaches of the Library of Babel, where every text is catalogued and multiply cross-referenced. In making this journey we are driven far out into the deep space, as we say these days, occupied by our orbiting texts. There objects pivot about many different points and poles. The objects themselves shapeshift continually and the pivots move, drift, shiver, and even dissolve away. Those transformations occur because "the text" is always a negotiated text, half perceived and half created by those who engage with it.

For several centuries—but only for several centuries—our models for knowing have been "scientific" and were cast in informational and expository forms. Those forms do not normally cultivate self-reflection, however deeply they may reflect upon matters they set apart from themselves to observe and interrogate, and least of all do they practice self-reflection on their medium of exchange.[8] But that kind of reflection is precisely what happens in imaginative work, where the medium is always the message, whatever else may be the subjects of the work.

Let's look at one other example—a short passage of four lines in one of the most famous poems in our canon of English verse. This is the opening of the second stanza of Keats's "Ode on a Grecian Urn."

> Heard melodies are sweet, but those unheard
>   Are sweeter; therefore, ye soft pipes, play on;
> Not to the sensual ear, but, more endear'd,
>   Pipe to the spirit ditties of no tone:

I want to focus on one aspect of these lines—the game of wit that carries the argument for the existence of "unheard" melodies. Keats is of course making a general allusion to the ancient idea that the phenomenal world is governed by a "music of the spheres," a system of transcendental and ultimately mathematical relations. This music, Keats's poem argues, is present and operating in the very poem he is writing and we are reading. In the poem we don't "hear" the melodies, we see them. Keats accomplishes this remarkable effect by exploiting some of his text's elementary bibliographical features. The words "unheard," "ear," and "endear'd" are rhyme words, as are the words "on" and "[no] tone." The fact that the phonemes of the end rhymes (lines 1 and 3 and 2 and 4) are different amounts to a figural representation of an unheard melody—as if the phonemic equivalent of these morphemic equivalences existed elsewhere, in some other musical order where "unheard," "ear," and "endear'd," or "on" and "tone," would all be (so to speak) *perfect* rhymes.

Note further how this particular effect is a function of the general material *form* of the stanza. Read at another another scale—recall the discussion in the last chapter of Byron's "To the Po"—we realize in a general way how that form might serve other functions: for example, how the stanza is in itself, and irrespective of its words, a narrativizing unit. The evolved set of conventions for coding verse in typographical space offer great resources to the artistic imagination bent upon developing complex autopoetic forms. Historical circumstances enrich the possibilities even further. Shakespeare's sonnets, for example, and Elizabethan poetry in general, develop remarkable effects by exploiting a nonstandardized orthographical situation. Or consider Emily Dickinson and the dazzling games she plays with the material forms of scripted letters. The poem beginning "Many a phrase has the English language" is particularly arresting. In one important perspective, for example, it is a poem "about" "the English language" in its special American dialect. To define her exposition—the poem *is* an exposition—Dickinson plays various games with codes of orthography and the bibliographical codes for representing verse.[9]

The passage from Keats foregrounds another matter of great importance. We do well to point out the symmetry Keats develops between these material forms of code and the signifieds that these forms attend upon—the poem's subject matter or thematic content, as we say. But note the *a*symmetry that leaps into play through the rhymes dominating the integrity of the third line. "Ear" and "endear'd" rhyme with each other for no apparent cognitive "reason," they develop what Susan Howe would call a "sumptuary value." Read at the scale of the "unheard" "ear/endear'd" textual unit, the rhyme words in line 3 comprise a symmetrical form, as we have seen. But the "law" of the line unit forces the two words into another relational order within line 3, where we (now, also) read them only in relation to each other. Seeing/hearing that particular rhyme unit we suddenly become aware that the text's phonemic arrangements and its thematic arrangements may as easily run cooperatively as independently, may merge into simultaneous symmetries and asymmetries.

The line exhibits in the clearest way what I mean by a quantum poetics. Aesthetic space is organized like quantum space, where the "identity" of the elements making up the space are perceived to shift and change, even reverse themselves, when measures of attention move across discrete quantum levels. The effect is especially notable because of the linguistic possibilities we can't fail to register in the word "endear'd" itself, at yet another change of scale. The words "end" and "ear" emerge full of sight and sound, if not fury, but signifying . . . what exactly? The text begins to spin off in a local moment of "wild surmise" as the word's letters dance their strange arrangements and forms.

Note that if we pursued the other notable tripartite rhyme unit in this passage—the words "on," "no," and "tone"—we would arrive at a similar set of observations. Indeed, the distinctive set of symmetries/asymmetries we might observe and track between this pair of triple rhymes exhibits yet another quantum measurement of the verse. The moral? Nothing in this space is self-identical *as such*.

Content in poiesis thus tends to involve more broadly "semiotic" rather than narrowly "linguistic" materials. The perceptual features of text are as apt for expressive purposes as the semantic, syntactic, and rhetorical features—at least so far as the poets and readers who make such texts are concerned. Every feature represents a determinate field of textual action, and while any one field might (or might not) individually (abstractly) be organized in a hierarchical form, the recursive interplay of the fields appears topological rather than hierarchic. The organization is more like a mobile with a shifting set of poles and hinge points carrying a variety of objects, many of an "opposite and discordant" character, as Coleridge might say.

Considered strictly in terms of bibliographical codes, then, poetical works epitomize a crucial expressive feature of textuality in general: that it can be seen to organize itself in terms of various relational segmentations and metasegmentations. Some elementary segmentations are sentences, paragraphs, chapters; in verse, lines, inter- and intralinear forms (rhyme, for example, and metrical forms), stanzas, cantos; in the page, the opening, the book. These segmentations may be usefully traced to the level of the individual character and, in general, to font and typeface design. Then, attending to different kinds and scales of segmentations—recall the example of Rochester above, and the Byron illustrations in the last chapter—we trace out further types of metasegmentations.

All of this phenomena exhibits quantum behavior. We distinguish a structure of relational segmentation in any text, but in autopoetic forms we observe as well that the segments and their relations cannot be read as self-identical. They mutate into different symmetries and asymmetries.

Which brings me back to Edward Tufte and the opening sentence of his influential book *Envisioning Information* (1990):

> Even though we navigate daily through a perceptual world of three spatial dimensions and reason occasionally about higher dimensional arenas with mathematical ease, the world portrayed on our information displays is caught up in the two-dimensionality of the endless flatlands of paper and video screen." (12)

So acute and arresting is Tufte's appreciation of textual graphics that we tend to pass over a crucial piece of *mis*information that his work has envisioned. Despite what he says, we do *not* "navigate daily through a perceptual world of three spatial dimensions," although it *is* true that we often think we do and even represent ourselves as doing so. Nor are we doomed, when we transact our books and our monitors, to "the two-dimensionality of the endless flatlands of paper and video screen." Even our daily movements are "multivariate" and n-dimensional, and when we imagine ourselves passing through a world of three dimensions we are merely surrendering to a certain type of perceptual filter. It is a filter regularly exposed and repudiated by an imagination like William Blake's, as my epigraph suggests. *Every* page, even a blank page, even a page of George W. Bush's ignorant and vapid prose, is n-dimensional. The issue is, how clearly has that n-dimensional space of the page—its "multivariate" character— been marked and released?

To see that truth about paperspace seems to me especially useful in an age fascinated to distraction by the hyperrepresentational power of digital technology. We want to remember that books possess exactly the same powers, and we want to remember not simply to indulge a farewell *nostalgia* at the twilight of the book. One of the great tasks lying ahead is the critical and editorial reconstitution of our inherited cultural archive in digital forms. We need to learn to do this because we don't as yet know how. Furthermore, we *scholars* need to learn because it is going to be done, if not by us, then by others. We are the natural heirs to this task because it is we who know most about books.

When we study the world of books with computers we have much to learn from our subjects. In crucial ways, for instance, a desk strewn with a scholar's materials is far more efficient as a workspace—far more *hypertextual*—than the most powerful workstation, screen-bound, you can buy. Or consider this: If these new machines can deliver stunning images to our view, the only images they understand are their own electronic constructions. Original objects—visual, audial—remain deeply mysterious to a computer. If a computer serves up, say, a facsimile of Rossetti's painting *The Blessed Damozel,* its most effective means for understanding that image—for analyzing it—are through sets of so-called metadata, that is, logical descriptions introduced into the electronic structure in textual form. Even when (some would say "if") that limitation gets transcended, logical ordering through metadata will never *not* be a part of computerized scholarship of literary works. The objects of study demand it—just as the physical sciences, for all their use of mathematical models, cannot do without empirical investigations.

And there are more serious problems. Scholars are interested in books and texts as they are works of "literature" and imagination, but those who design computerized tools sometimes seriously misunderstand their primary materials. So far as I can see, nearly all the leading design models for the scholarly treatment of imaginative works operate from a naive distinction between a text's "form" and "content." So in a recent essay the brilliant computer-text theorist Steven DeRose writes that "A book is 'the same' if reprinted from quarto to octavo and from Garamond 24 to Times 12 in all but a few senses."[10] Aldus and the fifteenth-century humanist printers knew better (and so, I am sure, does DeRose). Those "few senses" are never nontrivial, and in many cases—a list is too easy to develop—they carry the most profound kinds of "content."

DeRose's ill-judged remark is commonplace truth among those who are making decisions about how to design scholarly tools for the computerized study of literary works. Poems, for example, are inherently non-hierarchical structures that promote attention to varying and overlapping sets of textual designs, both linguistic and bibliographical. But the computerized structures being imagined for studying these complex forms approach them as if they were expository, as if their "information" were indexable, as if the works were *not* made from zeugmas and puns, metaphors and intertexts, as if the textual structure were composed of self-identical elements. Some textual information in poems is indexable, but nearly everything most salient about them is polyvalent. So far as imaginative works are concerned the equation remains: "a equals a if and only if a does not equal a."

Not to despair, however. Like the appearance of the codex nearly 2,000 years ago, like the advent of printing in the fifteenth century, the computer comes bearing great promise to literary scholars.

"But will we be assimilated? Is resistance futile?" There are no aliens here, no struggle between books and computers. From now on scholarship will have both, willy-nilly. The question is—the choice is—whether those with an intimate appreciation of literary works will become actively involved in designing new sets of tools for studying them.

Appendix to Chapter 6

"What Is Text?"

That question locates a set of issues dominating much of the most important debate and conversation in current humanities scholarship. History of
the book, theory of textuality, methods of knowledge representation, digital scholarship, even bibliography and theory of editing: All of these subject areas are now centers of the liveliest interest, most especially for
younger scholars. The interest is heavily interdisciplinary. It is also focused
on foundational matters. The advent of digital technology has, paradoxically, forced us to rethink the most basic matters relating to the nature of
texts and documents.

Addressing the question at a special panel in the 1999 joint meeting of
the Association for Computers and Humanities and the Association for
Literary and Linguistic Computing (ACH/ALLC), Allen Renear proposed
the following "five theses" about textuality, which he laid down in a brief
initial position paper.[1] In this argument texts are:

(1) Real: They have properties independent of our interests in them and
    our theories about them.
(2) Abstract: The objects that constitute texts are abstract, not material,
    objects.
(3) Intentional: Texts are, necessarily, the product of mental acts.
(4) Hierarchical: The structure of texts is fundamentally hierarchical.
(5) Linguistic: Texts are linguistic objects; renditional features are not parts
    of texts and therefore not proper locations for textual meaning.

That clear and succinct statement reflects an intensive involvement, over
many years, with the theory of text as it was being engaged by Renear and
his colleagues, principally at Brown University, as they were developing
TEI as a standard for electronic markup of humanities texts. That important practical tool implements the theory of text that Allen summarized in
his theses and that he went on to describe in this way:

> this account of text is rich in explanatory and predictive power, implied by
> our modal intuitions about cultural artifacts, and useful both in regulating
> further inquiry, and in guiding the development of tools and resources.
> Finally, and very importantly, I argue that this view has no serious com-

petitors. It is the best account of text that we have, and, fortunately, it is a good one.

The force of the first sentence in that passage is carried by the success of TEI as a disciplinary standard. But the two following sentences are not *in fact* true, though they have much truth in them. Renear's "account of text," while in certain respects a very good one indeed, has serious limitations. And "serious competitors" have been around for a long time.

My brief reply to Renear's view came as the following "position paper":

The question framing this ACH session involves a misconception. It assumes that "text" is a unitary phenomenon and that its concept can be thought as self-identical. But while both of these assumptions may be undertaken for heuristic purposes, neither represents what Wittgenstein called "the case."

In the field of Humanities Computing the idea of text has been dominated by conceptions practically realized in the TEI implementation of SGML markup. Several key theoretical papers published by Steve DeRose, Allen Renear, "et al." explain the ground of that implementation.

This ground, explicitly "abstract" (Renear, "Out of Praxis"), represents a view of text as essentially a vehicle for transmitting information and concepts (final cause). Text is "hierarchical" (formal cause) and "linguistic" (material cause), and it is a product of human intention (efficient cause).

Renear correctly insists upon the "platonic" character of this approach to textuality. That orientation, which traces its thought to the *Republic* in particular, helps to clarify the problems that arise when it addresses itself to "poetic" or noninformational forms of textuality. There is no question but that most of our textual archive is hierarchically organized. On the other hand, there is also no question but that poetical texts comprise a key, perhaps even a defining, part of the corpus of our humanities archive. When Plato called for the expulsion of the poets from the city, he was arguing for a certain theory of textuality.

Unlike expository text, poetry is not organized in a determinate hierarchy. TEI and SGML markup, therefore, while reasonably adequate vehicles for expository and informational texts, come up far short of rendering the features of poetic texts that are of greatest interest to those who read and use those texts. Poetical texts are recursive structures built out of complex networks of repetition and variation. No poem can exist without systems of "overlapping structures," and the more developed the poetical text, the more complex are those systems of recursion. So it is that in a poetic field no unit can be assumed to be self-identical. The logic of the poem is only frameable in some kind of paradoxical articulation such as: "a equals a if and only if a does not equal a."

This essential character of poetical text helps to explain why content in poiesis tends to involve more broadly "semiotic" rather than narrowly "linguistic" materials. The sonic and visible features of text are, so far as the poets who make these texts are concerned (or the readers who engage them), nearly as apt for expressive poetical purposes as the semantic, syntactic, and rhetorical features. Each of these features represent fields of textual action, and while each considered individually (abstractly) may be described in a hierarchical scheme, the recursive interplay of the fields produces works without a governing hierarchy. Of course a governing hierarchy can be imposed upon such works. TEI and SGML create, as Renear shows, a certain type of "linguistic" hierarchy, one that privileges text as a container for storing information. But even that linguistic hierarchy is highly specialized (it does not consider, for example, the rhetorical structures that overlap and infect the syntax and semantics).

The case of poetry in fact defines a kind of textual ethos, as it were, that may be seen to pervade genres not normally thought of as poetical. Certain kinds of philosophers lend themselves to a hierarchical approach—St. Thomas, Kant, Hegel. Others don't. Not without reason did the Bergen Wittgenstein project shy off TEI/SGML as a system for marking up the corpus of Wittgenstein's texts; and the scholars setting out now to "edit" the Peirce archive are well aware that TEI/SGML does not lend itself to an adequate treatment of Peirce's existential graphs. "Text" in Kant "is" one thing, but in Peirce it "is" something else again.

This represents a formulation of textuality I would not have been able to articulate in 1993, when I began to try to implement my ideas through the practical task of building *The Rossetti Archive*. Not that I had a different set of ideas about textuality in 1993, I just had a less determinate, a more fluid set. That inchoate state of mind was forced to greater clarity by the demands of our practical editing tasks. Because computers are a special race of idiot savant, we humans—or I should say we humanists—find it difficult to give them instructions that correspond to our thoughts and desires. Whereas we thrive in a world of analogues and fuzzy logic, computers exploit a different type of precision. How to engage a fruitful intercourse between these two forms of thinking defines the very heart of humanities computing.

I was lucky in 1993 to begin my work with computer scientists who understood the general problems far better than I did. These scholars and scientists were to be my "technical support," but the help they gave went out much farther and in much deeper. It began—in a way, was epitomized—in the first question put to me by the CS faculty person at the University of Virginia, Alan Batson, who was coordinating the computer support staff. "I want you to tell me and our CS people exactly what it is you do in your work as a humanities scholar. We'll listen and then try to tell you whether what *we* do can help you with your work." As it turned out, I found that I often didn't know precisely what I did as a textual scholar—or rather, that I was uncertain how to formulate what I did in ways that Alan and his associates—including his computers—could understand.

The discovery and the unpacking of that dysfunction has had a number of important consequences for our work. Most crucial has been the realization that humanities scholars are interested in textual forms that computers appear inapt to engage, as many critics who despise technology—and who commonly know even less about it than I do—regularly point out. When I began work on *The Rossetti Archive* I wanted a tool that could store, access, and analyze a large and complex body of textual and visual materials. We've been able to build that tool. But in the course of the work we also came to see the minimal levels of analysis we've been able to develop through textual theories driven by an informational model of textuality.

So if Alan Batson were to pose his question to me now, I would ask him some questions in turn: "Alan, how can electronic tools help to elucidate texts that we know are not and can never be self-identical, or composed of self-identical parts? Or how will those tools expose and explore the negative space of textuality? And can our computers help us deal analytically with all those crucial trans- and metalinguistic features of text so important to archivists and bibliographers—not to mention graphics designers, book artists, and many many poets. Are computers ready to have an interesting conversation with those kinds of texts?"

A few years ago I doubted that they were. Now, however, I see promising signs. An important move will be to exploit the difference between analogue thinking, which we do so well, and digital thinking, which computers do better than their human makers. A new level of computer-assisted textual analysis may be achieved through programs that randomly but systematically deform the texts they search and that submit those deformations to human consideration. Computers are no more able to "decode" rich imaginative texts than human beings are. What they can be made to do, however, is expose textual features that lie outside the usual purview of human readers.

That purview of reading is framed as a sympathetic exchange, or dialectic, between a specific text marked for reception by a general decoder. We decode only the message that we decide has been specifically sent. In imaginative works, our reading decisions are subject to revision or even erasure. These shiftings occur because the texts are multiply coded, and the multiples are so recursively arranged that we are always being teased beyond our decisive thoughts about what the text is "saying." Nonetheless, even in transacting imaginative texts our desire to close the sympathetic exchange is such that we make decisions about what we are reading, and those decisions occlude other kinds of awareness.

A computer with the same set of reading codes is naturally (so to speak) inclined to be less discriminating. That lack of discrimination in computerized reading is exactly what we want to exploit. We want to see what textual possibilities have been forbidden or made nugatory by the original act of textual encoding—that is, by the decisive and particular text that stands before us. The random access procedures of digital technology can bring those possibilities to view. The fact that many will appear to us, at that point, as *im*possible nonsense is exactly what holds out such promise, on two counts. First, not everything tossed up by the computer will seem nonsensical, and besides, people will differ. Second, however we judge the results, they will inevitably clarify our own thoughts to ourselves by providing a set of contrasts to throw our thinking into sharper relief.

Think of Emily Dickinson:

> Much Madness is divinest Sense–
> To a discerning Eye–
> Much Sense–the starkest Madness–
> 'Tis the Majority
> In this, as All, prevail–

But the Majority is not All. One wants to hear from those prevalent Minorities.

Chapter 7

Dialogue and Interpretation at the Interface of Man and Machine

> *The electric things have their lives, too. Paltry as those lives are.*
> —*Philip K. Dick,* Do Androids Dream of Electric Sheep

Trying to think about texts, documents, and their possible electronic transformations, I am going to begin at a severely oblique angle. I do this to set a visibly disorienting figure—obliquity—into the rhetorical structure of the exposition. We all know too much about texts and textuality. We need to think about them in different ways.

Knowing this move is being made, you may, I trust, willingly suspend your belief in it and instead work through its evident premeditation. My hope is that the exposed rhetorical illusion will set a clarifying frame around the issues, the way Brecht sets a clarifying frame around his theatrical investigations by exposing his use of them.

The discussion will begin through a return to G. Spencer Brown's remarkable 1969 book *Laws of Form*.[1] In his Introduction Brown notes that in writing his book "I found it easier to acquire an access to the laws [deliberated through the work] than to determine a satisfactory way of communicating them" (xxii). The comment seems at once, and paradoxically, both modest and outrageous, particularly for a book that takes as its point of departure and central subject "self-referential paradoxes." That modest/outrageous statement is as much a self-referential paradox as the famous one Brown cites in the preface to the American edition of his book: "This statement is false."

Brown's observation about his expressive difficulty cuts to the center of the laws of form his book seeks to elucidate, as I hope to demonstrate later in this chapter. Laws of form, it turns out, are expressive (trans)forms and are reflected—and reflexive—as such. And certain kinds of text—Brown calls these "injunctive" texts—reveal why it's difficult to communicate the laws they themselves realize.

This chapter will thus reconsider the issues taken up in *Laws of Form*. My purposes are, however, more narrow and more practical. I want to elucidate some key but neglected formalities of textual documents and to meditate satisfactory ways of communicating those formalities. I am particularly interested in documents that have been indispensable for traditional humanities disciplines: language and literature, history, philosophy, art.[2] Realizing the need to develop a reliable system for representing such documents in a form that lays them open to the power of digital analysis, humanities computing during the past 20 years has worked hard to develop a model for text markup with general applicability. Despite the problems its own implementation exposed, the model of TEI was developed and, as we've seen, has become a disciplinary standard.[3] But with increasing numbers of humanities scholars using digital tools in their research work, the realization is growing that TEI's problems are not technical but systemic. To address them properly we have to step back and think not about TEI but about "text" itself.[4]

What *is* text? I am not so naive as to imagine that question could ever be finally settled. Asking such a question is like asking "How long is the coast of England?" But now we have to ask it again because when the question was re-posed by our digital culture, the humanities response proved inadequate: on one hand a reactionary refusal to admit that this new culture had any right to ask such a question (Sven Birkerts); on the other, the emergence of TEI and the proposal that its view of text would serve the interests of humanities scholars for digital culture. Much is at stake here. Even now we are beginning the process of re-editing—of representing—in digital form the entirety of our received textual and documentary archive. How successful this effort will be depends on how clearly we understand the materials we have to work with. On one hand, digital tools often appear strange and wondrous, especially because they spawn and mutate so quickly into rich and surprising possibilities. Books and documents, on the other hand, seem stable and familiar. They are tools we have learned how to use, they are reliable. The question is, how well *do* we understand them?

Too well, I believe. They have become familiar to us and consequently have grown much more obscure. Brown's unusual approach to questions of form can help us think our way back into the problems of textual forms. But his work will itself benefit by a tangential move. To begin thinking about textuality with Brown, then, let's begin again further back, by thinking about textuality with Dante, whose grasp of the subject was acute. His way of thinking is especially useful in this case exactly because it is a premodern way.

Inner Infinities

In the *Vita Nuova,* Dante regularly attaches explanatory prose descriptions to the poems he imbeds in his famous autobiography.[5] These "divisions," as he calls them, are "made to open the meaning of the thing divided." Some of the divisions are so brief as to seem perfunctory. Others appear so simple and transparent that we wonder what use they might serve. Then again, in the case of one sonnet—an especially cryptic one as Dante himself acknowledges—no division is supplied because, Dante says, "a division is only made to open the meaning of the thing divided; and this, as it is sufficiently manifest through the reasons given has no need of division." The "reasons given" are the words in the text that explain "the occasion of this sonnet."[6]

I shall have to pass without remark much in these "divisions" that could be usefully taken up, even in the present context. My focus will be on a pair of related matters: the fact that dividing the poems into parts should seem to Dante a way of opening up their meaning; and the fact that the divisions Dante makes seem arbitrary. For example, after quoting the sonnet "Tutti li miei penser parlan d'Amore" Dante says that "This sonnet may be divided into four parts" ["Questo sonetto in quattro parte si può dividere"] and he then proceeds to do two things: First, he restates in schematic terms the prose sense of each of the designated parts; second, he then indicates where in the poem each part falls. Although the exegesis may in any particular case be more or less elaborate, this is the general double form that it always takes.

Note that in dividing this sonnet Dante *chooses* to distinguish four parts—that is to say, his partitioning represents a judgment Dante makes about what would be useful for the reader to know. The arbitrariness of his divisions leap to one's mind as soon as we see where the four parts separate from each other. In the case of this sonnet, part 1 comprises only line 1, part 2 includes lines 2–6, part 3, lines 7–8, and the last part covers the sestet. Looking at his divisions for the other poems in the text, we find that they too have little relation to their highly formalized metrical structures. The divisions cut across those structures in apparently random ways, as we see in the case of this sonnet. The randomness is all the more clear because Dante does not disguise from us the fact that the divisions have as much—perhaps more—to do with his purposes toward his readers as they do with the formal structure of the poems themselves.

We notice as well that the exegeses, even the elaborated ones, are spare to a degree. Unlike for instance in the *Convivio,* Dante gives no thematic or symbolic interpretations. Indeed, wherever the poems seem most obscure he typically retreats even further from explanations, even from the schematic divisioning process that marks his method here. So in the case of the sonnet that he doesn't divide at all, Dante says something remarkable. Though obscure and ambiguous words spring up, like tares among the wheat, in the passages "whereby is shown the occasion of this sonnet" in a clear way, Dante chooses not to provide a divisioning, for the difficulties, he says, can't be solved by anyone who doesn't have a deep insight into the issues in the first place: "And therefore it were not well for me to expound this difficulty, inasmuch as my speaking would be either fruitless or else superfluous."

Dante's method is perhaps most fully revealed in his prose division of the great canzone "Donne ch'avete intelletto d'Amore," the *Vita Nuova'*s central text. "That it may be better understood," Dante says, "I will divide it more subtly than the others." Then, having laid out an intricate set of divisions and subdivisions, he finishes his analysis with a remarkable set of statements:

> I say, indeed, that the further to open the meaning of this poem, more minute divisions ought to be used; but nevertheless he who is not of wit enough to understand it by these which have been already made is welcome to leave it alone; for certes, I fear I have communicated its sense to too many by these present divisions. . . .

From all this several things of importance seem clear. For Dante a process of divisioning could be carried on indefinitely, with a partitioning analysis moving to isolate further ranges of subdivision at any and all levels. Furthermore, if the divisions represent "objective" characteristics of the poetical work, they come to expose only a certain range or set of the poem's formalities—one reconstructed as a certain perspective on the poem taken by Dante. These divisions are, as we've already noticed, incommensurate with any metrical structure; they transcend sentence grammar; and they represent only what Dante himself thinks might or might not be useful for the reader. He seems to produce them as models or stimuli that might provoke readers with "wit enough to understand" and to search out meanings (and divisions) for themselves. Finally, Dante's divisions do little more than mark off places in the poems, as if each were a kind of field or area to be mapped rather than a complex linguistic event to be paraphrased or "interpreted" in the manner of the *Convivio* or of the "readings" we have cultivated in our twentieth-century exegetical traditions.

In setting out these divisions for his poems, Dante recalls us to a crucial primitive level of his work's textuality. The significance of Dante's divisionings can now be exposed further by considering them in relation to Brown's *Laws of Form*. These laws draw out the structural dynamic implicit in form as such. The elemental condition or manifestation of form is the appearance of a mark in an otherwise unmarked space. Brown calls this mark a "distinction" so that the elemental law of form is: a distinction can be drawn. Every conceivable formal world may be traced or tracked back to that elementary law.

Dante's textual divisions illustrate his understanding that the same law underwrites the making of poems. Each poem is a kind of world or universe to itself, and any set of poems—for instance, the set chosen for the *Vita Nuova*—may be conceived and fashioned into a meta-universe. So we might say—might show, as critics have done for centuries—that the *Vita Nuova* is usefully seen as part of other networks and textual universes. Or we might turn the direction of our tracing in the opposite direction, back into the subuniverses concealed, as it were, within the apparitions of the specific poems placed in Dante's autobiography. The latter is Dante's own procedure when he offers us his divisions and their arbitrariness points to the infinities of order that may be tracked inward of the poem, through the looking glass of its surface(s).

Argument by Bibliographic Code

Drawing on the ancient tradition of the Arts of Memory, Dante's textual *divisiones* point toward the inherently spatial conception he has of his textual field. The *Vita Nuova* is a "book of memory" shaped by visible rubrications so as to give a mirror image of the events it aims to recall. Indeed, it is for Dante only one section or division of a larger book clearly visible to his mind's eye as he undertakes its (re)construction: "In that part of the book of my memory before the which little can be read, there is a rubric, saying, *Incipit Vita Nova*. Under such rubric I find written many things; and among them the words which I purpose to copy into this little book."

Time itself for Dante occupies a space of events mapped on a grid of mathematical and astrological relations. Movement, textual as well as human, occurs within a fixed space where the relations of things is unimaginably deep and complex. One divides this space in order to mark a way into those complex relations.

Mark, space, direction: If we think of language in linguistic terms, these words as I've been using them appear to us as metaphors, figures of speech. But if we think of language in semiotic terms the same words take on a literality that can be extremely helpful for understanding how language works, and particularly—for my present purposes—how the language of poetic forms works. From that altered scale of attention we may then start to re-imagine, in the graphematic terms realized through digitization, analytic tools for our most complex semiotic devices.

It is useful to remember that the text we are transacting here and now on this page is not just a vehicle for communicating certain ideas. It is simultaneously a reflection of and on itself, an analysis of itself—to borrow from Dante, a divisioning of itself. The analysis is executed semiotically, that is, through the deployment of the forms of what might be called, after Robert Horne, its visual language. This language Horne describes as a composition of words and shapes and/or images. Useful as this definition is, it is not strictly accurate, and the loose feature of Horne's view is important since it pervades, as an assumption, nearly all approaches to textuality.[7]

The point is important and must be pressed. Horne sees visual language when he sees wordtext combined with shapes or wordtext combined with images or wordtext combined with both together. But graphically transmitted wordtext is always ab initio "visual" since there can be no wordtext without the presence of what Horne calls "shapes." According to Horne, images are optional to graphic text but shape is not. But in fact whether or not shape enters the pagespace as explicitly drawn boxes or arrows or circles or whatever—these are the forms Horne sees—shape is ever present. Graphically transmitted texts, by elementary "laws of form," automatically generate—perhaps "incarnate" would be the better term—shape, which emerges along with the primal "mark" that shapes Brown's demonstration.

So far as our common (visual) language is concerned, then, the elementary marks are an alphabet of letters, plus an accompanying set of signs—explicit or implicit—for reorganizing the letter marks into different scales and sets of relation. One can distinguish ("si può distinguere") the most common elementary textspace as the page itself (in contradistinction, for instance, to a scroll's textspace or to the nonlinear textspace of, say, a cave wall). This pagespace is elemental because it replicates at a different scalar level the same kind of distinction marked within the page space by the elementary letter and graphic marks. The relation between the elementary graphic marks and the elemental page space sets the parameters for all types of graphemic directionality. In the spatial conventions of the page regulated at two dimensions, the normative directions are horizontal left to right and vertical top to bottom (along with a normative line of directionality from upper left to lower right). So for the paperspace at two dimensions, a range of complex spatial options can be manipulated at the borders of the page space, between and within the lines of text, and as blocks of space and/or text formed within the main dynamical textspace area arbitrarily established by the margins, header, and footer. Variant forms of sequence and direction are developed through rule-governed deviations from these norms. In bookspace, pagespace variances emerge as a set of higher order conventions of three-dimensional relations: between page rectos and versos; between the single page and the page opening; and between sequences of pages gathered together. As more explicit shapes and/or images are introduced into the paperspace, that space will be pushed toward a space governed by rules of collage rather than by rules of textuality.[8]

A page of printed or scripted text should thus be understood as a certain kind of graphic interface. The complexity of the interface varies from a minimal use of the bibliographical codes open to a given paperspace— the text you are now reading is a good instance of such simplicity—to highly elaborated interfaces like those determined as poetic texts. Some of the latter exploit the bibliographical resources of paperspace to an extreme degree—Pound's *Cantos,* for example, or Dickinson's various writings— while others are satisfied to work within a set of basic and commonly used conventions. Whatever the specific differentials, however, a broad heuristic distinction separates informational from imaginative texts. The former aspire to transparency, the latter to noise, redundancy, repetition. One is vehicular, the other, iconic.

Exploiting bibliographical codes does not per se signal that poetic motives are governing a particular text, as the work of Tufte and Horne— as their own *books*—indicate. Both participate in a long tradition of "knowledge representation" that mixes textual and graphic forms (a tradition importantly advanced in the late work, the existential graphs, of Charles Sanders Peirce). It is crucial to realize that every text may choose, as it were, to engage that self-conscious tradition. We see this in the layout and general book design of Brown's *Laws of Form*. These apparitional features of the work show Brown's effort to meet the problem of effectively communicating himself. In the event, the rhetorical and design move would elucidate the laws of form at a much deeper level.

Figures 7.1 and 7.2 reproduce the first edition of chapter 1, "The Form," which begins with a statement of assumptions, an initial presentation of The Form's elemental definition, and a declaration of The Form's two primary axioms, the law of calling and the law of crossing.

Brown's root concept of "distinction" is thoroughly replicated in this text's bibliographical codes, in which various key differentials are developed through the manipulation of pagespace, changes of font, and the deployment of one simple, explicit shape (a line).[9] The layout constructs a graphic scene composed of related planes, colors, and textures. The simplicity of the elements can easily disguise the sophistication, even the elegance, of the graphical representations that transact every moment of Brown's conceptual exposition. In terms of the latter, this text's bibliographical codes exemplify—instantiate—The Form's elementary definition as well as axiom 1. The law of calling.

The text of chapter 1 does not instantiate axiom 2, the law of crossing, nor is that law exemplified at the bibliographical level in Brown's book anywhere in the first 11 chapters.[10] Of course Brown invokes and applies axiom 2 at a conceptual level throughout, but the axiom is never explicitly marked as such. We realize this remarkable fact about the book only in the culminant chapter 12, "Re-entry into the Form," where for the first time axiom 2 is instantiated. It gets marked in the text, however, not at the two-dimensional convention of the page but at the three-dimensional convention of the chapter, as the chapter title indicates. At the page level of the chapter, where a series of experiments are conducted, none of the experiments even invoke axiom 2, much less mark it.

That structure in Brown's book is extremely significant for understanding how laws of form operate in a textual horizon. The law of crossing governs reflexive functions, and in Brown's book reflexivity does not explicitly begin until the final chapter, whence it continues through the set of chapter notes and appendices that follow. How scrupulous Brown has been in constructing his text along the lines of his laws is underscored by the way those late chapter notes are (not) marked: Brown provides no links to them from within the chapter texts. The chapters draw and then draw out further and further distinctions until, at the conclusion of chapter 11, the process itself reveals "that the account may be continued endlessly" (68). At that point an implicit injunction becomes explicit in and as chap-

1

THE FORM

We take as given the idea of distinction and the idea of indication, and that we cannot make an indication without drawing a distinction. We take, therefore, the form of distinction for the form.

Definition

Distinction is perfect continence.

That is to say, a distinction is drawn by arranging a boundary with separate sides so that a point on one side cannot reach the other side without crossing the boundary. For example, in a plane space a circle draws a distinction.

Once a distinction is drawn, the spaces, states, or contents on each side of the boundary, being distinct, can be indicated.

There can be no distinction without motive, and there can be no motive unless contents are seen to differ in value.

If a content is of value, a name can be taken to indicate this value.

Thus the calling of the name can be identified with the value of the content.

Axiom 1. The law of calling

The value of a call made again is the value of the call.

That is to say, if a name is called and then is called again, the value indicated by the two calls taken together is the value indicated by one of them.

That is to say, for any name, to recall is to call.

G. Spencer Brown, *Laws of Form* (1969, first edition), page 1.

Equally, if the content is of value, a motive or an intention or instruction to cross the boundary into the content can be taken to indicate this value.

Thus, also, the crossing of the boundary can be identified with the value of the content.

Axiom 2. The law of crossing

The value of a crossing made again is not the value of the crossing.

That is to say, if it is intended to cross a boundary and then it is intended to cross it again, the value indicated by the two intentions taken together is the value indicated by none of them.

That is to say, for any boundary, to recross is not to cross.

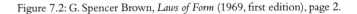

Figure 7.2: G. Spencer Brown, *Laws of Form* (1969, first edition), page 2.

ter 12, where we are called to reflection, that is to say, where we are called to cross back to chapter 1: "we return for a last look at the agreement with which the account was opened." In point of textual fact, it is the book's *first* last look back.

In the reflexive note to chapter 2 of his book Brown explains that "the primary form of mathematical communication is not description, but injunction. In this respect it is comparable to practical art forms like cookery [and] music" (77). Although Brown does not include text production among these practical art forms, he might and indeed should have done so, as his own book admirably demonstrates. Clearly Dante regards writing, including poetical writing, as injunctive. Dante's word would not be injunction, however, it would be—it was—rhetoric.[11]

As Brown's book shows, a primary textual injunction is to make and elaborate distinctions. If these distinctions are rigorously pursued they produce the realization "that the world we know is constructed in order (and thus in such a way as to be able) to see itself": "and so on, and so on you will eventually construct the universe, in every detail and potentiality, as you know it now; but then, again, what you construct will not be all, for by the time you have reached what now is, the universe will have expanded into a new order to contain what will then be" (106).

In a splendid act of wit Brown encodes this passage in the typographical convention of indented block quotation. But the passage is not a quotation in the ordinary sense; it is all Brown's own words. Setting it off as he does, however, Brown not only *marks* the text reflexively, he *names* himself one of those godlike "universal representatives [who] *can* record universal law far enough to say" what the passage says. These are altogether (and literally) lowercase gods, as Brown's text shows at a textual level that supervenes the typographical font. After rising to quote Brown's "universal" self in the block quotation, the text descends to its common margins to gloss that universal law as follows: "In this sense, in respect of its own information, the universe *must* expand to escape the telescopes through which we, who are it, are trying to capture it, which is us. The snake eats itself, the dog chases its tail" (106).

Injunctive Forms

That *Laws of Form* should display this kind of wit is perhaps not surprising. G. Spencer Brown—mathematician and philosopher—is after all also an imaginative writer—the latter under the pseudonym James Keys, whose strange autobiographical text *Only Two Can Play this Game* was conceived in the wonderlands of Borges, Abbott, and Carroll. *Laws of Form* does not resort to an imaginative genre. Nonetheless, an SGML or TEI markup that would adequately open such a work to digital analysis seems as unimaginable as it would be for the Alice books. The conceptual structure—the demonstration—of *Laws of Form* explains, *demonstrates,* why this dysfunction must occur in any case where laws of form operate—for instance, in language or any of its instances. Unbeknownst to itself until the moment when it turns reflexively back upon itself—and then it is too late—every form of thought is incommensurate with itself. Certain texts—and certain kinds of text—make that contradiction a primary focus of attention.

Not many works of philosophy demonstrate that paradox as elegantly as *Laws of Form*—perhaps Nagarjuna's treatise on "Emptiness" makes an apt comparison.[12] Some do it with greater force—Montaigne, Kierkegaard, Wittgenstein (especially in that relentless work known to us as *Philosophical Investigations*). How to "edit" such writers presents a constant challenge and adventure, and hence a recurrent opportunity to address anew the unanswerable questions they raise.

Works of imagination, however—let us say henceforth "poetry"—make the discourse of paradox and contradiction the ground of their semiosis. In terms of Brown's *Laws of Form,* this means that distinctions in poetic texts are elaborated in a space that (so to speak) has no intention of maintaining original integrity. As textual boundaries are defined and crossed, the marks of distinction constituting the boundaries are canceled or threatened with erasure, because new marks of distinction turn out to be phenomenal illusions, closely akin to mathematical transformations. New distinctions conceal algorithms—hidden injunctions—to cancel the same distinctions by recrossing the boundary initiated when the distinction first appeared to view.

Whereas everyone knows this about poetical texts, we are less clear about how and why this network of recursions unfolds. Yet clarity on the matter is particularly important in a digital horizon if we are to have any hope of building adequate electronic re-presentations of our received textual archive.

Modern linguistic analysis from Saussure to Hjelmslev to Segré develops a four-part analysis of the sign.[13] The signifier and the signified—the elemental dismantling and reconstruction of the ancient distinction of form from content—are each shown to replicate in themselves the form/content distinction because in any case both signifier and signified, in order to be recognized as such, have to be separately *marked.* The marking transaction creates, by the law of form, a new distinction—signifier versus signified—that dissolves a mistaken implication drawn from the earlier distinction of form/content. In the reconstructed sign both signifier and signified are not only "content constitutive," they are so precisely because of their "form function," because they have been marked.

What this otherwise useful analysis does not indicate—what it positively obscures, in fact—is the injunctive or rhetorical character of textuality. The structure of any text overgoes its own internal (signifier/signified) coherencies and/or contradictions. In Jakobsonian terms, this overplus is comprehended under the concept of "reference." The concept functions reasonably well in analyses focused on informational and nonpoetic texts, but its analytic force dissipates when directed toward poetry. This happens because a modern aesthetic understanding shapes our thought about "the literary text." Since poetical works are conceived as "communication *sui generis*" (or "language [oriented] toward the message in itself" [Segré, 28–29]), neither affirming nor denying anything beyond their internal relations, "reference" in the literary text turns (virtually) virtual. They are, as marxists used to say, "not among the ideologies."

Texts seen in this light turn dark and passive. They seem not to address us but rather to lie down and await examination, like corpses under autopsy or treasured secrets. That textual structure was fashioned in the rhetoric of romanticism, where a textuality was sought that would not appear to have "a palpable design upon" the reader. But all texts are generated through algorithms; romantic texts are coded with special instructions to obscure the design codes, or rather to make those codes appear not as reading instructions—not as *marked text*—but as pure character data.

The signifier/signified/referent structure implicitly poses two (related) questions to a text: "What is it saying?" and "What is it doing in saying what it says?" This second question points toward the injunctive feature that is open in every text and in every part of every text. Ultimately one would want to be able to describe and analyze what literary texts are doing, *sui generis,* in saying what they say—how they function in society and culture at large *as they are literary works.* To construct that kind of comprehensive analysis, however, we will have to undertake a thorough re-examination of their rhetorical and injunctive character at micro levels. The history of any text's emergence is both a record and an index of how it has been used, what it "meant." Those records should be recovered for a programmatic analysis of their injunctive features, which is to say for their Dantean "divisiones" and their Brownian "laws of form."

(In)Conclusion

But the historical record can only be "recovered" through acts that cover it yet again, by agencies of markup. Every text descending to us is not only marked text, it is multiply and ambiguously marked. The analytic usefulness of aesthetic texts lies exactly in their generic inertia to pursue and exploit multiple and overlapping formalities and divisions in explicit ways.

In such circumstances what is needed is a dynamic engagement with text and not a program aimed at discovering the objectively constitutive features of what a text "is." That dynamic requirement follows from the laws of form themselves, as Brown's work shows. But what equally follows is that the analysis must be applied to the text *as it is performative.* We begin with an understanding that text is always the marked or materially distinguished text—the text as image and/or audition—and that the textual analysis is itself part of the marking processes that governs the object of study.

The problem at this point becomes at once more clear and more difficult to address. One is perhaps reminded of Brown's observation that "I found it easier to acquire an access to the laws [deliberated through the work] than to determine a satisfactory way of communicating them." This difficulty arises because the act of communication promotes and re-energizes the original (historical) ambiguity of the textual signifiers. They are arbitrary forms, open to an indefinite range of significations. The more complex the form of the signifier the more deeply run the ambiguous options of meaning. In the visible state of language they scale up from letters and diacriticals to wondrous scriptural and bibliographical creatures.

In this situation the limitations of determinately marked forms can be exploited for more dynamic operations. The proposal I imagine here is directed at visible text only and involves approaching the text not in terms of its semantic "content" but as a physically shaped construction. We do this on the assumption that the physical arrangement of the text amounts to a reflection or interpretation—a marking—of its semantic meaning. The reflection will inevitably introduce a "deformance" of the work, and thus will appear in one or another perspective as what Joyce once called (in the opening chapter of *Ulysses*) "a cracked mirror": because even at the purely bibliographical level the semiosis of any specific set of signifiers will lie open to different possible readings. The text's non–self-identity extends itself through all marked levels precisely because it is the operation of marking that divides the text from itself.

The project imagined here attends only to the text's bibliographical codes in order to begin with a relatively simple set of rules for marking or interpreting textuality. We want to teach the computer a set of rules for reading texts. Trying to teach it higher order rules presents enormous difficulties. It seems possible, however, to develop an initial set of rules for bibliographical coding options and forms. Part of the programmatic operation is to implement these rules in order to expose and generate a more complex set of rules extending to higher orders of textual form.

The ultimate event in this program will be a dialogue between the computer and the human beings who are teaching it how to read. We want to study the bibliographical formations that appear out of the computerized readings. These readings will, we believe, inevitably constitute a set of (de)formations full of surprises for the rule-givers. What those surprising readings will be cannot be predicted, but that they will come is, we think, as certain as the fact that no text is commensurate with itself.

The more sophisticated we are the more we normalize textual incommensurates. We have internalized an immensely complicated, many-leveled set of semiotic rules and signs, and we control the contradictions of actual textual circumstances by various normalizing operations. We can hope to expose these normalizations—which are themselves deformative acts—by opening the conversation here being proposed between analogue and digital readers. We begin by implementing what we think we know about the rules of bibliographical codes. The conversation should force us to see— finally, to imagine—what we don't know that we know about texts and textuality.

At that point, perhaps, we may begin setting philology—"the knowledge of what is known," as it used to be called—on a new footing.

Conclusion

Beginning Again and Again: "The Ivanhoe Game"

Am I in earnest? Oh dear no! Don't you know that this is a fairy tale, and all fun and pretense; and that you are not to believe one word of it, even if it is true?
—*Charles Kingsley,* The Water-Babies. A Fairy Tale for a Land-Baby

The Aesthetic Interface

For a culture of the book such as ours, digital media have brought a great enlightenment. Of course many will be skeptical of that sentence. Computerization has often appeared like Byron's Giaour, "a thing of dark imaginings" sent by some alien god to raze, perhaps forever, the topless towers of our splendid codex world.

We are not facing the extinction of a species. We are involved in the historical convergence of two great machineries of symbol production and hence of human consciousness. Like any serious human intercourse, this convergence brings enlightenment from engaged differences. It also brings change. But we want to keep in mind, at this volatile and interesting moment, that nearly all these differences and changes—including the unforeseen, which predominate—unfold from human choices and ideas. At every moment different ideas are in play or conflict, and certain among them manage to build a grammar of assent.

In our current enthusiasms and uncertainties about books and computers we might stop briefly to consider an important literary event of about a hundred years ago. I refer to the climactic moment in the career of

Stéphane Mallarmé when he conceived that amazing prophetic revelation of the culture of the book, *Un coup de Dés*.

Let's briefly recall what he did with that work. The chief object, he told André Gide in 1897, was to make "the rhythm of a word group . . . imitate the action or object in question."[1] He expands on that idea in his essay "The Book: A Spiritual Instrument" by comparing the structure of the book to a musical score. Mallarmé conceives the alphabet, as well as (any of) a book's bibliographical and typographical formations, to have a kind of Orphic power. The work he has in mind will only be realized when it is composed in at least three senses simultaneously: a typographical sense, a musical sense, and a poetic sense. The book that emerges is a machine for executing the orders that bring it into existence at each of those three orders.

We mislead our imaginations when we think of the book as a carrier of information, according to Mallarmé. The key move in shattering that positivist illusion is the typographical move—the decision to expose the soul that lives in the physique of text. The Mallarméan book comes forth as a set of figurations behaving like sentient and purposive creatures, constituting and calling forth their world(s), which include all of the book's readers, living and dead, actual, possible, imaginary. Text as a musical score to be played in a space populated—defined—by all "the noble living and the noble dead"; text as a type of self-engendering creature/creation. Text passed forward to be played again.

Mallarmé was well aware that this way of thinking about the book was uncommon. Within cultures of modernity, Blake was perhaps the first to adopt and execute such a view of text. Born before historical circumstances could provide a clarifying framework for his work, however, he would not become an important cultural presence until the English advent of Mallarmé's generation—until the coming, that is to say, of D. G. Rossetti, A. C. Swinburne, and William Morris. From our still later vantage we can see how such a view emerges as the dialectical fate of journalistic and narrowly instrumental ideas about language that had been developing since the seventeenth century. In the United States, Dickinson and Whitman—both in their very different ways—were playing with comparable imaginations of books and texts.

More important for this moment of ours, however, we may also begin to see how much of the specifically Mallarméan imagination of the book forecasts key terms by which we now characterize digital media. Take these basic "forms of digital life" (as Wittgenstein might have called them):

Simulation Medium
Interaction/Interoperability
Accessible Memory
Programs and Protocols

How remarkable that these commonplaces of digital culture should so correspond with the most advanced self-conceptions of book culture. So the Mallarméan book's linguistic and graphical elements resemble algorithms, and *Un coup de Dés* a systems program for realizing "the spiritual instrument" it instantiates. So the reader must execute the score that is at once the book and the reader's world called into being (action) by that very score. So the contents of that world are memory simulations, encodings of encodings as Plato long ago lamented. Mallarmé's first textual proposals for his great work are each separate performances. No text is "data," every text has been marked and parsed. Every text, having thus been *played,* is henceforth riven with ancient memory, which we may hear, if we try, in a new way.

We are talking here not in terms of identities but of differences, that is to say, of tropes and figures. To realize *that,* however, is to glimpse the reciprocal illumination that a book culture can bring to our textual illusions, digital as well as bookish. The idea of "data," for example, or the ideal of a noise-free communication channel—finally, their underlying imagination of a primal self-identity: All three are derivative, not primitive, conceptions, projects formed to gain a certain kind of instrumental mastery over the mysteries our loves and fears have known, and will always know, far more intimately. Such ideas already function in vehicular conceptions of the book, or in views that imagine book design and typographical forms—what we now call "interface"—as "trivial" semiotic phenomena.

Conceived in this way, the great power of the book, when set beside digital functionalities, is its ability to promote and develop self-reflection. It has served other important purposes as well, of course—most significantly, to store and transmit messages and information. The latter comprise two of the great aptitudes of IT instruments, and this functional overlap has precipitated tension between digital and bibliographical cultures, as we know. The tension is raised to a higher level because of the computer's remarkable powers of simulation and analysis. We have reason for thinking that digital machines can be made with the self-reflexive and creative capacities of the Mallarméan book.

But perhaps not *every* reason to think so, as we shall see in a moment.

The Frankenstein (or Faustian) dream of the artificial intelligence (AI) community may well be the self-contradiction it has appeared to many. The contradiction need not matter in the short or even the long term, as Mary Shelley's famous book makes clear. Both monster and novel—the dream of creating a human being by scientific artifice as well as the artistic representation of that dream—have served us well in our quest for self-consciousness and self-reflection. We possess no more powerful means by which to see and study ourselves, our actions as well as our dreams, than our mirrors of art. Second only to them, in this respect, have been our reflections on these reflections: the critical works—historical, scientific, philosophical—that preserve and polish the primary aesthetic mirrors.

We have had some centuries of experience with our bookish mirrors—mechanisms that simulate with a difference—and we aren't done with them yet, if we ever shall be. In any case, we would do well to remember that history as we try to imagine what we have in mind for these new, digital, tools for simulation.

Difference Engines

No one ever imagined, except in conscious imagination, that a book might be capable of thinking. Today lots of people know that machines have that capacity, at least in some important sense, and many pursue a quest to develop not just thinking machines but cyborgs. These pursuits implicitly declare that while books are prosthetic instruments, digital media might operate differently. The difference measures the (possible) capacity of computerized creatures for human, self-conscious thought, for affection, and—most important—for creativity (the ultimate Turing test for these imagined AI beings). Or perhaps for some new kind of affective thought—transhuman—that will emerge through a kind of Hegelian leap to another order of being altogether.

Drawing a distinction between two classes of servomechanism, we tend not to imagine that book technology—its history and its functional forms—has much to contribute to the development of this presumably higher-order machine. But until our electronic instruments do acquire cognitive and affective functions of a human kind, we might well think of them as prostheses after all (rather than as emerging beings). In this connection, their relation to the prosthesis of the book can be illuminating.

To the degree that we imagine the book, the library, and their network of relations as a complex vehicle for storing, organizing, transmitting, and connecting information, these traditional instruments all speak a language that computers can master. So we see that the computer's ability to manage this network of data has already outstripped our traditional instruments. Such achievements are impressive enough, as we recognize in the remarkable transformations taking place in our libraries, as well as in the computerized editorial and archival works now being built by various scholars and teams of scholars.

Given successes at these foundational levels of humanities studies, one might expect the scholarly community to be deeply invested in these new tools. The opposite is the case, as we know, and we have examined some of the practical and day-to-day reasons why this is happening. But another important factor is in play here. Only a few, usually very specialized, literary and humanities scholars are seriously involved with archiving, with the methodology of scholarly editing, or with investigations into the material operations of their own critical tools. Most of us are interested in questions of meaning and interpretation—of the literary and cultural works "themselves" or of the inter- and extratextual contexts and relations that these works (as it were) half create and half perceive. Our interests in "literary and cultural studies" have preserved the book as the critical tool of choice for the humanities community. When it comes to processes of reflection, digital tools lag far behind the technology of the book.

The example of Mallarmé and his idea of the book force themselves on our attention at this point. Much as we depend upon it for our critical work, the book remains in many respects an undiscovered or misperceived country even to those who are far traveled in its realms of gold. But the striking congruences between digital and Mallarméan ideas of text and book suggest that our traditional critical procedures may themselves be lagging behind our most interesting ideas about books and texts.

The true complexity of bookspace becomes shockingly apparent, as we have seen in earlier chapters, exactly when one tries to map the space with digital tools. "Shockingly" because these new tools, we are urged to believe, are so much more powerful at managing knowledge and information. But our efforts to gain digital mastery of the book have so far discovered at least as much failure as success. John Unsworth, who knows more about these matters than most, is stimulated rather than dismayed by this fact. So in a celebrated essay he champions what he calls "The Importance of Failure."

Two failures were particularly important in my own case. Although involved in the study of textuality for my entire intellectual life, the intransigence of the book before the analytic enginery of the computer was a sobering lesson. It demonstrated in the clearest way that in fact I did not know what I thought I knew about books and the textual condition in general. So exposing and clarifying the semiotics of traditional textuality became imperative as we tried to design digital scripts for processing such materials. Those pursuits, in their turn, revealed how far removed our work stood from the central interpretive interests of humanities scholars. Hence arose into ever clearer view a question that had been haunting our work from the beginning: How could we exploit digital tools to augment critical reflection both on and within bookspace?

Thinking in practical ways about the differences between textual space and digital space—that is to say, actually building *The Rossetti Archive*—finally brought us to think *through* those differences. It seems not within our capacity to build true cyborgs. We create such machines only in our imaginations. But it is definitely within our capacity to build machines that produce simulated forms of meaning—that is to say, machine-generated interpretive forms that can augment our own processes of critical reflection.

We want to work with digital tools as we have always worked with our tools for making simulations—for instance, with all our semiotic tools, and pre-eminently with the book. Critical reflection emerges in the mirroring event that develops at simulacral interfaces, of which the book is the one we are most used to using. With the coming of digital instruments we encounter (and create) a new genre, so to speak, within our sciences of the artificial—a new kind of interface between the human and the machinic.

How do we—we humans—exploit this situation *if our interests are primarily intellectual rather than instrumental*—that is to say, if we want to use these tools the way we use books made for critical and reflective purposes? The question is not often posed, and is sometimes not even permitted, among those who work most actively at this new human/machine interface. What dominates the work are efforts to create machines that would replicate our procedural, as opposed to our reflexive, powers and faculties.

Consider Project BRUTUS, the "Storytelling Machine" developed by Selmer Bringsjord and David Ferrucci. This foray into artificial intelligence and literary creativity was undertaken to examine the possibility of simulating imaginative creativity (rather than computational or problem-solving capabilities). Even as they succeeded in making their storytelling machine, however, Bringsjord and Ferrucci also came to a remarkable conclusion.

The machine could tell stories that would pass graduated Turing tests—that is, it could learn to make better and better stories. But in all these cases the stories would exhibit only what Bringsford calls "weak creativity."

BRUTUS is the direct descendant of that equally remarkable creature built some ten years ago by Harold Cohen, AARON, the program that makes fine art paintings. Both are examples of what Douglas Hofstadter calls "Computer Models of the Fundamental Mechanisms of Thought" in his discussions of his own similar explorations with the programs COPY-CAT and JUMBO.[2] All of these programs exhibit self-reflection, that is to say, they are designed to generate textual forms and transforms by studying and elaborating on their own processes. Hofstadter isolates four of the most important features of these kinds of programs under the general heading "Dynamic Emergence of Unpredictable Objects and Pathways":

- creation of unanticipated higher-level perceptual objects and structures
- emergence of a priori unpredictable potential pathways of exploration (via creation of novel structures at increasing levels of abstraction
- creation of large-scale viewpoints
- competition between rival high-level structures

(Hofstadter 267)

Simulating these kinds of activity is an impressive achievement, as Hofstadter is eager to say. But in a "Somewhat Skeptical" concluding set of reflections on "Computers and Creativity" (467–491) Hofstadter presses a recurrent problem. Starting with AARON, Hofstadter asks what it could mean for a program to draw pictures of phenomena it has no experience of. More trenchantly he suggests "that it would be more appropriate for Aaron to draw pictures not of people but of its own kind. . . . Indeed, perhaps Aaron's most appropriate subject would be itself . . . such as itself drawing itself drawing itself . . ." (468–469). He follows a similar critical line in his comments on the prose/poetry generating machine RACTER. Though its output is "quite amazing" and "pretty remarkable," Hofstadter points out that these reactions are a function of a previous understanding we have about such texts, "which leads us to read into the prose . . . all sorts of intentions and ideas" (473). Because "one doesn't know what goes on behind the scenes" we are unjustified in imagining what our pleasure and sense of amazement suggest: that this behavior is an index of the machine's conscious agency. The conscious agents, throughout, are the humans who design the program, tweak it, and then select from its output those materials that exhibit the closest analogy to human creative acts (473–475).

"To whom should the credit go?" for the output of these programs, Hofstadter asks. The question is important because *how* these works are made is as important as the *fact* that they are made. "I feel a need to have a sense for [their] provenance, in some manner or other" (Hofstadter 481). Hofstadter might have elucidated more clearly the import of that "feeling," for it locates the core issues here, and why all of these works exhibit what Bringsjord calls "weak creativity." One explanation would observe that to set out to make models of the brain or of cognitive activity is per se to make a commitment to simulations that are less than human. Another would remark that to ask "how" events unfold is implicitly to declare that an event can be reduced to facticity only by an arbitrary intrusion. The "multivariant" and "incommensurable" character of events and phenomena is the frame of reference that exposes why *what* we know and experience is a function of *how* we do so.

Summarizing his view of this marvelous AI scene, Hofstadter makes an interesting suggestion. "There are two avenues by which one can obtain knowledge of the mechanisms of a computer model of some aspect of cognition. One . . . is by reading a description of the program's architecture" (481–482). He rejects this method, essentially, because it only *appears* to address the problem of "how." He then goes on:

> The other avenue is less ambiguous but more indirect—it is simply by *interacting* with the program over a period of time in an unrestricted manner. In this way, one can make a long and systematic series of probes and thereby discover for oneself in what ways the program is flexible and in what ways it is rigid. (482)

Organizing this kind of interaction—indeed, making it a demand and then seeing to the demand—remains the office of the human agents. The interaction is a matter of human, not machine, interest. We easily imagine a moment when this functional relation would be reversed—science fiction is replete with such imaginings—and perhaps these imaginations forecast a historical order beyond human history. However that may be, here and now we must still deal with our immediate interests. And the interaction that Hofstadter lays before us is the sign of the simple but clear truth that it is we who want to use these tools and that we want to use them in order to understand ourselves more clearly—to understand not how the machines work but how we work when we make, use, and interact with machines of this kind.

Concealed in the cool codes and charming surfaces of projects like

AARON, BRUTUS, and RACTER lie our own unrealized critical possibilities. Let's try to think about using such creatures the same way we use traditional paper-based instruments—as vehicles for self-awareness and self-reflection. Though Plato warned against books and writing as dangers to the mind seeking self-knowledge, human beings have developed elaborate strategies for using those (now ancient) tools for just such uses (as well, of course, for more instrumental uses like storing and accessing information). Human beings found ways of using certain tools as mirrors in which to see and study ourselves at a slight but critically significant differential. The same opportunity awaits us, creatures of flesh and blood, in digital silicon. The computational, simulating, and interactive capacities of these new machines should be taken up as mirrors of the same kind as our traditional texts and other semiotic manifolds.

"The Ivanhoe Game" and the Precisely Indeterminate Text

The volatile scene of humanities computing between 1993 and 2000 precipitated the issues that "The Ivanhoe Game" would try to engage and clarify. During those years, our work at IATH was focused on a set of projects that used digital technology to implement very traditional humanities scholarship. *The Rossetti Archive* was just one of the projects supported by IATH. As we've already seen, it was developed with a double goal in mind: on the practical side we wanted to build a scholarly tool that would marry the hitherto separated functions of critical and facsimile editing; on the theoretical side we wanted to use the process of building the archive as a laboratory for investigating the nature of texts and textuality. Nothing even remotely like "The Ivanhoe Game" came into view until very late—until 1999, in fact; and when the idea for the game arose, it did not come as a digital imagining. The first form of the game was paper based, though we played those experimental rounds in e-mail exchanges. The determination to enlist digital technology for the game's interpretational purposes only emerged during our discussions about those first rounds of gameplay.

Briefly, "The Ivanhoe Game" explores a new approach to acts of critical interpretation based in game models. The procedure is performance based and collaborative and operates in the discourse field of specific historical or literary works or events. The game pursues critical self-awareness in the doubled social space of the work(s) taken up and the persons and institutions that had been collectively involved in transmitting and elucidating those works in the past. Its central object is to make explicit the assumptions about critical practice and textual interpretation that often lie unacknowledged, or at least irregularly explored, in a conventional approach to interpetational practice. To achieve this goal, a game strategy is deployed within a field of interrelated textual, visual, cultural, and critical artifacts. The game "moves" involve the production (the writing) of texts that integrate with and simulate the materials in the discourse field of the game. Players produce text in response to the opportunities and problems raised by the texts produced by the other players.

The game actually began out of a critical exchange between myself and Johanna Drucker on the subject of literary-critical method and our dissatisfaction with received forms of interpretation. We wanted to develop a more imaginative critical methodology, a form closer in spirit and procedure to its subject matter, original works of poetry and literature. The first phase of play took place under the auspices of Oulipean models and the whole of what we saw as the 'Pataphysical tradition of writing and thinking.[3]

From the start the premise of the game—and of our critical ideas in general—was (is) that works of imagination contain within themselves, as it were, multiple versions of themselves. This multiplicity, widely recognized, is now regularly treated as a function of the perceiver rather than being inherent to the work as such. That perceiver-oriented approach marks a break with classical theories of reality. In these new romantic theories, readers are not seeking a poem's (inherent) meaning but, rather, examining the poem for patterns and forms we judge to be satisfying or interesting. Note that in both cases, classical and romantic, either the perceiving subject or the perceived object is artfully stabilized for purposes of an interpretive action. In what I would call a quantum approach, however, because all interpretive positions are located at "an inner standing point," each act of interpretation is not simply a view of the system but a function of its operations.

Artifices of reality as they propose to be, imaginative systems simulate what Humberto Maturana and Francesco Varela call an "autopoetic" reality that sustains itself by communicating with itself.[4] In this view of the matter, the figure of the inquiring interpreter obscures both the locus and the form of an interpretive action. The action does not take place outside but inside the object of attention. It is therefore not so much a perceived "meaning" as a line of the (interactive) system's own developmental possibilities, within which the "interpreter" is immersed. Its most important function is not to define a meaning or state of the system as such—although this is a necessary function of any interpretation—but to create conditions for further dynamic change within the system. Understanding the system means operating with and in the system. The more this "meaning" can be defined, the more capabilities it has for generating different lines that are latent but undeveloped by the system. "The Ivanhoe Game" was invented to expose and promote this view of imaginative works.

The game is played by two or more players. It is called "The Ivanhoe Game" because Drucker and I first played it with Walter Scott's romance fiction *Ivanhoe*. That initial game involved replaying the discourse field determined by the book Scott wrote. By discourse field we understand the entirety of the reception and transmission histories that transact the work for us. The players engage with this discourse field in the same way one engages in any critical exercise, by making use of primary and secondary bibliographic and historical documents. The object is to explore and elaborate significant features of the materials that constitute the discourse of *Ivanhoe*—and to explore these, first, as a way to uncover latent texts within this field and/or the work itself; and second, as a procedure for heightening one's own critical self-awareness. It is in other words a game of literary criticism and appreciation, and perforce a game of cultural criticism as well. In contrast to the preponderant body of received literary exegesis, its critical method is procedural rather than expository.

Why play the game in the discourse field rather than focus on "the work itself"? Because that field comprises a reflection and intervention in a supervening social space. As such, it implicitly declares that all critical moves, including moves made in "The Ivanhoe Game," are immersed in the same field. Topological models and metaphors are particularly useful for conceiving this kind of field. The discourse field of *Ivanhoe*—Scott's romance—is itself what topologists call a "basin" of dynamic order arbitrarily (consciously) taken out of an encompassing and indeterminate social space. That space is pervaded by "strange attractors" that organize around themselves local dynamic basins of order.[5] Any particular edition would be conceived as another basin of order operating at another "place" in the field, at another scale. An idea like "the work itself" here will be exposed as a figure of speech suggesting that the work possesses *in se* a determinate identity. This is not a critical view we want to encourage as a premise of the gameplay, where the concept "work" is replaced by a "field" concept. (In that change of conception, "the work itself" appears as *a* critical view of the field—a certain topological basin—and as such might be consciously taken up as a framework for a series of interpretive actions in the discourse field.)

The first experimental round of the game was played by Drucker and myself using a particular edition of Walter Scott's romance *Ivanhoe* as our discourse field. We played the game with no explicit rules other than the requirement that our textual moves lie open to reciprocal engagement. This loose situation quickly revealed how inexplicit assumptions were driving our gameplay. We had not thought to specify, for example, the point of view that was governing our moves. This obscurity led us to realize that our moves were in fact constellating around a more or less coherent "role" that we were playing as we made our moves. In my case, I could see my moves were emerging from a kind of Byronic reading of Scott's fiction. I also saw how closely this interpretive strategy resembled a dominant earlier approach to the book. Many Victorian readers were dismayed that Rowena rather than Rebecca married Ivanhoe at the end. Indeed, Rebecca's problematic position in the book produced numerous Victorian spin-off works—theatrical as well as textual—that essentially rewrote the story to different fabulous desires. Some 30 years after the book was published, Thackeray published what is probably the most famous, as it is certainly the most distinguished, rewriting in his witty "romance upon romance," *Rebecca and Rowena.*[6]

Following this we were led to formulate some basic gameplay rules for the next round we were preparing to undertake. This initial set of rules was kept, deliberately, simple.

(1) That all game moves by a player get executed under the auspices of a particular and explicit "role" to be taken by the player. This role is like a mask that the player puts on, an assumed "character." Its purpose is to shape the intentional field of a player's acts and provide players with a form of objectivity by which to generate and assess their own moves.

(2) That each player keep a "player-file" (unavailable to the other players during the gameplay). This file will contains the player's explicit description of his/her assumed role as well as the player's own interpretations of each move he/she makes and sees being made by the other players. Thus the game involves two "lines" of material: the line represented by the player's moves (always a fully public line) and the line represented by the player-file, which documents the player's commentaries on the moves being played in the game. (Players may decide to put their player-files into game play, as public moves in the game. If such a play was made, however, the rules require the player to create a nonpublic player-file on that now public material.) Our initial thought was that these player-files would be opened at the end of a game round for critical discussion by the various players.

The point of the game is for players to hypothesize and then extrapolate ideas about the discourse field of *Ivanhoe* within a performative and dynamic intellectual space. The point is not *as such* to arrive at a reading or interpretation of *Ivanhoe* but to refashion and reshape its discourse field in ways that bring to the fore "possible worlds" latent in the work and in the materials that transmit the work to us. Implicit in this act of reshaping will be an interpretational view that the player is to make explicit in the non-public player-file.

Precise and consciously determinate as the game moves have to be, the game puts the moves into an open and indeterminate playing field. This means that the critical explication of the moves—the texts generated in the player-files—will be seen by everyone to represent strategic rather than generic understandings. The game encourages and expects from the players a conscious and purposive involvement with the discourse field of *Ivanhoe*. The playing space is thus occupied and transacted by various dynamic forces, sympathetic as well as resistant, which are brought to bear through the player moves.[7]

An actual demonstration of gameplay offers perhaps a clearer explanation of the game's rationale. In the appendix to this chapter, therefore, I give the ten game moves and the player-file that comprised my part in our second round of experimental gameplay (with *Wuthering Heights*).

Very soon after we had begun the first phase of gameplay, Drucker and I realized the critical opportunities that would open up if the game were played in digital space. A computerized environment could hold the entirety of the gameplay open to random or structured transformations. The implications of that capacity were important if one wanted to pursue a critical investigation of a discourse field. The computer could store and reconfigure the data generated by the human players, as well as its own reconfigurings, in a datafield that would grow and develop exponentially. As in any computer game, the machine would thus be itself an active agent in the gamespace. It could intervene and constrain the human players in various ways and it could as well generate gameplayers of its own.

Note, however, that even in such a digital reconception "The Ivanhoe Game" is not primarily a problem-solving game but a space structured for critical reflection. Although sophisticated strategy games like *SimCity* encourage thinking about the game process, the effect of moves, and the impact of decisions that allocate virtual resources within the game, they do not formalize the process of decision making and interpretation within the substance of the play. "The Ivanhoe Game" is not a video game to be bested but a difference engine for stimulating self-reflection through interactive role-playing.

Dialogues of the Mind with Itself

We must study closely this decision to reconceive the game in digital form since the matter bears upon critical and aesthetic questions that command a broad cultural interest. Though the decision was made by Drucker and myself together, I inevitably perceive it from my own vantage point. In that view, the move involved a clarification of issues that were preoccupying my work for almost 30 years. The significance of "The Ivanhoe Game" hangs upon the importance of those issues for humanities studies in general, and in particular for interpretational theory and method.

For some time various scholars have been seeking after disciplined critical methods that could exploit much greater ranges of conscious subjectivity.[8] The impact of the rise of science during the past 200 years has had its inevitable effect on humanistic pursuits of knowledge. The scholarly edition in its various forms and the expository critical essay—whether theoretical or empirical—exhibit the influence of science very clearly. The neoclassical impulses of twentieth-century modernism—it has other impulses—were perhaps most apparent in this area. New Criticism and New Bibliography both held out for themselves scientific, not to say scientistic, procedural models.

The first clear—that is to say disciplined and self-conscious—revolt against these methods of critical inquiry came at the end of the last century. We locate this revisionist move in the work of Alfred Jarry, though it seems apparent that Lautréamont had anticipated his key ideas by several decades. However that may be, Jarry's work gave an explicit locus and name—'Pataphysics—to the proposal for a new, paradoxical kind of "science": "the science of exceptions." The program sketched by Jarry would get resurrected more than a half-century later, in our own day, in the work of the OULIPO group, most notably in the writings of Perec, Queneau, Mathews, and Calvino. Two important things to keep in mind are: first, that a "science of exceptions" must inevitably be related to statistics; second, that 'pataphysical work has largely assumed imaginative rather than critical forms.

Though a serious (or unserious) interest of mine since the late sixties, I did not perceive OULIPO's scholarly relevance to questions of critical method until late 1998, when Drucker arrived at the University of Virginia. Among other things, she brought with her a long-standing interest in the 'pataphysical tradition. This would prove crucial throughout the various stages of development of "The Ivanhoe Game."

In 1970, however, I framed my interests quite differently. Three matters seemed important (they remain so for me). First, the usual scholarly essay or monograph or edition adopts and cultivates a critical point of view that is set outside the object of interest and attention. Second, the work adopts and cultivates *a* critical point of view to which all its ideas and procedures are subordinately related. Third, having taken those positions, the critical work is left with few if any resources in itself to refashion itself or rethink itself.

To evade these constraints I began thinking about the resources of non-Socratic dialogue. Just as this work was beginning, however, it was set aside for some 15 years while I was involved in the study of the history and theory of editing and textuality.[9] That work proved quite useful for the dialogue project, which I returned to from 1987 to 1993 with a series of dialogues and theatrical writings. The form was attractive, first, because it was performative and hence could fashion arguments from "an inner standing point." Furthermore, if properly managed dialogue could accommodate multiple argumentative positions and views. Finally, you could bring a dialogue to closure while simultaneously preventing closure to its topics of discussion—indeed, while positively exposing the topics to further levels of difficulty.

The first of these dialogues was written as an explicit self-critique ("Marxism, Romanticism, and Postmodernism: An American Case History"), the last was "The Alice Fallacy," the most theatrical and performative of these works. In the vantage of historical hindsight, they clearly forecast the issues addressed by "The Ivanhoe Game." Performance, simulation, and a contest of ideas are the vehicles of the dialogues' critical method, which installs an approach to aesthetic exegesis modeled on Wilde's dialogues and the hoaxes of Edgar Allen Poe.

Unlike "The Ivanhoe Game," however, "The Alice Fallacy" is what Matthew Arnold long ago called a dialogue of the mind with itself. True, it offers an image of real—that is to say, of open—dialogue. But while the dialogue develops many roles, it has only one active player. In this respect its simulation resources are limited. That particular limitation—there are others—is not as such a function of the dialogue's discourse field—as if its paper and theatrical existences were less dynamic and "interactive" than if it had been built in a digital environment. The limitation is personal, historical, and finally conceptual. The dialogues as originally written and presented did not *require* the presence of others—"the real presence," as Christian theology puts the matter. By contrast, "The Ivanhoe Game" simply cannot be played alone. It also can't be won or lost (though it can be played well or badly). Those features of the game implicitly constitute the premises of the kind of critical thinking both theorized and practiced in the game.

The first round of Ivanhoe gameplay exposed both the symmetry and the asymmetry between the performance involved in dialogue and the performance involved in game. Considered as a critical tool in this context, game is dialogue raised to a higher power. A world of difference separates an intellectual challenge made in literary dialogue and challenges made through the gameplay of different persons. That realization quickly brought about a wholesale rethinking of "The Ivanhoe Game" and, eventually, a name change signaling this shift.[10] "IVANHOE: A Game of Interpretation" would be computerized.

IVANHOE: A Game of Interpretation

Let me recall here a passage from this book's preface:

> To date . . . digital technology used by humanities scholars has focused almost exclusively on methods of sorting, accessing, and disseminating large bodies of materials, and on certain specialized problems in computational stylistics and linguistics. In this respect the work rarely engages those questions about interpretation and self-aware reflection that are the central concerns for most humanities scholars and educators. Digital technology has remained instrumental in serving the technical and precritical occupations of librarians and archivists and editors. But *the general field of humanities education and scholarship will not take the use of digital technology seriously until one demonstrates how its tools improve the ways we explore and explain aesthetic works—until, that is, it expands our interpretational procedures.*

IVANHOE is being developed to begin such a demonstration. Its purpose is to bring computational resources to bear on elucidating the noninformational—the aesthetic and rhetorical—aspects of texts. These features operate both bibliographically—in the material physique of text—and linguistically. Imaginative works are inherently transformational and multivalent, and their dynamic potential is a function of the ways human beings interact with such works, which by design solicit transformation or reinterpretation. IVANHOE proposes to open up the transformational structure of imaginative works by promoting a dynamic connection between the digital pattern-analysis capacities of computational tools and the analogue pattern-making capacities of human beings.

The game is to be played in a digital environment by human players and the computer interacting in the play. The human players initiate the action by intervening in, and reorganizing in purposive ways, the discourse field—a given dataset of visual and textual artifacts that is the initial play environment. As we have seen in relation to its precursor "The Ivanhoe Game," these "moves" represent performative interpretations of that field made from within that field by the roles adopted by the players. In IVANHOE, however, every move, when made, itself gets added to the initial discourse field, which in this case is the computational database. The database therefore grows from three sets of additions: the public moves made by the players, their nonpublic analytic moves located in the player-files, and the computer's interventions in the gameplay. (Two of Johanna Drucker's schematic diagrams of IVANHOE's structure—see figures C.1 and C.2 below—are perhaps useful representations of how the game is being functionally organized.)

IVANHOE represents a considerable expansion of the basic ideas developed in "The Ivanhoe Game." The game space is extended to include a MOO, where the player roles can execute their dialogical moves in real time;[11] a chat room, where the players can discuss the course of the game play; and various other functionalities, including dynamically generated analytical displays of the gameplay as it stands at any point in time.

Two kinds of computational intervention are provided for, both a function of the computer's emergence software.[12] On one hand, the computer will be licensed to constrain the acts of the players in various ways, much like ordinary computer games. On the other hand, the computer will map patterns and relationships in the database as it goes through its dynamic changes.

Computational resources alter the gameplay in certain crucial respects, all a consequence of the differences between analogue and digital mapping protocols. Whereas the human players will organize and manipulate the data at analogue levels, the computer's digital mappings will "see" the "same" data in radically different ways. The computer's digital views have to be returned to human awareness—in this case, to the game players—in readable interface forms. To do this the computer will be forced to deliver what it takes to be disambiguated results from a body of inherently ambiguous data.

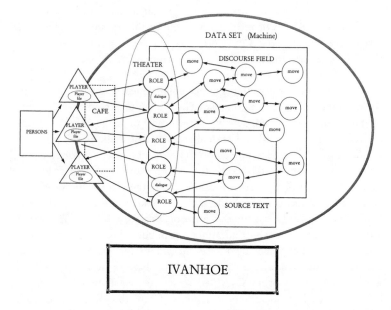

Figure C.1: **Diagram of the Basic Dynamical Structure of IVANHOE**. This is a sketch of the elementary behavioral organization of gameplay in IVANHOE. The diagram shows the relations of game players to their roles and the game moves executed under the masks of those roles. The diagram superimposes the structure on a diagram of the game's elementary spatial fields, most importantly the computational "data set."

As we already saw in discussing projects like RACTER, AARON, and BRUTUS, most AI projects using emergent consciousness software involve efforts to overcome the gap between the disambiguating processes of data analysis and the ambiguating character of human thought and perception. The same impulse governs every approach to text and data markup: A formal "language" is imposed upon a natural language or on real objects that licenses a computer to manipulate the marked materials. Whatever is not formally marked is not merely unapparent, it is computationally nonexistent. The ideal of a markup system that would be as flexible as natural language but logically unambiguous is equivalent to the AI dream of creating a true cyborg.[13] But text—even printed or scripted text—is foundationally ambiguous. The ambiguity results not merely from the formidable complexity of every material textual form but because such forms only function in use.

Seen in one perspective, this gap between digital and analogue commu-

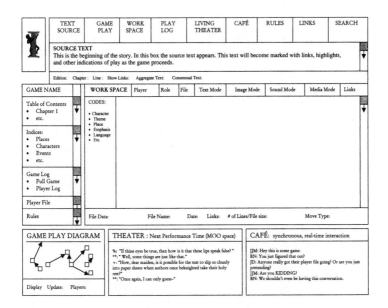

TEXT SOURCE	GAME PLAY	WORK SPACE	PLAY LOG	LIVING THEATER	CAFÉ	RULES	LINKS	SEARCH

SOURCE TEXT
This is the beginning of the story. In this box the source text appears. This text will become marked with links, highlights, and other indications of play as the game proceeds.

Edition: Chapter :   Line :   Show Links: Aggregate Text: Consensual Text:

GAME NAME		WORK SPACE	Player	Role	File	Text Mode	Image Mode	Sound Mode	Media Mode	Links

Table of Contents
• Chapter 1
• etc.

Indices:
• Places
• Characters
• Events
• etc.

Game Log
• Full Game
• Player Log

Player File

Rules

CODES:

• Character
• Theme
• Place
• Emphasis
• Language
• Etc.

File Data: File Name: Date: Links: # of Lines/File size: Move Type:

GAME PLAY DIAGRAM	THEATER : Next Performance Time (MOO space)	CAFÉ: synchronous, real-time interaction

Display   Update: Players:

%: "If thine eyes be true, then how is it that these lips speak false? "
**: " Well, some things are just like that."
+ : "How, dear maiden, is it possible for the text to slip so cleanly into paper sheets when authors once beknighted take their holy rest?"
**: "Once again, I can only guess–"

JJM: Hey this is some game.
BN: You just figured that out?
JD: Anyone really got their player file going? Or are you just pretending?
JJM: Are you KIDDING?
BN: We shouldn't even be having this conversation.

Figure C.2: **Diagram of IVANHOE Functions**. This sketch gives an idealized presentation of the general functional elements of IVANHOE as they might appear in framed spaces on a monitor. The Text Source is the literary work that is the focus of the game play (for example, Walter Scott's romance fiction *Ivanhoe*). The Work Space is the area where basic moves are made, in whatever mode (textual, pictorial, etc.). The Game Play Diagram is the dynamically generated display of the state of the gameplay at any given moment—a diagrammatic presentation of the moves made. The Living Theatre is a MOO space where certain kinds of real time moves can be made, and the Café is a chat room (outside the computational area of the game) where players can meet to discuss the game. Various functions and some basic menus are also indicated.

nication can cause frustration and dismay. Seen in another it supplies reasons for thinking computational resources have nothing substantial to contribute to the understanding of cultural forms. But the gap may be read—may be used—in a different way. IVANHOE's object is to cultivate that gap—to replicate and develop it and in the process, to expose to our thinking aspects of our own thought that would have otherwise remained only intuitively or randomly available to us. Keats called those things "unheard melodies," and he revealed them, in that famous passage, to an ear—to an intelligence—we often hardly believe we possess.

Quantum Poetics

That kind of thinking has been widely exercised in other-than-digital media for as long as human beings have existed, I suppose. If it cannot be completely systematized, it need not be imagined as simply a mystical gift or afflatus, a grace to be looked for rather than a cultivated discipline. Rigor and discipline are not the privilege of science alone. When we specialize our thought for the technical purposes of science, we set a privilege on problem-solving models. It is a privilege we are happy to grant because of the enormous practical rewards that scientific models of thinking have both promised and delivered.

Until recently, the language of those models was marked by the following characteristic features, according to the distinguished Italian physicist Giuseppe Caglioti: It is analytic, rational, precise, controlled, objective, and esoteric. As the discourse of science moved into the twentieth century, however, some of the features by which we could distinguish it from poetical discourse began to evaporate. Relativity, quantum mechanics, and non-Euclidean geometries all realize a world marked by the same kind of ambiguities, transformations, and incommensurable features that we take for granted in Ovid and Lucretius, Dante and Petrarch, Blake and Byron. In that event, as Caglioti argues, we come to a point "where science and art converge" and the features of science undergo the kind of apparitional shift that so fascinates Caglioti. Now the language of the scientist, seeming to merge into the language of the artist, "becomes analytic and synthetic, precise and vague, rational and instinctive, esoteric and exoteric at the same time. In a word, it becomes *ambiguous*" (137).

Despite their evident aesthetic features, however, digital environments are regularly filed in the discourse of science. More than that, their commonest identifier—"digital technologies"—marks them with a forbiddingly instrumentalist label. But rigorous conception and coding are no more or less important for aesthetic work than they are for computerized media, as we have seen throughout this book. Furthermore, in each case the codes are marvelously apt for generating rich arrays of structural and phenomenal transformations.

IVANHOE is one proposal for integrating digital tools with our received textual instruments in order to promote critical self-consciousness. The awareness we are after would move along any or all of the three axes by which the game is ordered: the axis of the literary work (*Ivanhoe, Wuthering Heights,* and the data of their discourse fields); the axis of digitization and its tools of analysis, display, and transformation (the software);

the axis of the gameplay with its text, sound, and image outputs and their new, second-order data. Because the game environment commands interaction across the entirety of this field, the data is forced into continuous transformations.

One does not have to play such games. If played, however, the game can only be a game of critical reflection, a game to study the symmetries and asymmetries of the transformations and come to judgments about them. The performative character of those judgments, situated in dynamic gamespace, marks them not so much as "provisional" or "incomplete" but as algorithmic and rhetorical. They are like measurements taken in a quantum dynamical field. The digital axis—the new feature in what is recognizably a very ancient game—comes to alter the game's cognitive scale and thus to challenge the human players by increasing the range and momentum of the transformations. In this respect IVANHOE is not at all dissimilar to the games of wit often pursued by poets and scholars, perhaps most spectacularly (in the West) during the Renaissance.

But the digital architecture locates a statistical and probabilistic order at the very heart of the game. That order inclines one to theorize the game in quantum mechanical terms like those invoked by Caglioti in his chapter on "Structural Transformations and the Role of Symmetry Breaking in Poetry, Music, and the Visual Arts," or in terms of the topological, "catastrophic" geometries elaborated by René Thom. Each investigates what Caglioti calls "The Dynamics of Ambiguity," that is, the play of continuity and discontinuity, of symmetry and asymmetry, in systems (like art and poetry) "characterized by time-dependent energy operators" (109). These are the "strange attractors" of topology, the systemic elements of a probabilistic universe that simultaneously licenses order and disorder.

Though we don't usually think of a poetic field as probabilistic, this is because we measure the significant elements of such fields at gross—even Newtonian—levels. Traditional textual analysis takes virtually no account of anything but a poem's linguistic codes, and even those codes are conceived in macroscopic terms.[14] The atomic units of the language, for interpretive purposes, are assumed to be the words of the dictionary. But the truth is that even the most pedestrian scrap of prose text—oral or typographical—might *and should,* for critical purposes, be investigated with a passion for fine, for microscopic, for subatomic discriminations. Poets do this "intuitively," we are told. Perhaps many do, but in certain cases—Dante, Poe, Mallarmé come immediately to mind—the level of attention is so concentrated and acute that poetic intuition appears to function at a breathtaking level of awareness. Breathtaking because, in their cases, the poetic field is so manifestly complex and (as a physicist might say) energetic.

IVANHOE is a proposal for a critical apparatus that will not *rationalize* in macroscopic terms the complex and energetic field of imaginative text. Its function is rather to help *reveal* the field's particular dynamic repletions—its unheard melodies and otherwise invisible forms. The proposal comes, first, with the demand that the data of the field be raised to statistically significant levels. This effect will necessarily emerge as a function of gameplay in a digital environment. Second, the game insists that critical reflection on the field of attention—that is to say, measurement of the field—will be located within the field itself. IVANHOE is performative and interactive "at an inner standing point."

The difference between revealing and fixing significance is perhaps the crucial thing. Listen to Giuseppe Caglioti on the "quantum structure" of aesthetic phenomena:

> What counts in the conceptual synthesis therefore isn't so much the energy as the information, which is the quality of the energy. At the level of conceptual synthesis, a structure appears qualitatively symmetrical until the moment in which, following a scansion of the structure itself, a dynamic instability of the perceptive process is produced: and one realizes that he has extracted information, or given a new meaning, or has been enlightened by an idea.
>
> Breaking the sym.metry then is equivalent to shattering a com.mensurate equilibrium of structural relationships of a dynamic, geometric, rhythmic, acoustic, conceptual, etc. nature.
>
> In the artistic field, inserting elements of symmetry into a structure is a primordial, aesthetic need. Elements of symmetry are incorporated in a work of art or in poetry more or less latently: on the other hand, this is the way the artist is able to give himself, or perhaps with the observer's active participation—as occurs when perceiving ambiguous structures—give, the pleasure of breaking symmetry. (110)

"Perhaps with the observer's active participation." Perhaps, rather, *not* perhaps. In a quantum understanding, works of art and language are not discrete phenomena, separated from their users—that is to say, from the activities of what we sometimes misleadingly call their "observers." The subject of IVANHOE, after all, is not the subject of (say) physics or computer science—the natural world, digital order—it is the mind of those who have imagined and created those kinds of intellectual prostheses, the mind of *Ivanhoe* and IVANHOE. We want a framework in which such forms can be regularly and self-consciously examined as "facts" that are also consciously seen as illusions of reality. We want a framework that will fracture our facticities—in this case, the actual phenomena generated in the gameplay—until they become refracting mirrors.

"The observer's active participation" is a figure of speech that will be read, in the context of IVANHOE, as the actual play that gets played in the discourse field—the player-generated texts that realize "the pleasure of breaking symmetry" and that from those breaks offer new symmetries for further intervention. The form of interpretation to be sponsored is emergent, reappearing in a surprising series of deformations and transformations. "Game" and role-playing are thus crucial features of the process since the object is not to arrive at essential meanings and final interpretations but to generate these as hypothetical forms to be self-consciously reflected upon. Like art it is a game of mirrors in which (like engineering) actual things get made; but like science it demands that the made things be studied to expose their structure and their "laws." The latter must also be *made* as artistic, illusionistic forms put into gameplay. What emerges is a discourse field shaped as an evolving scene of human cognitive and affective exchange: a repertory of what we know and think we know and hence also a set of negative images and spaces for imagining what we don't know—for all that remains "still art and part" of these processes, though they remain yet to be realized.

Appendix to the Conclusion

A Round of Moves in "The Ivanhoe Game"

Collected here are the materials I generated during the second round of our experimental gameplay with "The Ivanhoe Game," which was played during August 2000 with Emily Bronte's novel *Wuthering Heights*. Four players were involved in this round: Johanna Drucker, Beth Nowviskie, Steven Ramsay, and myself.

The materials here are of two kinds: (1) the actual game moves I made; (2) my player file notes explicating those moves. The moves of the other players can be found online at the following location: http://www.people.virginia.edu/ ~ bpn2f/ivanhoe.html.

I. Game Moves

MOVE 1 (jjm)

30 July 1915. So once again the day comes and I may look at these amazing documents. Each year they seem yet more wondrous. Perhaps—surely!—because they appear to me alone, like some special theophany. God knows we inhabit a botched civilization. Emily's ferocious retreat more and more seems a forecast of what we are and what we keep becoming. And the lust to possess fragile remains like these—even the damned recollect what they have lost and long to regain it. Vainly of course. And so come men like Clement, John, Harry—myself: hyenas of glory. Worse than that—its salesmen and investors. But these precious remains I hold back, and when I die they shall die with me, I'll see to that.

What wouldn't any one of them give just to see these things, to know they exist. That fool Clement had them in his hands 20 years ago but when Nicholls brought out that trove of his—well, depth of passion is not always measured by excitability. Extreme and manifested feeling in a god like Catherine is one thing. As you plunge toward the quotidian—Hindley, Isabella—it turns to curse and torment. And when it reaches the like of us it is folly alone. Clement's hands shook as he turned over each of those priceless leaves. Priceless! That exactly—and I at any rate may aspire to that kind of truth, to know and to preserve for ever that pricelessness. So trembling with pleasure and excitement—like that other fool of fiction Jeffrey Aspern—he could not see what I did not try to hide. I merely had to draw no special attention to myself, merely lift that packet and put it away in my satchel. Nicholls saw nothing but the happiness and sorrow of those memories Clement is so clever at working upon when he is bent on rifling a gravesite. And Clement was absorbed in his corrupt double pleasures of swindling and possessing.

And so here they are, these relics of a spiritual world, brought out in this yearly ceremony performed by the only priest of a religion that has no adherents and never shall have.

What will be the readings of this day's liturgy?

MOVE 2 (jjm)

[A MS leaf, undated, written on both sides, approx. 8"x10", with a small note pinned to the upper right in another hand, dated and signed.]

Note leaf:

"This is EB's holograph, normal size, fair copied and remarkably with no erasures or corrections. No watermark and without date, the paper uniform with some of the Diary papers. Date uncertain but sometime during 1845–46. TJW 10/1/01"

MS:

—"What is that you hold behind your back, Cathy?"

—"It's something I found in father's old trunk in that room upstairs over the kitchen."

—"Hindley said he'd thrash us if we went in there."

—"Oh Hindley's a beast. He hates anything that pleases me. Look." She smiled in that way of hers, Nelly, so careless and consumed by what held her attention, and tossed the thing to me. I grasped it and saw it was a mask. It was black, a half mask very like the one we put on Punchinello when we play at puppet theatre.

—"Put it on, Heathcliff. It will improve your looks. And I've some questions to put to you. When you wear that mask you may hide your scowling face and show me your true soul."

—"When have I never showed you that—to my cost often enough."

—"Poor Heathcliff! What kind of soul do you have, that's the question. It doesn't bleed, I think—at least I've never seen its blood. But perhaps it simply doesn't bleed for me."

—"If you could see anything but your own will and pleasure you'd have seen the truth, Cathy. I am crucified very day on that wicked tongue of yours. And you know it, you pretend otherwise, you laugh. But I know you, Cathy, and if that's what you want of me, that's what you shall have. What does Joseph say—that Jesus hung on his cross for three hours dying?

Three hours are nothing. You've hanged me on a cross for days and days for no reason but to study my pain."

—"You're wicked to talk that way. Stop it!" She pouted and bit her lip and looked hard at me. "Put on the mask."

—"Cathy is a perverse and willful girl, Heathcliff. You should resist those whims of hers, for her good if you don't care for your own where she's concerned. As I fear you don't and never will."

—When I put it on, that dark willfulness seemed to run off under her skin and her eyes went flat and bright, the way they look when we reach the top of Penniston Crag and they lose themselves in gazing out across the western moors. Those eyes were passing through me then, looking somewhere else, and she said: "What have those lonely mountains worth revealing, Heathcliff?"

—"Grief and glory." The words raised a brief smile that she was sending somewhere else, I know, because it quickly perished as she seemed to waken. This time she looked directly at me with her small crooked smile and said: "And what should I do with Heathcliff when he behaves badly and vexes me?"

—"Reason with him, and if he won't listen to reason, beat him." She burst out laughing. "I will, oh Heathcliff, I will."

—"You will do exactly as you please, no more or less. You will ignore me if that suits you or tell tales to Hindley just to watch him break into fury and do your beating for you. Or you will do something else you haven't yet thought of. And now I've obeyed you, Cathy, it's your turn." I pulled the mask from my head and thrust it in her hands. She looked at it and then at me and she said: "I will," and she put it on.

MOVE 3 (jjm)

[This MS (designated MS.TJW1) is copied neatly on both sides of a single foolscap sheet, undated, unwatermarked, in the hand of T. J. Wise.]

—"What do you see when you look across the moors from the top of Penniston Crag?"

—She didn't answer right away, Nellie, she stood silent and still as that statue of the angel guarding Sowden's grave in the back of the church-yard. Then she began to speak. The words came out each one by itself like a complete thought and her lips seemed to set them in the air like cut blocks of stone, as if building a building—a great hall somewhere or a fortress. "I see nothing at all until the wind comes down streaming through its firmament. Then the bogs and stones and furze bestir themselves and rise to his call.

'Return now and dwell with me today' he says, and his voice runs like rain and fire through the brush and trees and all the blown heathflowers.'His lightenings enlighten the world, the earth sees and trembles.' So the thaw-wind's cold fires bring new life from these kindled and perishing embers. Clouds are racing from the west across the sun's slow path, they meet and meet again like battalions of Forlorn Hopes hurling themselves along this relentless crag, scattering in splintered pieces of tumbling dark and fleet brightenings. As they all gather and race away I see their white faces and their burning eyes dissolving in mysterious and fevered flight, and the viewless wind freeing them from their iron earthen chains drives them along, legions and legions with silver swords and silver lyres, all singing wild words of an ancient song:

> 'We come with western winds, with evening's wandering airs,
> From that venomed heart of heaven that brings the darkest stars,
> Winds, take our maddened souls—stars, plunge us in your fire!
> Come visions—shake and change and kill us with desire.'

If you were there, Nellie, you would have scarcely thought she spoke, she stood so still and tranced. It was as if her whole body were an Aeolian-harp set on Penniston itself, and the wind torn to shreds of words as it passed through her.

—You're more mad than that wicked girl to speak this way. What demon world has she drawn you to?

—You're a fool to think so. I have seen what she has seen, we have *been* there, Nellie. And that day as I watched her I nearly choked to death with terror that she would leave me here. I threw myself weeping at her feet and circled her ankles with my arms. "Stay Cathy, or take me with you." But she was feeling and hearing and seeing elsewhere, I knew, from words that continued to pour through her. "Hush, Heathcliff," she said, "listen, look: he for whom I wait thus now is come to me! Strange Power, I trust thy might, trust thou my constancy." Then the crag began to tremble and as I looked toward Crow Hill bog it seemed to plunge and labor and groan with pain. Suddenly the whole moor broke itself apart, erupting in a black and viscous torrent that overtook the horizon like a glacier of peat and began thundering toward us. Stones of immense size ran before that solid oncoming front of dark and upheaved earth. It was as if the whole top of the moor turned itself over on its side and thought to change its ancient place. Not to go far, as people reading books sometimes think to do, just to move a mile or so farther along toward Saltonstal. But in making that move it cared for nothing that might stand in its way. So this convulsion of nature sank in tumult across a mile and more of flowered waste and desolation, choking up each intervening watercourse and burying for ever all that iron stunted moorland fauna. Three stone bridges were carried to their earthy origins ere this inexorable monster ceased its subterranean heavings. Call you this a demon world, Nellie? I tell you all this time a host of skylarks wheeled in the sky, their songs crossing each other in a strange and haunting lacework of sounds heard clear above that rolling din below.

MOVE 4 *(jjm)*

1 December 1908. Clement's books have gained their object, their celebrity. But reading them I think of my treasure and have to smile—how much he doesn't know he doesn't know. But suppose he could read these texts of mine, would he be able to decipher them better than I? Thirteen years have left them as uncertain for me as ever. The mask scenes in particular. Where did she intend to put them—I mean where *exactly?*! And why did she leave them out? And when in fact did she write them? All those echoes from Clement's MS. B poems ought to explain something anyway. But they only deepen the ambiguities. Most fascinating, most maddening, are those miscegenations of real and fictional places and events. No one doesn't know WH for the amazing personal apocalypse that it is. But what finally do we see of her in those bold and shocking texts, the published ones as well as these precious remains that haunt my mind? She seems still as clear and mysterious as a star. As my self! No, there she is far more clear. Even her texts, like cleansed doors of perception. Even I can see that, though their clarity is my daily shame. And yet, in the country of the blind the one-eyed man is king. That is my office, I am a dark creator—a vacancy absorbing the false spaces of scholarship and imagination. All those majestic lights! So we say, but we know nothing, we pretend we watch those vanished stars. And so I have come to light some few *ignes fatui* for the fat and fatuous.

When I am dead they will know me for what I am—dark star, black hole, anti-matter. Some clever fellow will come along and start examining those wicked children of mine, will go burrowing around and drag them to the light for his righteous inquisition. And when it happens—as it will, it always does—I will become a monster! I only hope I'm not already across the bar when that day comes. I'll lose my second and darker joy if it turns out so.

I'm dead already, of course, in a way—having chosen, as I have done "with clear and sound mind," to corrupt the roots of my life and my work and all my loves. "And for what," some will ask, "for nothing but some perverse private pleasure." Hardly that—the pleasure is the least of it, a mere sop to my mortal nature. For what? For a knowledge otherwise ungainable and unknowable, a knowledge of what we might call the nothing that is not there and the nothing that is. You think knowing nothing is nothing. The dead are prophets. When you read these words—this text I shall *not* destroy—you will *see* what I can see. Not myself, least of all those gone great ones. But you—all of you, who know nothing and think otherwise— you I despise and foresee.

And now, reflecting thus, I can see something else that I must do. I must make copies of these precious relics—at least some of them. And leave them with these "diary papers" of mine, these wretched imitations of those glorious originals that arose from the hands of original angels.

MOVE 5 (jjm)

30 July 1909. Another thrilling day spent alone with EB, my annual devotional visit—breathtaking as ever, if also laborious. I've now made copies of everything I have and I can already see how I shall use them when my enemies descend. But mostly when I am no longer here.

But enough of that. For now I record my notes on the day's principal investigative activity: trying to sort out the odd discrepancies between the two MSS with the two mask episodes.

It must be that EB hadn't integrated the first mask episode (Heathcliff en masque) with the second (Cathy's visionary mask event). The text of the second, as we have it in my MS, has material that clearly overlaps certain materials in the first. Most conspicuous here is the repetition, though with variances, of Heathcliff clasping Cathy's legs. Two possibilities suggest themselves, and each probably involves lost MS materials. 1. EB wrote a different version of Cathy's vision, one that merged properly with the text of the Heathcliff masking MS, and/or a different version of the Cathy vision episode, with a correspondingly correct jointure. These MSS, if either or both existed, have not appeared. 2. EB wrote the Cathy vision text first, and then as she wrote the second she began to contemplate a different way of joining the two—a way evidenced in the final lines of the Heathcliff masking text.

MOVE 6 (jjm)

[This MS (designated MS.TJW2) is copied neatly on both sides of a single foolscap sheet, undated, unwatermarked, in the hand of T. J. Wise; paper identical to MS.TJW1.]

That evening Heathcliff did not take supper. When I asked Mrs. Heath-

cliff where he was she replied "Dead, I trust, in hell, both, either." As if
these words were an incantation to summon him forth, Heathcliff himself
appeared as she was finishing her brief curse.

—"Not yet, my dear wife, but let them come and we shall see how
Death or the Devil like my company. Poorly perhaps. Death may beware,
I have my eye on him. If it is he that keeps Catherine from me I'll hunt
him out and raze every foot of his proud world, and weigh him down with
pains he never knew, till he yield her up to me again. Or if she be in
hell"—his eyes seemed to burn more fiercely at this reflection—"yes,
where else *should* she be, better still—lost for ever to everyone but me. Ah
Satan, call your legions, I think you shall need them."

—"Monster! Monsters both, she worse than you perhaps for making
you the beast you are." Mrs. Heathcliff spat the words and turned away, and
as she made to ascend the stairs to her room she stopped and uttered a brief
cry of fright. Throttler lay across the bottom steps and began a low menacing snarl as she approached what he had recently made a favorite loung-
ing place. Her fright ran quickly to frustration and then fury, and she
whirled around at Heathcliff. "That dog was another being when he lived
at the Grange. Now see what a sullen and savage thing he has become. You
have monstered the very air we breath Out of my way, you filthy cur!"
Heathcliff laughed in a low guttural as the dog began to bristle, though it
did not move except to raise its head slightly and fix a menacing look on
Mrs. Heathcliff. "Ah woman, look how he cowers before your will!"

—"I am going to my room *now,*" she said, looking a hurricane of hatred
at her husband. "And if that brute hinders my purpose by the fraction of
an instant he shall regret it." As Heathcliff roared with laughter Isabella
advanced toward the staircase and Throttler leapt to his feet, growling
loudly now through bared gums and teeth, his thick neck distended. He
seemed readying to attack her there in her own house, but ere he could
execute his unnatural purpose Mrs. Heathcliff flew at him like an animal.
Her eyes glowed out of the paleness of her face, her lips compressed to
stone. Instantly the dog's menace and hostility turned to a wary and perhaps no less dangerous fright as she descended on him like a minor fate.
She seized his heavy collar with her left hand and began dragging him from
the staircase, his hind legs now not poised to spring but set in a hard effort
of stiff resistance, which she broke when she grasped the scruff of his
heavy neck with her free hand. Neither Heathcliff nor I spoke as she
hurled the enraged and terrified beast into the corner by the kitchen door,
and before the brute could recover his resources she fell on him again, her
hand quickly back on the collar, this time forcing his head up so that their

eyes seemed to meet each other in mutual fear and hatred. Then she raised her right arm and drove her fist against those fierce red eyes, again and again repeatedly, punishing him till the sockets bled and swelled and finally closed in pain. Mrs. Heathcliff then dropped the blind and stupefied beast and walked without a word across the hall and up the stairs.

—"Merciful heaven," I thought to myself, "his madness is maddening us all."

MOVE 7 (jjm)

30 July 1896. These past months—I shall never experience anything like them again. I expected the usual labors deciphering and then organizing what one knew would be a difficult sheaf of MSS. But how could anyone have anticipated what that customary tedious, if also always fascinating, process would reveal? Nicholls—pious and sweet man—clearly could not have studied these documents or realized their contents. I still recall the shock that some of these texts caused when their contents gradually began to unfold themselves in my private study during these months—a shock I feel even now, reflecting on them. When WH first appeared its reviewers—most of them—were as troubled by the book's tale as they were impressed by its style, and when it became clear that its author was a woman, the difficulty increased. CB and Gaskell did much to mitigate the public murmur, and then we passed into our new and odd age with our new and odd men and women. Now if our books and our art works and our ideas do not carry some kind of shock wave with them they scarcely register or carry public credit at all.—But some things even *we* continue to cherish and try to protect!

What a sensation would be stirred were it known that a great part of the first version of WH has been preserved in MS! The version that Colburn in 1846 did not—and I (at least) now know *would* not and *could* not—publish. And then, were these remains of that abandoned work actually revealed. . . . Well, even in this epicene and jaded time, *quelle horreur*. The incest theme alone, so explicit and so resolutely pursued across three generations as well as along an unexpected genteel tangent! How different must now appear to us the novel's remarkable and seductive gaps—teasing us into and out of thoughts about what those gaps withhold from our direct view. The first book would have been far less haunting, perhaps, but far more naked and terrible—such a book, indeed, as Zola himself could not have contemplated writing, much less publishing—and least of all any of those more refined sensualists from Gautier to our own bad boy Oscar Wilde. One wonders: is it possible that EB and her siblings managed to divine the deep and imageless truth, still forbidden to be told fully in public, about Byron and Augusta? Byron looms like a dark god over the work of EB and her siblings, but especially EB, whose work involves, in my judgment, a more profound meditation on Byronism than what we find even in Baudelaire, Melville, or Nietzsche. Stowe's scandalous and pinched sermon didn't appear until years after death brought peace and oblivion to EB and her breathtaking—what other word will do?—imaginative explorations. We know that an oral history preserved the precious truth of Byron's life, its splendours and its miseries, its evil—another word to be taken at face value here—and its good. A history that could keep the truth alive by keeping it from a public that simply would not hear of it. Did that oral history make its way into Hayworth?

Holding these papers in my hands tonight I realize what this special lust of mine holds in store for me. A lifetime's pursuit of questions that shall lead on only to other questions, on and on until the questions break like waves against some forbidden, Masoretic wall. Last week I dreamed of that wall in a dream that took me on an agonizing journey through vast Piranesi-like chambers, endlessly leading on one to the next, until I seemed finally pitched into an ultimate hall of ruined grandeurs—and at its opposite end was this looming wall. The whole room shook and throbbed as if it were holding off some vast and powerful enginery just outside itself. The air resounded with a dull roar from these engines, whose principal locus was just beyond that wall. As I walked up to it I saw at its base a great metal door, and I knew that if I were to open that door the questions would cease—but that I would die.

Tonight I know, I fear, I shall never have the courage to open that door.

Yet knowing that dreadful truth about myself, I hereby make this vow: that every year on this day I shall take out these papers and study them. Why? Because if they shall never yield up the secrets of themselves, if those secrets are to remain beyond my power to grasp, they shall at any rate hold a mirror to my soul and reflect back to me its wretched truths. If I am damned I shall at any rate observe my corruptions with the most perfect care and fidelity I can give to them.

MOVE 8 (jjm)

[E-mail letter to Jarred Huonnack from Cora Jegmann, 30 July 2000.]
Dear J,

I know you've seen (or heard about) that listserve announcement by Anne Mack about the newly discovered T. J. Wise *Diaries* and associated papers. The excerpts she posted are truly remarkable, no doubt there. But all that secrecy and circumspection about their location and present owner is infuriating! I suppose we're all to suppose it can't be helped—at least for now. Happily, everything will be revealed "in the fullness of time," as Wise himself discovered—even in his own nefarious lifetime. As the poet has remarked somewhere or other: "If life is short, and art is long / All craft is punishment."

Craft. That's my word for the day and the reason I'm writing. Here's the thing—and I want to know, *need* to know—what you think about this. I BELIEVE THE WHOLE THING'S A HOAX.

Period, end of story? Not to be thought of! I want your judgment on this because I mean to write it up and either post what I think about these materials or send the piece to a journal for publishing, or both. There's much more at issue here than the question of whether any or all of these announced documents are genuine or not. Myself I think they're not, but it might well be that some—even all—*are* what Mack represents them to be. Whatever, since Wise is involved the question of authenticity looms large; and addressing THAT question—something critics, if not scholars, rarely do when they pursue their games of "reading" and interpretation— opens up the entire subject of the relation between original and secondary textualities.

But let me leave that subject for the essay and just lay out for you some of my reasons for suspecting foul play here.

Understand, I'm not saying that Anne Mack is the avatar of that odi- ous TJW, a very satan of the profession the honor of which he cast into disrepute. She MAY be involved in some kind of hoax but she may also simply be the victim of her own enthusiasm and critical naivete. I'm rather inclined to this latter view since she chose to make her "discovery" known via the internet. I mean, REALLY! You can say or propose ANYTHING in this venue and give it an appearance of gospel truth. You can also get your ideas circulated rapidly and widely. Her production mode, as the Marxists would say, is not I think the best one to choose if you want to perpetrate a successful hoax. It's rather an index of something more or less enthused and even spontaneous—more like this letter I'm writing to you now, with its (I admit) petty obvious *negative* enthusiasm (that "petty" is a typo for "pretty," but I leave it intact as a sign of my desire for candor and honesty—even if it IS a Freudian sign).

The evidence for hoaxing stands clear whether Anne Mack is involved or not. It appears in the "texts themselves," as scholars used to say before the coming of our various "hermeneutics of suspicion." (Is this letter a document from that hermeneutical archive? Perhaps, but let me not digress.) Instead, let me lay out the evidence for my suspicions.

First of all, the method by which this "discovery" was made known to the scholarly community. Nothing so momentous, surely, would be reported in such a loose and unexamined way. We're talking here about MS materials and an early version of one of the half dozen most important novels in the English canon.

Second, who can believe that such materials would have been held back this long? These were not LOST documents, like the lost Byron and Shelley MSS found in that trunk in Coutts's bank. We're told they were documents known for what they were since TJW first had them in his hands in 1895.

Third, suppose they were/are what that wretch Wise says they are (in those "Diaries" said to be his—but more on THAT subject in a moment!). Is it even remotely believable—I admit it is possible!—that TJW, of ALL people (note I do not say "of all SCHOLARS"), would have held these materials in secret and never capitalized on them either for money or for fame or both? Or that he would have destroyed them, as he tells us he intended to do? That fetishist DESTROY original EB MSS? I don't THINK so! What else did that monster care about except money and fame—and that peculiar and disgusting sensual delight he took in handling MSS?! HAN-DLING! When I think of it my whole body shivers with repulsion.)

Fourth (and finally), NOT ONE SINGLE FEATURE OF THESE MATERIALS, IF THEY EVEN EXIST, CAN BE SHOWN TO BE UNEQUIVOCALLY GENUINE. Why is that the case? Because according to the tale we are being asked to credit here, the actual original EB MSS no longer exist. Mack's revelations tell us that we have now only TJW's so-called diaries plus the copies HE made of the original EB MSS.

I admit there are problems here. If those TJW diaries are authenticated we shall have to rethink much of what we—let us say I and all scholars who take their profession seriously—now take for granted about the despicable TJW. We shall even have to reconsider the case for the authenticity of the EB MSS TJW said that he intended to destroy. But the authenticity of the diaries and associated MSS also leaves open the possibility that Wise was planning a hoax more horrid and infamous than any of the ones we now know about. A hoax from beyond the grave, and one that would, he imagined, NEVER be finally exposed. Never be able to be exposed!

This last possibility leaves me aghast with a fear that goes to the ground of everything I hold true and dear. If this proves to be the situation, my judgment of that man will have been shown to be truer—more terribly true—than I ever dreamed (or "nightmared"). We would in that case see that the true purpose of his life and work was this: to destroy for good and ever any ground of objective authority for the work that we do!

x

Cora.

MOVE 9 (jjm)

12 August 2000

Dear Jarred,

This comes to you as snailmail since I clearly can't even HOPE for a serious response from you in that electronic medium. I thought your long-standing interest in puzzles and hoaxing would have inspired your critical imagination—you used to have one, I seem to recall—but instead it triggered your old slapstick habits. You're really impossible sometimes. Men! I've no idea what flimsy traces of actuality cling to that fabric of trivial nonsense—whether you were at any party at all and saw McGann, whatever. It's so LIKE you, piling a travesty set of hoaxes on top of these matters—turning everything into a kind of burlesque theatre. *My Emily!!* And publisher's blurbs thereon! Gag. Stop blowing bubbles for a minute and THINK about this thing. The problem can be simply and clearly stated even though what follows from the problem—whatEVER follows from it, whatever we make of it—opens what the derrideans used to call, in their rather self-important and now happily-gone glory days, a *mise en abime*.

WHAT IS TO BE GAINED BY PRESERVING ANY CONCEPT OF TEXTUAL AUTHENTICITY IN AN ACT OF LITERARY-CRITICAL REFLECTION? or;

ARE THE PROCEDURES AND CONCEPTS OF BIBLIOGRAPH-ICAL ANALYSIS AND TEXTUAL CRITICISM CATEGORICALLY THE SAME AS THE CATEGORIES OF HERMENEUTICS? or;

THE SEMANTIC REQUIREMENT FOR A GRAMMAR OF CRITICAL ASSENT IS A VOCABULARY THAT NEED REFERENCE ONLY (A) THE INTENTION OF THE "SPEAKING" SUBJECT AND (B) THE DELIBERATION OF A WILLING INTERLOCUTOR or;

THE CONCEPT (AND HENCE THE FACT) OF A DOCUMENT IS AN ACT OF FAITH IN THE TRUE PERSISTENCE OF HUMAN INTERCOURSE.

I could multiply these kinds of apothegms at some length but in your present mood you probably register only an amused recoil from such reflections. But haul out all your 'pataphysical apparatus and test what I'm saying in its light (or dark). For instance, consider this: that if the object of critical reflection is enlightenment and critical clarity, then this case shows why documentary authenticity, in the traditional sense, has no necessary privileged or foundational status?—shows, in fact, that its assumed privilege and foundation—sometimes called its "pre-critical" status—is nothing more than an imaginative hypothesis.

Now if you (or any of your cronies) care to weigh in on these matters in some SERIOUS way—and I don't mean BEETLE-BROWED, JUST *SERIOUS* IN THE SENSE OF INTELLECTUALLY SALIENT (as opposed to that flip and inconsequent manner you put on in your last two notes)—I'd be, as I'd very much like to be,

Your humble and obedient servant,

Cora

MOVE 10 (jjm)

30 July 1911

Nothing in this library, nothing I could ever hope to gain for it (perhaps not even a copy of Byron's lost *Memoirs!*) touches or shall touch the precious and terrible character of these few pages. Each year they yield up to my persistent attentions a few more of their secrets and mysteries. Unlike those more or less integral units—the masking episode for instance—the power of these fragments is a direct function of what fate has torn away from them. They are, I now see quite clearly, the scattered residue of the original narrative of what EB reworked into our received chapters 7–10.

This afternoon's investigation into that maddeningly enigmatic scrap beginning "me—I started and after a moment's bewilderment" has convinced me of this. The piece—I am sure of it!—is all that remains of Catherine's *original* remarks to Nelly Dean following the visit Heathcliff makes to Thrushcross Grange immediately after his three years' absence. The fragment shows that in the original version of the story Catherine left the Grange that evening and met Heathcliff on the moors. In the published novel Catherine wakens Nelly Dean in the middle of the night because, she says, "I cannot rest, Ellen" [page 76]. Now we understand much more about that restlessness as well as the full import of the midnight conversation between Ellen Dean and Catherine Linton.

Here is how the fragment would have been situated [see pages 75–76]:

"[About the middle of the night . . . and pulling me by the hair to rouse] me—I started and after a moment's bewilderment managed to ask 'Mrs. Linton, what are you doing here at such an hour?'

—'Did you not hear the wind tonight, Ellen?'

—'I heard nothing unusual.'

—'Perhaps at such times it only speaks to us. It came and I knew Heathcliff was waiting for me, so I went to him, I had to go, and there he was.'

—'If you had not come, Cathy, no power on earth or in heaven would have stopped me from carrying you where you belong—away from the life of that ridiculous house and its ridiculous characters, and out here with me. You cannot have forgotten what we found so many times together in this place—what you first discovered to me, for me, when I was not yet 14 years old! "Come to me Heathcliff"—that was what you said the very first time, I shall never forget or let you forget—"This is our life-in-death, our death-in-life, no one else can know us as we will know ourselves." And you were right, I came and died then, and was born again in another world where I learned to die many times since. Our world, *this* world.'

—And oh Ellen he rapt me away and *this* other world dissolved and disappeared and we were there together again—beyond the Grange and the Heights and everything that seems to be. And now I am back and I want some living creature to try to understand my happiness. Not Edgar, he would only sulk and[. . .]."

And there the fragment ends.

But the implications of this passage! Young Catherine, we are surely meant to understand, is the child of Heathcliff and Cathy, born prematurely, if Nelly Dean's chronology is correct.

And whenever Cathy or Heathcliff speak about death and their desire for it, they are using as it were a different, a kind of prelapsarian, language. Their idea of death is an idea of consummate love—indeed, of consummated love! Well and good, if also unspeakable. What seems truly uncanny is how EB manages to reveal in those moments of her book the childlike *literality* of C's and H's ways of speaking. Death seems no stranger to them, death seems for them to be, to have been, a way of life, an intense and uncontaminated existence "that has been and shall be again."

Player File: J. McGann

My role: Thomas James Wise (scholar, collector, bibliographer, forger).

MOVE 1

Several determinate historical references are included here, including various persons (Harry Buxton Forman, Clement Shorter, and John Henry

Wrenn, all friends of Wise); Arthur Bell Nicholls, the husband of Charlotte Bronte and principal source of the MS remains that descend to us. "Twenty years" refers to the single most important moment in Bronte scholarship, the day in 1895 when Shorter and Wise visited Nicholls and saw—and made arrangements to purchase for a disgraceful song—those materials that Charlotte's husband had husbanded. We are in 1915 in order to be "into" the beginning of WWI.

Role Rationale:

This role allows me to move along three lines simultaneously. I can write in a justified historical sense virtually any kind of original Brontean materials. I can also reflect upon the first (mythic) period of Bronte criticism and scholarship from an "inner standing point," so to speak. Finally, that inner standing point allows me to "fictionalize" for critical and reflective purposes the initial scene of Bronte scholarship, when nearly all the received lines of criticism and interpretation were put into play—not excluding the most recent lines out of deconstruction and feminism.

Let it be stated here, at the very outset, that I intend to make a "leap" after four or five moves. The leap will involve the introduction of another role, a contemporary (with us) critic/scholar, fictitious as TJW is not, named Cora Jegmann. This person will wade in to "interrogate," as we say these days, the TJW materials—and perhaps (we shall see!) the materials produced by others in the game. Her role will begin with a letter on these subjects to her friend Jarred Huonnack.

Sources:

John Collins, *The Two Forgers. A Biography of Harry Buxton Forman and Thomas James Wise.* Scholar Press: Aldershot, 1992.

Fanny Ratchford, ed., *Letters of Thomas James Wise to John Henry Wrenn.* Knopf: New York, 1944. (see especially pp. 162–163)

T. J. Wise and J. A. Symington, eds. *The Brontes: Their Lives, Friendships and Correspondence.* 4 vols. Shakespeare Head Press: Oxford, 1932.

Notes:

Shorter and Wise used to lunch together every week (see Collins, 117). This will be referenced. Also to be referenced are a pair of known facts: 1. that Emily left at her death the fragment of another novel—because these remains have not appeared, it is assumed that Charlotte destroyed them; 2. the Bronte sisters regularly produced what later scholars, led by Wise and Shorter, have come to call "Diary Papers"—more or less coherent units of diaristic writing that mix fictional materials (typically from Angrian and Gondolian contexts) with personal and/or topical references to the daily thoughts and doings of the sisters.

MOVE 2

Sources:

For "the room upstairs over the kitchen" see Edward Chitham, *A Life of Emily Bronte* (Basil Blackwell: Oxford, 1987), 14–17.

For the mask episode see Patrick Bronte's letter to Elizabeth Gaskell, 30 July 1855 (NB—Emily's birthday!).

For the initial question and answer see "Stanzas" ("Often rebuked, yet always back returning")

MOVE 3

Sources:

Clement Shorter, *The Brontes: Life and Letters.* 2 vols. Hodder and Stoughton: London, 1908.

MOVE 4

Sources:

For Sowden's grave and the churchyard see the map of Haworth in Chitham, Appendix B.

For Cathy's vision see the reports of the Crow Hill bog eruption of 2 September 1824, reported in Horsefall Turner, *Bronteana* (Bingley, 1898), 201–219.

For other parts of Cathy's vision see various poems by EB.

MOVE 5

No new or special sources. This move takes up the "challenge" sent out to me by JD on 2 August. However, it will be useful at this point to recapitulate the rationale of my moves to date, especially because this challenge-response will be folded into my ongoing plan of moves.

The response will be TJW's, a diary entry in which he speculates on the textual situation—the overlapping materials—that arise because of JD's insertion. Here I show that I have accepted the simultaneous existence of the two MSS and hence of their overlaps/discrepancies. Both documents, according to TJW, are real and in his secret possession.

MOVE 6

Sources:
Elizabeth Gaskell, *The Life of Charlotte Bronte* (1857), 183–185; quoted in Chitham, 157–158.

MOVE 7

Sources:
The poem quoted is by Jerome McGann, from *Air Heart Sermons*—I forget which poem in that book it's from.

MOVE 8

This role switch was announced in my first player-file notes. Its exegesis is pretty self-explanatory. Now, with these 2 roles in play, I mean to explore some "serious" issues in theory of interpretation—in a wildean mode of course.

What's especially important here, in my view, is that these literary-critical commentaries are cast within the same imaginative space as all the other texts. They function at the same "level," so to speak, as the public game moves *as well as the level of EB's original imaginative materials.*

MOVE 9

This move continues the critical line begun in the previous move. Both are intended to introduce a reflexive vantage on the whole previous set of interpretive moves, and to raise some fundamental interpretive issues about different forms of critical explanation.

MOVE 10

This move returns us to the TJW materials. The point, however, is to use the two intervening moves—with their explicit contemporary critical and theoretical point of view—to establish a differential context for critically exposing both the earlier materials (real and imaginary) and our immediate critical/theoretical situation.

Notes

Introduction

1. The archive is online accessible at http://jefferson.village.virginia.edu/rossetti/.
2. The topic was made the subject of a double issue of *Computers and the Humanities* 27, no. 5–6 (1993–1994), in an issue titled "A New Direction for Literary Studies?," edited by Paul A. Fortier.
3. Though OULIPO is the most prominent exponent of this kind of writing, it has become widespread in the twentieth century.
4. See Ian Hacking, *Representing and Intervening*.
5. The URL for IATH is http://jefferson.village.virginia.edu/home.html.
6. See Roberto Busa, *Fondamenti di informatica linguistica* (Milano: Vita e Pensiero, 1987); Luciano Gallino, ed., *Informatica e scienze umane. Lo stato dell' arte,* Collana 885/76 (Milano: Franco Angeli, 1991).
7. For a useful presentation of this matter see R. Howard Bloch and Carla Hesse, eds. *Future Libraries Representations* 42 (Special Issue, spring 1993).
8. The best introductions to SGML , TEI, and other markup procedures are online. A useful collection is available in the "Related Resources" section of *The Rossetti Archive*'s homepage. The URL is http://jefferson.village.virginia.edu:2020/resources.html.
9. The "inventor" of the web, Tim Berners-Lee, has recently published an account of its early history and implementations in *Weaving the Web.*
10. This fact is evident from a review of the papers that were given at the annual ACM Hypertext conferences in 1993–1995.
11. For good treatments of these matters see Gérard Genette, *Paratexts;* Jerome McGann, *The Textual Condition.*
12. The basic bibliography on SGML can be found at http://www.oasis-open.org/cover/biblio.html. The developers of SGML have written some

of the most important critical materials on its problems: see, e.g., David T. Barnard, Lou Burnard, and Michael Sperburg-McQueen, "Lessons from Using SGML in the Text Encoding Initiative," Technical Report 95–375 (Kingston, Ontario, Canada: Department of Computing and Information Science, Queen's University, March 2, 1995); and especially Allen Renear, Elli Mylonas, and David Durand, "Refining our Notion of What Text Really Is: The Problem of Overlapping Hierarchies," available online at http://www.stg.brown.edu/resources/stg/monographs/ohco.html. See also Ian Lancashire, "Early Books, RET Encoding Guidelines, and the Limits of SGML" (Paper presented at The Electric Scriptorium. Approaches to the Electronic Imaging, Transcription, Editing and Analysis of Medieval Manuscript Texts: A Physical & Virtual Conference, University of Calgary, Calgary, Alberta [physical conference], November 10–12, 1995). The event was sponsored by The University of Calgary, Calgary Institute for the Humanities, and SEENET, and was coordinated by Dr. Murray McGillivray, Thomas Wharton, Blair McNaughton, and Robert McLean (available online at http://www.ucalgary.ca/ ~ scriptor/papers/lanc.html). See also two essays of my own, "The Rossetti Archive and Image-Based Electronic Editing" and "Comp[u/e]ting Editorial F[u/ea]tures," both available online at http://jefferson.village.virginia.edu:2020/resources.html. An important related problem, not often enough discussed, is the refusal of programmers to build software that might implement SGML because of the mathematical difficulties involved; the emergence and rapid success of XML (which has its own set of problems) is a direct function of this refusal. But from the point of view of the present essay, SGML is a markup syntax designed for texts that are imagined as information repositories, not for texts whose cognitive resources are coded aesthetically (i.e., through linguistic recursions and repetitions, on one hand, and graphical arrangements, on the other).

13. For Greg Crane's *The Perseus Project* see http://perseus/tufts/edu; for George Landow's *The Dickens Web* see http://eastgate.com/catalog/dickens.html.

Chapter 1

1. See Gerald Graff, *Teaching the Conflicts.*
2. See Stanley Burnshaw's influential New Critical book *The Poem Itself.*

Chapter 2

1. An earlier publication of this chapter, in *The Electronic Text: Investigations in the Method and Theory of Computerized Textuality,* ed. Marilyn Deegan and Kathryn Sutherland (Oxford: Oxford UP, 1997), 19–46 contained a series of graphical illustrations of *The Rossetti Archive.*

2. The simplest definition of hypertext is Theodore Nelson's "nonsequential writing" (*Literary Machines* [Sausalito, CA: Mindful, 1990], sec. 5, 2). Nelson's book is a classic introduction to hypertext. For other introductory information about hypertext and hypermedia, and about the projects mentioned in this and the next paragraphs, see *Hypertext/Hypermedia Handbook,* ed. Emily Berk and Joseph Devlin (New York: Internet Publications, McGraw Hill, 1991); *The Digital Word. Text-Based Computing in the Humanities,* ed. George P. Landow and Paul Delany (Cambridge MA: The MIT Press, 1993); *Hypertext:The Convergence of Contemporary Critical Theory and Technology* (Baltimore: Johns Hopkins UP, 1992); *Hypermedia and Literary Studies,* ed. George P. Landow and Paul Delany (Cambridge MA: MIT Press, 1991); Jay David Bolter, *Writing Space: The Computer, Hypertext, and the History of Writing* (Hillsdale: Laurence Erlbaum, 1991).

3. See *The Poems and Songs of Robert Burns,* ed. James Kinsley (Oxford: Clarendon Press, Oxford UP, 1968) I. 435–436.

4. See for example the ballad "Tam Lin" (Kinsley no. 558, II. 836–841).

5. This revaluation of Dickinson studies was sparked by the great facsimile edition of the poet's original fascicles, edited by R. W. Franklin, *The Manuscript Books of Emily Dickinson.* Since then the work of Susan Howe and her students has been only slightly less significant, especially the edition of Dickinson's fragments edited by Marta Werner (Ann Arbor: U of Michigan P, 2000) and the essay by Jeanne Holland, "Scraps, Stamps, and Cutouts." Howe's seminal essay is indispensable:"These Flames and Generosities of the Heart." See also Paula Bennett, "By a Mouth that Cannot Speak: Spectral Presence in Emily Dickinson's Letters," *The Emily Dickinson Journal* 1 (1992): 76–99 and my own "Emily Dickinson's Visible Language," *The Emily Dickinson Journal* 2 (1993): 40–57. Martha Nell Smith is currently the head of the Emily Dickinson Editorial Collective, a group of scholars committed to seeing Dickinson's work re-edited so as to expose its "sumptuary values," i.e., the scripts and visible designs that are such an important feature of the writing.

6. See Andrew Boyle, *An Index to the Annuals,* vol. I (vol. II never printed) (London: privately printed by Andrew Boyle, 1967); F. W. Faxon, *Literary Annuals and Gift Books: A Bibliography 1823–1903* (1912, reprinted Boston: Pinner, Private Libraries Assoc., 1973); Anne Renier, *Friendship's Offering. An Essay on the Annuals and Gift Books of the 19th Century* (London: Private Libraries Assoc., 1964); Alison Adburgham, *Silver Fork Society. Fashionable Life and Literature from 1814 to 1840* (London: Constable, 1983).

7. Arthur Henry Hallam, "On Some of the Characteristics of Modern Poetry, and on the Lyrical Poems of Alfred Tennyson," reprinted from the *Englishman's Magazine* (August 1931) in *The Writings of Arthur Hallam,* ed. T. H. Vail Motter (New York and London: Modern Language Assoc. of America, 1943), 182–197.

8. Quoted from Bruce Sterling, "Internet," *The Magazine of Fantasy and Science Fiction*, Science Column no. 5 (February 1993). I quote here from the text of the column that was made available through a network mailing list.

9. For discussion of the structure of hypertext (and a critique of rather loose representations of its decentralized form) see Ross Atkinson, "Networks, Hypertext, and Academic Information Services: Some Longer Range Implications," *College & Research Libraries* 54, no. 3 (May 1993): 199–215.

10. Textual scholars will understand that this chapter stands in a consciously revisionist relation to W. W. Greg's great essay "The Rationale Of Copy-Text."

Chapter 3

1. "The Importance of Failure," *The Journal of Electronic Publishing* 3, no. 2 (December 1997).

2. The images discussed here cannot be reproduced in this book. They can be found, however, in my online essay "Imagining What You don't Know."

3. I discuss this aspect throughout my recent study of Rossetti, *Dante Gabriel Rossetti and the Game that Must be Lost* (New Haven: Yale UP, 2000).

4. "The science of imaginary solutions" is Alfred Jarry's own definition of his 'pataphysical project.

Chapter 4

1. See the previous chapter's discussion of the "praxis of theory."

2. See William Blake, *The Marriage of Heaven and Hell*, plates 21–22, as well as his "Annotations to Boyd's Historical Notes on Dante."

3. Had the interpretive method displayed by St. John of the Cross, in his commentaries on his own poems, become as influential for us as Dante's methods have been, we might think very differently about interpretive analysis. St. John's commentaries are flagrantly subjective. Invoking the entirety of a Judaeo-Christian discourse, they nonetheless keep us aware that the interpretations stand in a partial and idiosyncratic relation to the poems. The absolute status of the poems is both assumed and reinforced by the commentaries—as if the poems had been, as Blake would later say, "dictated from Eternity."

4. See Anthony Grafton, *Forgers and Critics: Creativity and Duplicity in Western Scholarship* (Princeton: Princeton UP, 1990).

5. Kathy Acker's fictional recastings of canonical texts are well known. More naive literary travesties circulate in the academy as comical anecdotes but are not normally treated with the seriousness we think they deserve. See the student discussion of Keats's "Ode on a Grecian Urn" recapitulated above in chapter 1.

6. See, for example, Randall McLeod's recent essay "Information on Information."

7. A discussion of these deformances can be found in chapter 3. See also my online essay "Imagining What You Don't Know."

8. In *A Homemade World,* Kenner calls Stevens "a mere poet," criticizing what he sees as Stevens's preference for "saying" (subject matter) over "making" (form), and at the same time complaining about the way Stevens's verbal world is wholly removed from the "real" world (see especially 50–57, 67–75). B. J. Leggett, on the other hand, finds Stevens's world a place to take seriously, a place for philosophical and systematic theorizing: see *Early Stevens* and *Wallace Stevens and Poetic Theory.*

9. Charles Olson, "The Escaped Cock. Notes on Lawrence & the Real," in *Human Universe and Other Essays,* ed. Donald Allen (New York: Grove Press, 1967), 123.

10. This (so to speak) pre-emptive status of poetical and imaginative work licenses freedom of engagement and interpretation. Everyone who reads poetry or responds to art will and should have the authority of personal "taste." Expert and educated responses are a special genre, nothing more (and nothing less). Choosing to frame expression under the sign of the imagination is a defining gesture that does not in itself raise the question of "goodness" or "badness." It simply sets the audience in a special relation to the medium and the gestures being made. This situation is what makes it possible—perhaps even imperative—to generate elaborate interpretations of imaginative works that might be widely judged to be "minor" or "inferior." Such interpretations are efforts to give an "objective" status to a serious subjective engagement. For examples see the readings of Kilmer's "Trees" and of Hemans's "The Homes of England" in (respectively) chapter 1 (above) and "Literary History, Romanticism, and Felicia Hemans," in Wilson and Haefner, 210–227.

11. This kind of toggling back and forth between poetizing prose and prosing poetry has been carried out before in critical texts. Two examples: In *Metre, Rhyme, and Free Verse* (London: Methuen, 1970), 17–18, George Fraser lineates a prose passage as free verse; and in *Poetic Artifice* (New York: St. Martin's Press, 1978), Veronica Forrest-Thomson lineates a newspaper paragraph as free verse and as a kind of bipart structure visually similar to alliterative verse.

12. See the appendix to chapter 4 for some further examples of deformative operations, including a reordered reading of Coleridge's "Limbo."

13. McLeod is the most textually deforming "mainstream" critic we know. But a substantial and growing tradition of twentieth-century "experimental" criticism enacts various kinds of performance, deformance, and subjectivity. This criticism is carried out almost exclusively by those who are primarily known as creative writers: a partial list includes Gertrude Stein (*How to Write*), some

of Ezra Pound (*Guide to Kulchur,* for example), Louis Zukofsky (*Bottom: On Shakespeare*), John Cage (see *Silence. Lectures and Writings by John Cage*), Susan Howe (*My Emily Dickinson*), and Bob Perelman (ed., *Writing/Talks*). See also the double issue of *Chain* 3, nos. I and 2 (1996), edited by Jena Osman and Juliana Spahr; and *A Poetics of Criticism* edited by Spahr et al. A fuller treatment of deformative criticism will involve some examination of these twentieth-century critical engagements. For our present purposes, it has seemed more pressing to situate deformance in the context of earlier interpretive histories.

14. Deformative criticism can be a very successful pedagogical counter to the problems of interpretive criticism. Deformance helps students to interact with the physiques of the poem: for example, with the problematics of parts of speech, which often come to be revealed as metaphorical when the poem is dislodged from its original orderings. Such interaction can also help students to overcome their common fixation on authorial intention and to see their roles as *makers* of poetic meaning in the act of reading.

15. See "The Rejection of Closure," in Perelman, 270–291. Hejinian is in turn echoing the sense of language's fractured sufficiency that we see in Wittgenstein.

16. See "Preface" to Riding, *Progress,* 10.

Chapter 5

1. Drucker has written about this frequently, but perhaps the most important piece is the unpublished essay I have referred to at various times, "Metalogics of the Book."

2. See Part III chapter 7 where the work of G. Spencer Brown is used to demonstrate how states of identity are a function of states of difference and not—as in classical theory—the other way round. This view yields the axiom: a equals a if and only if a does not equal a. In poetical works, where ambiguities are often deliberately set in "controlled" play, a field of meta-ambivalences emerges to expose in the sharpest fashion the general textual condition.

3. It's important to remark here that throughout this study I have specifically excluded the phonological aspects of textuality from the discussion. This exclusion reflects nothing more than my own lack of scholarly expertise to deal with the matter, and not any lack of awareness of its central importance. The phonological—and for that matter, the tactile—aspects of textuality are intrinsic to its total physique. Digitization, of course, has a uniform system for treating any of these features of traditional textuality.

4. Allen Renear, "What is Text, Really?" with Steve DeRose, David Durand, and Elli Mylonas, *Journal of Computing in Higher Education* 1, no. 2 (winter 1990).

5. For further discussion of this see the following three chapters.

6. See Part I chapter 3.

7. See Ascher and Ascher, *Code of the Quipu;* Joyce Marcus, *Mesoamerican Writing Systems. Propaganda, Myth, and History in Four Ancient Civilizations* (Princeton: Princeton UP, 1992); Elizabeth Hill Boone and Walter D. Mignolo, eds., *Writing Without Words. Alternative Literacies in Mesoamerica and the Andes* (Durham: Duke UP, 1994).

8. Don D. Roberts, *The Existential Graphs of Charles S. Peirce* (The Hague, Paris: Mouton, 1973).

9. See below, Part III chapter 7, where this text is discussed and analyzed in some detail.

10. MS. M and MS. B actually differ slightly in their titles ("To the Po. June 2 1819" v. "To the Po. June 1819"). The difference is small but, given the *gestalt* of the poem, much could be made of it.

11. Because several rhymes get repeated, the description of the continuous rhyme scheme does not proceed simply ababcdcdefefghgh etc.

12. See *Lord Byron. The Complete Poetical Works,* 4: 210–211, 496–499.

13. I use the word "scripts" here in a double sense; it carries a conscious reference to its meaning in the discourse of programming, where a "script" is a unit of programming instruction.

14. Brenda Laurel's work (see *Computers as Theatre*) offers stimulating ideas about how to exploit the simulacral capacities of digital tools.

Chapter 6

1. For *The Perseus Project* see: http://www.perseus.tufts.edu/; the homepage of the Institute for Advanced Technology in the Humanities is: http://jefferson.village.virginia.edu/.

2. See Tufte's *Envisioning Information,*

3. See Part I chapter 2.

4. See Part I chapter 3.

5. The exception is the theory developed by Galvano della Volpe: see above, Part II chapter 4.

6. I've given attention to this kind of elementary bibliographical "expressivity" for two reasons. First, it gives a simple but arresting reminder of the determinate materiality of every language form. (An example for an oral event of language would not be difficult to construct). Second, although the matter is beyond the scope of this essay, I believe that an analysis of these kinds of visible features of text holds promise for exploiting computerized resources for the interpretation of imaginative works. A more detailed treatment of this matter is given in a paper (unpublished) being written in tandem with this one. The latter lays out the theoretical basis for a set of experimental operations presently being carried out by several people at the Institute for Advanced Technology in the Humanities.

7. For a discussion of this poem and its attribution problems see Vieth, 199–203.

8. The twentieth century has produced a number of notable exceptions among scientists from Einstein and Gödel to G. Spencer Brown and Roger Penrose. Brown's *Laws of Form* (1969) is particularly important, not least because of Brown's self-conscious use of textspace to develop his argument. See Part III chapter 7.

9. For a discussion of this poem and of Dickinson's material codes in general see my *Black Riders*, 26–41, esp. 28, and Susan Howe's brilliant "These Flames," 134–155.

10. See DeRose, "Structured Information."

Appendix to Chapter 6

1. Renear was presenting a synthesis of ideas for which he was already a well-known advocate. See his "Out of Praxis" and "What is Text, Really?"

Chapter 7

1. I quote from the first English edition (London: Allen and Unwin, 1969) throughout. The several later reprintings all reproduce the format of the first edition—a crucial bibliographical fact.

2. I will have little to say here about visual and graphical works. The representation of such objects in digital form is, however, a crucial subject and one deeply related to the (primarily) textual subject of this book, as I think will be apparent from the way I will be handling the whole question of textuality. For a good recent survey of the field see Jorgensen, "Access to Pictorial Material: A Review of Current Research and Future Prospects," 293–318.

3. See the TEI homepage (http://www.hcu.ox.ac.uk/TEI) and the special double issue of *Computers and the Humanities* 33, nos. 1–2 (1999).

4. A number of the sessions at the 1999 meetings of the ACH/ALLC addressed, in different ways, the need to revisit the most basic issues of text analysis and text markup. This broadly distributed critical interest was brought to a sharp focus in Susan Hockey's special session "What is Text?" (http://www.iath.virginia.edu/ach-allc.99/proceedings/hockey-renear2.html). See above, Part II chapter 5, chapter 6, and the appendix to chapter 6.

5. The translations of Dante's *divisiones* are those made by William Michael Rossetti for his brother Dante Gabriel's translation of *La Vita Nuova,* which he published in his 1861 collection *The Early Italian Poets.* For a good introduction to Dante's *divisiones* see D'Andrea, 30–40.

6. The sonnet is "Con l'altre donne mia vista gabbate."

7. This is odd but true. It is odd because Saussurean linguistics, and Derridean commentaries that depend from it, emphasize the materiality of language and its "graphemic" foundation. Nevertheless, commentaries and interpretations that profess to these approaches to textuality almost never seek to explore or expose the signifying acts of a work's bibliographical codes.

8. For a good recent discussion of montage and collage in the context of hypermedia see George Dillon, "Data Photomontage and net.art Sitemaps."

9. Because the text runs over two pages and occupies a place in the work's bookspace, the chapter also exploits—minimally—the three-dimensional resources of such space.

10. It might be thought that the repetition of certain graphic elements—the boldface type, for instance, or the italics—are bibliographical illustrations of the law of crossing. Those repetitions are not, however, recrossings. They are calls made again.

11. Dante's understanding that writing is performative is commonplace in a classical view of textuality. This view was occluded for us by romantic aesthetics, where the rhetorical structure of texts was neglected for an interest in subjectivity. Romantic sincerity is itself a textual rhetoric, but it is a rhetoric programmatically occluded in romantic forms of textuality.

12. See Streng, *Emptiness*. See Streng's appendix A for his translation of Nagarjuna's key work, "Mulamadhyamakakarikas" ["Fundamentals of the Middle Way"]; Appendix B gives a translation of the closely related "Vigrahavyavartani" ["Averting the Arguments"].

13. See Segré, *Introduction,* which offers a lucid and comprehensive summary of the Saussurean/Jakobsonian synthesis on textuality.

Conclusion

1. Quoted in *Mallarmé: Selected Prose Poems, Essays, and Letters,* trans. with an introduction by Bradford Cook (Baltimore: Johns Hopkins UP, 1956), 105. The remark was made specifically in reference to Mallarmé's work on *Un Coup de Dés.* The essay "The Book: A Spiritual Instrument," written in 1895, also bears directly on the poem (Cook's translation appears at pages 24–29).

2. See Hofstadter.

3. Many good resources for studying OULIPO are available. Online see: http://www2.ec-lille.fr/ ~ book/oulipo/info/. See Motte, *Oulipo* and especially Mathews and Brotchie, *Oulipo Compendium.*

4. Humberto R. Maturana and Francisco G. Varela, *Autopoiesis and Cognition: the Realization of the Living* (Dordrecht, Holland; Boston: D. Reidel Pub. Co., 1980); Francisco J. Varela, Evan Thompson, Eleanor Rosch, *The Embodied Mind: Cognitive Science and Human Experience* (Cambridge, MA: MIT Press, 1991).

5. For a good general introduction see Courtney Brown, *Chaos and Catastrophe Theories* (Thousand Oaks, CA: Sage Publications, 1995); more serious is the great work by René Thom.

6. [Thackeray], *Rebecca and Rowena.*

7. See http://www.people.virginia.edu/ ~ bpn2f/ivanhoe.html for a record of one of our initial trial runs of gameplay. In practical terms this trial, and the other two as well, were played as a series of email exchanges. Our game moves—in concrete terms, the texts we produced and exchanged—were stored for study and access by the players in a freeware program called BLOGGER. Using email and then BLOGGER proved useful since both set a certain distance between the players as well as between the players and their role-played moves. The performative and the reflexive imperatives of the game were, it seemed to us, enhanced by these arrangements.

8. This kind of work, even if we confine ourselves to English language writings, appears everywhere, even in works that pretend to a kind of scientific objectivity, as in many of Pound's works or, more spectacularly perhaps, in Graves—*The White Goddess,* for example. The impulse grows even stronger, perhaps, in the last 20 years or so. Exemplary works here include Howe's remarkable *My Emily Dickinson;* much of Bernstein's critical writings, including *My Way;* and the collection *A Poetics of Criticism,* edited by Spahr et al.

9. The extended dialogue *Swinburne: An Experiment in Criticism* (Chicago, 1972) was written in 1971, the year I began work on *Lord Byron: The Complete Poetical Works* (Oxford, 1980–1993).

10. The new name was suggested by Worthy Martin in the course of several months' discussions about the digital architecture of the game.

11. A MOO is a MUD, "Object Oriented." A MUD "is a network-accessible, multi-participant, user-extensible virtual reality whose user interface is entirely textual." This is the brief definition of a MUD given by the inventor of MOOs, Pavel Curtis. It is quoted in John Unsworth's excellent general introduction to MOO environments "Living Inside the (Operating) System."

12. See Pribram, ed., *Rethinking Neural Networks;* Honavar and Uhr, *Artificial Intelligence;* Hameroff, "Quantum Coherence"; Chalmers, *Towards a Theory of Consciousness;* and his essay "Facing Up," available online at: http://www.u.arizona.edu/ ~ chalmers/papers/facing.html.

13. This statement refers to rigorous formal logical systems, not to "loose" and nonlinear logics.

14. The reference here is to the distinction between "linguistic" and "bibliographic" codes that I developed in the 1980s in the aftermath of *A Critique of Modern Textual Criticism* (1983).

Bibliography

Paper Materials

Aarseth, Espen. *Cybertext: Perspectives on Ergodic Literature*. Baltimore and London: Johns Hopkins UP, 1997.

D'Andrea, Antonio. *Il nome della storia*. Napoli: Liguori, 1982.

Albright, Daniel. *Quantum Poetics: Yeats, Pound, Eliot, and the Science of Modernism*. Cambridge: Cambridge UP, 1997.

Ascher, Marcia and Robert Ascher. *Code of the Quipu: A Study of Media, Mathematics, and Culture*. Ann Arbor: U of Michigan P, 1981.

Barbi, M., ed. *Vita Nuova*, in *Le Opere di Danti: Testo Critico della Societa Dantesca Italiana*. Firenze: R. Bemporad e figlio, 1921.

Berners-Lee, Tim. *Weaving the Web*. With Mark Fischetti. London: Orion Business Books, 1999.

Bernstein, Charles. *My Way*. Chicago: U of Chicago P, 1999.

Blake, William. *The Complete Poetry and Prose of William Blake*. Ed. David V. Erdman, with commentary by Harold Bloom. Rev. ed. Berkeley and Los Angeles: U of California P, 1982.

Bloch, R. Howard and Carla Hesse, eds. *Future Libraries. Representations* 42 (special issue, spring 1993).

Bloom, Harold. *The Anxiety of Influence: A Theory of Poetry*. New York: Oxford UP, 1973.

Bolter, J. David. *Writing Space: The Computer in the History of Literacy*. Hillsdale, NJ: Lawrence Erlbaum, 1990.

Brooks, Cleanth and Robert Penn Warren, eds. *Understanding Poetry*. New York: Holt, Rinehart, and Winston: New York, 1938.

Brown, [G.] Spencer. *Child's Game, On a Journey, and Other Poems*. New Rochelle, NY: The Elizabeth Press, 1979.

——. *Laws of Form*. London: George Allen and Unwin Ltd., 1969.

Buchanan, Robert ["Thomas Maitland"]. "The Fleshly School of Poetry: Mr. D. G. Rossetti." *Contemporary Review* 18 (October 1871): 334–350.

Burckhardt, Sigurd. *Shakespearean Meanings.* Princeton: Princeton UP, 1968.

Burnshaw, Stanley. *The Poem Itself.* New York: Holt, Rinehart, and Winston, 1960.

Busnelli, G. and G. Vandelli, eds. *Convivio.* 2 vols. Firenze: Felice le Monnier, 1937, 1957.

Buzzetti, Dino. "Rappresentatione Digitale e Modello del Testo," unpublished essay [1–17].

Byron, George Gordon, Lord. *Lord Byron: The Complete Poetical Works.* Ed. Jerome J. McGann. 7 vols. Oxford: Clarendon Press, 1980–1993.

Cage, John. *Silence; Lectures and Writings.* Cambridge, MA: MIT Press, 1969.

Caglioti, Giuseppe. *The Dynamics of Ambiguity.* Berlin: Springer-Verlag, 1992.

Chalmers, David J. *Towards a Theory of Consciousness.* Cambridge, MA: MIT Press, 1995.

———. "Facing Up to the Problem of Consciousness." *Journal of Consciousness Studies* (1998). Available online text: http://www.u.arizona.edu/ ~ chalmers/ papers/facing.html.

Chernaik, Warren, Caroline Davis, and Marilyn Deegan, eds. *The Politics of the Electronic Text.* Humanities Communications Publication No. 3, Centre for English Studies, U of London. Oxford: Oxford Computing Services, 1993.

Coleridge, Samuel Taylor. *The Poems of Samuel Taylor Coleridge.* Ed. E. H. Coleridge. London: Oxford UP, 1912.

Collins, Harry and Martin Kusch. *The Shape of Actions: What Humans and Machines Can Do.* Cambridge, MA: MIT P, 1998.

DeFrancis, John. *Visible Speech: The Diverse Oneness of Writing Systems.* Honolulu: U of Hawaii P, 1989.

Dickinson, Emily. *The Poems of Emily Dickinson.* Ed. Thomas H. Johnson. 3 vols. Cambridge, MA: Harvard UP, 1955.

Dillon, George. "Data Photomontage and net.art Sitemaps." *Postmodern Culture* 10 (January 2000).

Dreyfus, Hubert L. *What Computers Can't Do: The Limits of Artificial Intelligence.* Rev. ed. New York: Harper Colophon Books, 1979.

Drucker, Johanna. "Notes." (Unpublished essay).

———. "The Metalogics of the Book." (Unpublished essay).

———. *The Visible Word: Experimental Typography and Modern Art, 1909–1923.* Chicago: U of Chicago P, 1994).

Forrest-Thomson, Veronica. *Poetic Artifice: A Theory of Twentieth-Century Poetry.* New York: St. Martin's Press, 1978.

Fortier, Paul A., ed. "A New Direction for Literary Studies?" *Computers and the Humanities* 27, nos. 5–6 (Special Double Issue, 1993–1994).

Foster, K. and P. Boyde, eds. *Dante's Lyric Poetry.* 2 vols. Oxford: Clarendon Press, 1967.

Franklin, R. W., ed. *The Manuscript Books of Emily Dickinson.* Cambridge: Belknap Press, 1981.

———. *The Poems of Emily Dickinson.* Cambridge: Belknap Press, 1999.

Fraser, George. *Metre, Rhyme, and Free Verse.* London: Methuen, 1970.

Frost, Robert. *The Poems of Robert Frost.* New York: Random House, 1946.

Gabler, Hans Walter, ed. *Ulysses: the corrected text.* Random House: New York, 1986.

Genette, Gérard. *Paratexts: Thresholds of Interpretation.* Trans. Jane E. Lewin with a foreword by Richard Macksey. Cambridge and New York: Cambridge UP, 1997.

Graff, Gerald. *Teaching the Conflicts.* New York: Garland, 1994.

Grafton, Anthony. *Forgers and Critics: Creativity and Duplicity in Western Scholarship.* Princeton: Princeton UP, 1990.

Grandgent, C., ed. *La Divina Commedia.* Rev. ed. Boston: Heath, 1933.

Greg, W. W. "The Rationale of Copy Text" [1950], reprinted in *The Collected Papers of Sir Walter W. Greg.* Ed. J. C. Maxwell. Oxford: Oxford UP, 1966.

Greetham, D. G. *Theories of the Text.* Oxford and New York: Oxford UP, 1999.

Hacking, Ian. *Representing and Intervening: Introductory Topics in the Philosophy of Natural Science.* Cambridge: Cambridge UP, 1983.

Haken, H. *Synergetics: An Introduction.* Berlin: Springer, 1977.

Hameroff, S. R. "Quantum Coherence in Microtubules: A Neural Basis for Emergent Consciousness?" *Journal of Consciousness Studies* (1998): 91–118

Hockey, Susan. *Electronic Texts in the Humanities.* Oxford: Oxford UP, 2000.

Hofstadter, Douglas. *Fluid Concepts and Creative Analogies: Computer Models of the Fundamental Mechanisms of Thought.* New York: Basic Books, 1995

Holland, Jeanne. "Scraps, Stamps, and Cutouts: Emily Dickinson's Domestic Technologies of Publication." *Cultural Artifacts and the Production of Meaning.* Ed. Katherine O'Brien O'Keeffe and Margaret J. M. Ezell. Princeton: Princeton UP, 1993. 139–182

Honavar, Vasant and Leonard Uhr, eds. *Artificial Intelligence and Neural Networks: Steps Toward Principled Integration.* Boston: Academic Press, 1994

Howe, Susan. *My Emily Dickinson.* Berkeley: North Atlantic Books, 1985.

———. "These Flames and Generosities of the Heart: Emily Dickinson and the Illogic of Sumptuary Values." *Sulfur* 28 (1991): 134–155.

Illich, Ivan. *In the Vinyard of the Text: A Commentary on Hugh's Didascalicon.* Chicago: U of Chicago P, 1993.

Johnson, Ronald. *RADI OS.* With an afterword by Guy Davenport. Berkeley: Sand Dollar, 1977.

Johnson, Steven. *Interface Culture: How New Technology Transforms the Way We Create and Communicate.* New York: Basic Books, 1997.

Johnson, Thomas H. and Theodora Ward, eds. *The Letters of Emily Dickinson.* 3 vols. Cambridge, MA: Belknap Press, 1958.

Jorgensen, Corinne. "Access to Pictorial Material: A Review of Current Research and Future Prospects." *Computers and the Humanities* 33 (1999): 293–318.

Kane, George and E. Talbot Donaldson, eds. *William Langland: Piers Plowman: The B Version*. London: Athlone Press, 1975.

Keats, John. *The Poems of John Keats*. Ed. Jack Stillinger. Cambridge: Harvard UP: 1978.

Kenner, Hugh. *A Homemade World*. New York: Morrow, 1975.

Kilmer, Joyce. *Trees and other Poems*. New York: George H. Doran Company, 1914.

Krieger, Murray. *Ekphrasis*. Baltimore and London: Johns Hopkins UP, 1992.

Lachmann, Karl. *T. Lucreti Cari De rerum natura libri sex*. Georgii Reimeri: Berolini, 1853.

Lakoff, George. *Women, Fire, and Dangerous Things: What Categories Reveal about the Mind*. Chicago: U of Chicago P, 1987.

Landow, George. *Hypertext: The Convergence of Contemporary Critical Theory and Technology*. Baltimore: Johns Hopkins UP, 1997.

Laurel, Brenda. *Computers as Theatre*. Reading, MA: Addison-Wesley, 1993.

Lautréamont, Compte de [Isadore Ducasse]. *Maldoror (Les Chants de Maldoror)*. Trans. Guy Wernham. New York: New Directions, 1943.

Leggett, B. J. *Early Stevens: The Nietzschean Intertext*. Durham: Duke UP, 1992.

————. *Wallace Stevens and Poetic Theory: Conceiving the Supreme Fiction*. Chapel Hill: U of North Carolina P, 1987.

Marigo, Aristide, ed. *De Vulgari Eloquentia*. 3rd. ed. Firenze: Felice le Monnier, 1957.

Marillier, Henry Currie. *Dante Gabriel Rossetti: An Illustrated Memorial of his Art and Life*. London: Bell, 1899.

Mathews, Harry and Alastair Brotchie, eds. *Oulipo Compendium*. London: Atlas Press, 1998.

McGann, Jerome. *Black Riders: The Visible Language of Modernism*. Princeton: Princeton UP, 1993.

————. *A Critique of Modern Textual Criticism*. Chicago: U of Chicago P, 1983.

————. "Marxism, Romanticism, and Postmodernism. An American Case History." *South Atlantic Quarterly* 88 (Summer, 1989): 605–632.

————. *The Textual Condition*. Princeton: Princeton UP, 1991.

McLeod, Randall. "Information on Information." *TEXT* 5. Ed. D. C. Greetham and W. Speed Hill. New York: AMS Press, 1991. 241–284.

Motte, Warren F., Jr. *Oulipo: A Primer of Potential Literature*. Lincoln: U of Nebraska P, 1986.

Murray, Janet H. *Hamlet and the Holodeck: The Future of Narrative in Cyberspace*. Cambridge, MA: MIT Press, 1999.

Nagy, Gregory. *Poetry as Performance*. Cambridge: Cambridge UP, 1996.

Nelson, Theodor Holm. *Literary Machines*. Swathmore, PA: Theodor Holm Nelson, 1987.

Nicolis, G., I. Prigogine. *Self-organization in Nonequilibrium Systems*. New York: Wiley, 1977.

Nietzsche, Friedrich. *The Gay Science*. New York: Vintage Books, 1974.

Olson, Charles. *Human Universe and Other Essays*. Ed. Donald Allen. New York: Grove Press, 1967.

Olson, David R. *The World on Paper: The Conceptual and Cognitive Implications of Writing and Reading.* Cambridge: Cambridge UP, 1994.

Osman, Jena and Juliana Spahr, eds. *Hybrid Genres/Mixed Media. Chain* 3, nos. 1, 2 (special double issue, 1996).

Pater, Walter. *Appreciations.* Macmillan: London, 1889.

Patterson, Lee. "The Logic of Textual Criticism and the Way of Genius: The Kane-Donaldson *Piers Plowman* in Historical Perspective." *Textual Criticism and Literary Interpretation.* Ed. Jerome J. McGann. Chicago: U of Chicago P, 1985. 55–91.

Penrose, Roger. *The Emperor's New Mind: Concerning Computers, Minds, and the Laws of Physics.* Oxford: Oxford UP, 1989.

Perelman, Bob, ed. *Writing/Talks.* Carbondale: Southern Illinois UP, 1985.

Phillips, Tom. *A Humument: A Treated Victorian Novel.* London: Thames and Hudson, 1980.

Porter, Theodore M. *The Rise of Statistical Thinking 1820–1900.* Princeton: Princeton UP, 1986.

Pound, Ezra. *Cantos.* New York: New Directions, 1970.

———. *Guide to Kulchur.* London: Faber and Faber, 1938.

Pribram, K. H., ed. *Rethinking Neural Networks: Quantum Fields and Biological Data.* Hillsdale: Lawrence Erlbaum, 1993.

Prigogine, Ilya and Isabelle Stengers. *The End of Certainty: Time, Chaos, and the New Laws of Nature.* New York: Free Press, 1997.

———. *Exploring Complexity: An Introduction.* New York: W. H. Freeman, 1989.

Renear, Allen. "Out of Praxis: Three (Meta)Theories of Textuality." *Electronic Textuality: Investigations in Method and Theory.* Ed. Kathryn Sutherland. Oxford: Oxford UP, 1997.

Renear, Allen, Steve DeRose, David Durand, and Elli Mylonas, "What is Text, Really?" *Journal of Computing in Higher Education.* 1, no. 2 (winter, 1990).

Riding, Laura. *Anarchism Is Not Enough.* London: Jonathan Cape, 1928.

———. *Progress of Stories.* Deja Mayorca: Seizin Press, 1935.

Rossetti, William Michael, ed. *The Works of Dante Gabriel Rossetti.* London: Ellis, 1911.

Ryan, Marie-Laure, ed. *Cyberspace Textuality: Computer Technology and Literary Theory.* Bloomington: Indiana UP, 1999.

Samuels, Lisa. "Poetry and the Problem of Beauty." *Modern Language Studies* 27, no. 2 (spring 1997): 1–7. (Special issue edited by Samuels and devoted to the subject *Poetry and the Problem of Beauty.*)

Segré, Cesare (with the collaboration of Tomaso Kemeny). *Introduction to the Analysis of the Literary Text.* Trans. John Meddemmen. Bloomington: Indiana UP, 1988.

Shelley, Percy Bysshe. *Poetry and Prose.* Selected and edited by Donald H. Reiman and Sharon B. Powers. New York: W. W. Norton and Co., 1977.

Shillingsburg, Peter. *Scholarly Editing in the Computer Age: Theory and Practice.* Athens: U of Georgia P, 1986.

Simon, Herbert. *The Sciences of the Artificial.* Cambridge, MA: MIT Press, 1969.

Soderholm, James, ed. *Beauty and the Critic: Aesthetics in an Age of Cultural Studies.* Tuscaloosa: U of Alabama P, 1997.

Sontag, Susan. *Against Interpretation.* New York: Dell Publishing Company, 1966.

Sowa, John. *Knowledge Representation: Logical, Philosophical, and Computational Foundations.* Pacific Grove, CA: Brooks Cole, 1999.

Spahr, Juliana et al, ed. *A Poetics of Criticism.* Buffalo: Leave Books, 1994.

Stein, Gertrude. *How to Write.* Paris: Plain Edition, 1931.

———. *Tender Buttons.* New York: Claire Marie Press, 1914.

Stevens, Wallace. *The Collected Poems of Wallace Stevens.* New York: Knopf, 1967.

———. *Harmonium.* New York: Alfred A. Knopf, 1923.

Streng, Frederick J. *Emptiness: A Study in Religious Meaning.* Nashville: Abingdon Press, 1967.

Surtees, Virginia. *The Paintings and Drawings of Dante Gabriel Rossetti.* 2 vols. Oxford: Oxford UP, 1971.

Swinburne, Algernon Charles. *Notes on the Royal Academy Exhibition, 1868.* Part II. Hotten: London, 1868.

[Thackeray, William Makepeace]. *Rebecca and Rowena: A romance upon romance.* By Mr. M. A. Titmarsh. With illustrations by Richard Doyle. London: Chapman and Hall, 1850.

Thom, René. *Structural Stability and Morphogenesis; an Outline of a General Theory of Models.* Translated from the French edition [1972], as updated by the author, by D. H. Fowler. With a foreword by C. H. Waddington. Reading, MA: W. A. Benjamin, 1975.

Tufte, Edward. *Envisioning Information.* Chesire, CT: Graphics Press, 1990.

Unsworth, John. "The Importance of Failure." *The Journal of Electronic Publishing* 3, no. 2 (December 1997). Available online at http://www.press.umich.edu/jep/03–02/unsworth.html.

Vieth, David M. *Attribution in Restoration Poetry: A Study of Rochester's Poems of 1680.* New Haven: Yale UP, 1963.

Virginia Pilot and Norfolk Leader.

della Volpe, Galvano. *Critica del Gusto.* SC/10 no. 4. Milano: Feltrinelli, 1960.

———. *Critique of Taste.* Trans. Michael Caesar. London: New Left Books, 1978.

Waller, Robert H. W. "Graphic Aspects of Complex Texts: Typography as Macropunctuation." *Processes of Visible Language 2.* Ed. Paul A. Kolers, Merald E. Wrolstad, and Herman Bouma. New York: Plenum Press, 1980. 241–253.

Werner, Marta, ed. *Radical Scatters: Emily Dickinson's Fragments and Related Texts 1870–1886.* Ann Arbor: U of Michigan P, 2000.

Whitman, Walt. *Walt Whitman: The Complete Poetry and Selected Prose.* Ed. James E. Miller, Jr. Boston: Houghton Mifflin Co., 1959.

Wildgen, Wolfgang. *Process, Image and Meaning: A Realistic Model of the Meanings of Sentences and Narrative texts.* Amsterdam and Philadelphia: John Benjamins, 1994.

Wilson, Carol Shiner and Joel Haefner, eds. *Re-Visioning Romanticism: British Women Writers 1776–1837.* Philadelphia: U of Pennsylvania P, 1994.

Wordsworth, William. *Poetical Works*. Ed. Thomas Hutchinson. London: Oxford UP, 1904.

Zeeman, E. C. *Catastrophe Theory*. Reading, MA: Addison-Wesley, 1977.

Zukofsky, Louis. *Bottom: On Shakespeare*. Austin: Ark Press, for the Humanities Research Center, U of Texas, 1963.

Online Materials

Ayers, Edward. *The Valley of the Shadow: Two Communities in the American Civil War.* http://jefferson.village.virginia.edu/vshadow2/

Buzzetti, Dino. "Ambiguità diacritica e markup. Note sull'edizione critica digitale." http://bice.philo.unibo.it/ ~ buzzetti/pavia/ambiguita.html

———. "L'Argomento Dominante e la posizione di Scoto a proposito di un 'errore' interpretativo di Jules Vuillemin." http://bice.philo.unibo.it/ ~ buzzetti/pozzi/vuillemin.htm

Crane, Gregory. *The Perseus Digital Library*. http://www.perseus.tufts.edu/

DeRose, Steve. "Structured Information. Navigation, Access, and Control." http://sunsite.berkeley.edu/FindingAids/EAD/derose.html

Eaves, Morris, Robert Essick, Joseph Viscomi, eds. *The William Blake Archive*. http://www.iath.virginia.edu/blake/

Landow, George. *The Dickens Web*. http://www.eastgate.com/catalog/Dickens.html

McGann, Jerome, ed. *The Complete Writings and Pictures of Dante Gabriel Rossetti: A Hypermedia Research Archive*. http://jefferson.village.virginia.edu/rossetti/

———. "Imagining What You Don't Know: The Theoretical Goals of the Rossetti Archive." http://jefferson.village.virginia.edu/%7Ejjm2f/chum.html

McGann, Jerome and Johanna Drucker. "The Ivanhoe Game: An Introduction." http://jefferson.village.virginia.edu/%7Ejjm2f/IGamehtm.html

Nelson, Theodor Holm. "What's On My Mind?" http://www.sfc.keio.ac.jp/ ~ ted/zigzag/xybrap.html

———. *ZigZag Software*. http://www.xanadu.net/zigzag/

Pitti, Daniel and John Unsworth. "After the Fall—Structured Data at IATH." http://www.iath.virginia.edu/ ~ jmu2m/ach98.html

Robinson, Peter. ". . . but what kind of electronic editions should we be making?" http://gonzo.hd.uib.no/allc-ach96/Panels/Finneran/robinson.html

———. *The Collate Software*. http://www.cta.dmu.ac.uk/projects/collate/

Sowa, Cora. *The MINERVA System for the Study of Literary Texts*. http://www.best-web.net/ ~ sowa/minerva/index.htm

The Text Encoding Initiative (TEI). http://www.hcu.ox.ac.uk/TEI

Unsworth, John. "Living Inside the (Operating) System: Community in Virtual Reality." http://www.iath.virginia.edu/pmc/Virtual.Community.html#4

———. "The Only Responsible Intellectual is One Who is Wired." http://www.iath.virginia.edu/ ~ jmu2m/tori.html

Index

added deformance, 117
Adobe Photoshop, 84, 86
aesthetic interface, 209–12
aesthetic space, 183
aesthetic texts, 206
aesthetics of digital media, 171–72
"Alice Fallacy, The," 15, 24
  dramatic presentation, 29–52
altered deformance, 117, 133–35
analogue thinking, 190, 225–27
analytic mechanisms, 56
analytical material, 88
antithetical reading models, 106–7
artificial intelligence, 214
artwork, 84–87. *See also* digital
  images; images
audial elements, 58–61, 185
automated computational analysis, 175
autopoetic forms, xiv, 182, 184, 218

backward reading, 106–10, 116–18, 120,
  126, 131
ballads, 59, 61, 179
bibliographic code, 197–203, 206–7
bibliographic space, 179
book culture, 210–11
books
  computers and, xii, 168, 170–71,
    209–10, 212
  electronic format, 57
  as machines of knowledge, 54–57

study of, 55, 82
technology and, 147, 165, 167–68,
  212–14
bookspace, 199, 213, 214

CD-ROM disks, 58
classical scholarship, 69
codex-based tools, 55–57, 63, 67–68, 79,
  82
computer games, 158–60, 217
computerized imagination, 89
computers
  books and, xii, 168, 170–71, 209–10,
    212
  data management, 213
  humans and, 190–91
conceptual interpretation, 109, 111, 118
conscious subjectivity, 222
copyright issues, 92
creativity, 214–16
critical deformance, 116, 126–30, 173–74
critical editions, 56, 60, 62, 68, 77–79,
  170, 222–23
critical interpretation, 128
critical performatives, 114–15
critical reflection, 221, 222, 224, 228,
  230, 231
criticism, 114, 181. *See also* New
  Criticism
Critique of Modern Textual Criticism, A, 12,
  23, 25–26

cultural studies, 213
cybertexts, 147–48, 158–60

databases, 88
decentered text, 70–74
decentralism, 71–74
decoders, computers as, 191
deformance
    critical dialetics and, 126–30
    interpretation and, 101–3, 105–30
    performance and, 113–16
    of poetry, 117–33
    reveal codes and, 144
deformative diagramming, 123–24
deformative procedure, 131–35
deformative scholarship, 114–15
dialogue project, 223–24
digital art, 17, 69, 84–86, 88, 92, 94
digital culture, 1–19, 210–12
digital environments, 147
digital facsimiles, 92
digital images, 69, 84–86, 88, 92, 94
    handling of, 141, 173–75
digital imaging, 17, 69
digital media
    advantages of, 209
    aesthetics of, 171
    culture of, 1–19, 210–12
digital space, xi, 214
digital technology, xi–xii
    games and, 158–60, 217
    humanities computing and, 10, 194,
        217
    revulsion to, 139–40
    for studying texts, 151–52, 170, 224
    World Wide Web (W3) and, xii, 10, 169
    See also digital tools
digital textuality, 81
digital thinking, 190, 225–27
digital tools, 2, 8–9.
    aesthetics of, 171
    book technology and, 147, 165,
        167–68, 212–14
    integrating with textual tools, 228
    scholarly editing and, 170
    simplicity of, 141–42
    understanding, 194
    See also digital technology; IT tools

digitized images, 17, 69
discourse field, 219–21
distinctions, concept of, 200–204
distorted images, 84–86
divisions, of poems, 195–97
Document Type Definitions (DTDs). *See*
    DTDs
documentary networks, 58, 72–73
DTDs (Document Type Definitions), 69,
    90–92
    for images, 95
    for text documents, 96

editing
    codex-based tools, 55–57, 63, 67–68,
        79, 82
    theories of, 26, 79–81
    See also hyperediting; scholarly editing
electronic text, 57, 58, 68–69, 70–74, 82.
    See also hypertext
electronic tools. *See* digital tools
electronic transparencies, 94–95
encyclopedic properties, 147
ergodic texts, 148
experimental analysis, 129
experimental projects, 139–40, 143–46
    scanners and, 137, 144–46

facsimile editions, 56, 62
failure
    importance of, 26, 83, 213–14
    rewards of, 82–87, 141–43
fiction, 64
form, laws of, 193–94, 197, 198, 200–206
four dimensions, 146

game space, 225
games
    digital technology for, 158–60, 217
    interpretation and, 231
    See also "Ivanhoe Game, The"
gnosis, 83
graphemes, 152–53
graphical transformations, 155

hard copy, 56–57, 73
holograph manuscripts, 153
holographic projection, 146

HTML (Hypertext Markup Language), 5, 16, 88
humanities, and digital culture, 1–19
humanities computing, 6–10, 102–3, 139, 175, 194, 217
humans, and computers, 190–91
hyperediting, 57–58, 68. *See also* editing; scholarly editing
hyperfiction, 16–17
hypermedia, xiii
  hyperediting and, 57–58
  hypertext and, 88, 140, 168
  necessity of, 59–68
  Rossetti archive, 68–70, 172
hypermedia programs, 57–58
hypertext, 4–5
  decentralization of, 70–74
  hypermedia and, 88, 140, 168
  rationale of, 53–74
  structure of, 71–72
Hypertext Markup Language (HTML), 5, 16, 88
hypertext programs, 57

IATH (Institute for Advanced Technology in the Humanities), xiv, 3, 4, 6
  expectations of, 8–9
  idea of, 7–10
  outcome of, 9–10
image-editing operations, 174
imagery, 65–66
images
  digital format, 69, 84–86, 88, 92, 94
  filtering of, 84–86
  handling of, 141, 173–75
imaginative creativity, 214
imaginative works
  deformance and, 105–16, 172–73
  games and, 159
  interpretation and, 129
  poems, 181
  textual documents, 142, 185–86
  See also literary works
imaginings, 82–83, 85
information technology (IT) tools. *See* IT tools
injunctive elements, 203–5

inner infinities, 195–97
Inote, 94, 95, 97
Institute for Advanced Technology in the Humanities (IATH). *See* IATH
interface, 74, 88
  aesthetic elements, 209–12
  book formats, 211
  design models, 146
  graphic formats, 199
  of man and machine, 193–207, 216
  structure of, 141
internal dialogue, 129
Internet structure, 72
interpretation
  act of, 218–19
  conceptualization, 109, 111, 118
  deformance and, 101–3, 105–30
  game-playing and, 231
  as performance, 109–13
  of poems, 106–13, 117–30
  of textual documents, 140, 207
interpretational methods, 164, 222
interpretational theory, 222
interpretive limits, 115
intuitive thinking, 227, 229
invisibility, of literary works, 167–91
isolated deformance, 117, 120–21, 124, 126, 132–33
IT (information technology) tools, 2, 8–9
  aesthetic resources of, 171
  benefits of, 211
  book technology and, 147, 165, 167–68, 213–14
  scholarly editing and, 170
  simplicity of, 141–42
  See also digital tools
"Ivanhoe Game, The," xv,19, 24, 209–48
  diagram of, 226, 227
  electronic format, 165, 222, 224–27
  game moves, 232–45
  object of, 219, 221
  origins of, 218
  player file, 245–48
  purpose of, 159–60, 217, 224
  rules for, 220
  strategy of, 218

Laws of Form, 193–94, 197, 198, 200–206
libraries, 2, 3, 72
linear texts, 148
linguistic codes, 151, 229
linguistic material, 183, 189
linguistic space, 151
literary studies
    hypermedia and, 59–68
    scholarly editing and, 77–79
    tools for, 55–56, 185–86, 213
literary works
    deformance of, 206
    digital tools and, 55
    function of, 172
    physical character of, 54
    study of, 55–56, 185–86, 213
    visibility of, 165–91
    See also imaginative works

machines
    man and, 193–207, 216
    thinking abilities, 214–17
manuscript text, 154–57, 168–69
marked texts
    formal structures, 96–97
    graphics, 138
    markup language, 4, 89, 139, 187
    textual analysis of, 206–7
    See also HTML; SGML
metaphoric transformations, 153
multimedia, xiii, 58, 68. *See also* hypermedia

n-dimensions, xiv, 184
New Bibliography, 5, 10, 222
New Criticism, 4, 5, 10, 165, 222
novels, 64

OCR (Optical Character Recognition), 137, 144–45
OHCO thesis, 139, 141
Omnipage, 144
online publishing, 26–27
Optical Character Recognition (OCR), 137, 144–45
ordered ambivalence, 137
ordinary texts, 148

orthography, 182
Oxford English Dictionary, 55, 57

pagespace, 149, 199
paper-based text, 147
    changes in, 70
    converting, 82
participatory properties, 147
'pataphysics, 222–23
performance, 59
    deformance and, 113–16
    interpretation and, 109–13
philology, 207
phonemes, 152–53
pictorial deformation, 116
picture-poem, 64–66
poems, 64–66, 78–79
    divisions of, 195–97
    editing, 80
    features of, 189
    interpretation of, 106–13, 117–30
    logic of, 175, 188–89
    as prose, 122, 195
    symmetries/asymmetries, 182, 183, 184
    transformations of, 154–55, 181
poetic deformation, 117–30
poetic discourse, 228
poetic intuition, 229
poiesis, 83, 110, 112, 113, 120, 127, 130, 183
printed text, 154–57, 168–69, 178. *See also* texts
procedural properties, 147
prose descriptions, 195–97
prose format, 122
prose/poetry generating machine, 215–16

quantum behavior, 184
quantum models, xiv–xv
quantum poetics, xv, 161–66, 183, 228–31
quantum space, 183
quid, 87, 128

rationale
    of hypertext, 24–26, 53–74
    of textual documents, 137, 138
reading backward, 106–10, 116–18, 120, 126, 131

reference, concept of, 205
reordered deformance, 117, 131–32, 134–35
rethinking textuality, 54, 103, 109, 137–60
reveal codes, 144
rhetoric, 109, 112, 113, 149, 205
role-playing games
  digital technology, 158–60, 222
  interpretation and, 164, 231
  See also "Ivanhoe Game, The"
Rossetti Archive, The, 1–3
  building, 91–94, 140–41
  changes in structure, 92–93
  electronic edition, 82–84
  history of, 11–12
  hypermedia and, 68–70
  interpretive methods and, 24, 25
  model of, 12–17
  publishing online, 26–27
  purpose of, 170, 217
  scholarly editing and, 10–14
  structure of, 83–84

scanner experiments, 137, 144–46
scholarly editing
  codex-based tools, 55–57, 63, 67–68, 79, 82
  literary studies and, 55–56, 61, 77–79
  Rossetti archive and, 10–14
  technology and, 170
scholarly editions, 222–23
scientific discourse, 228
semiosis, 102
semiotic codes, 151
semiotic forms, 165
semiotic material, 183, 189
semiotic space, xiii, xiv, 151
SGML (Standard Generalized Markup Language), 4, 14, 16, 17, 57–58, 69, 88–91, 94, 139, 140–41, 187–89
songs, 59, 61
spatial conception, 147, 197–98
spatial units, 178
Standard Generalized Markup Language (SGML). *See* SGML
storytelling machine, 214–15
subjective aesthetic engagement, 86

symmetries/asymmetries
  game-playing and, 224, 229
  of poems, 182, 183, 184

technology. *See* digital technology
TEI (Text Encoding Initiative), 4, 14, 89–90, 139, 140, 143, 187–89, 194
text, defining, 102–3, 187–91, 194
Text Encoding Initiative (TEI). *See* TEI
texts
  audial elements, 58–61, 185
  editing, 55, 80–81. *See also* editing; scholarly editing
  electronic format, 57, 58, 68–69, 70–74, 82
  paper-based format, 70, 82
  traditional format, 148–49, 158–60, 229
  visual elements, 58, 62
textspace, 149–51, 157–59, 198–99
Textual Condition, The, 23
textual deformance, 102, 145
textual documents
  bibliographic formats, 138, 145, 149, 155, 168, 182, 197–203, 206–7
  experimental projects, 139–40
  graphic formats, 138, 143–45, 168, 184, 198–99
  marking, 4, 89, 96–97, 138, 139, 187, 206–7. *See also* HTML; SGML
  theses on, 146–47
  See also textuality
textual forms, 165
textual interpretation, 140, 207
textual materials, xv, 59–61, 97
textual space, xiv, 214
textual studies, 55, 56
textuality
  determinations of, 166
  digital format, 81
  injunctive forms of, 203–5
  interfaces, 193–95
  interpretation of, 140, 207
  nature of, 2–3
  rethinking, 54, 103, 109, 137–60
  theories of, 12
  theses on, 187
  See also textual documents

thematic interpretation, 107, 109
three dimensions, 184, 199
traditional texts, 148–49
  analysis of, 229
  distinguishing from cybertexts, 158–60
transformations
  electronic elements, 193, 224–25, 229
  graphical elements, 155
  metaphoric elements, 153
  of poems, 154–55, 176–77, 181
two dimensions, 184, 199

University of Virginia, xiv, 3, 6–7, 10
user interface, 74, 88

verbal space, 118
verse presentation, 154–56
video games, 17. *See also* computer games
virtual documents, 56–57, 72–73
visibility, of literary works, 165–91
visual elements, 58, 62, 185
visual language, 198
visualized models, 146

weak creativity, 215, 216
World Wide Web (W3), 4–5
  coding of, 88
  digital technology and, xii, 10, 169
  documentary networks, 58, 72–73